THE POLITICS OF THE CARIBBEAN COMMUNITY
1961–79

To Jill

ANTHONY PAYNE

The Politics of the Caribbean Community 1961–79

Regional Integration among New States

St. Martin's Press
New York

© A. J. PAYNE 1980

All rights reserved. For information, write:
St. Martin's Press, Inc., 175 Fifth Avenue, New York, N.Y. 10010
Printed in Great Britain
First published in the United States of America in 1980
ISBN 0–312–62874–9

Libary of Congress Cataloging in Publication Data

Payne, Anthony, 1952–
  The politics of the Caribbean community, 1961–79.

  Bibliography: p.
  Includes index.
  1. Caribbean area—Economic integration. 2. Caribbean area—Politics and government. I. Title.
  HC155.P39   1980   37.1'729   80–10500
  ISBN 0–312–62874–9

Computerised Phototypesetting
by G.C. Typeset Ltd., Bolton, Greater Manchester

CONTENTS

Preface	*page*	vii
Abbreviations		xi

Introduction. The paradox of regional history in the Caribbean — 1

PART I. Origins and establishment

1	The vision of an economic community	26
2	Free trade *v.* production integration	56
3	The establishment of CARIFTA	89
4	The first four years	112
5	From crisis to CARICOM	140

PART II. Analysis and evaluation

6	Economic integration	166
7	Functional co-operation	194
8	The co-ordination of foreign policy	208
9	The style of regional decision-making	225
10	Political integration	254

Conclusion. The politics of regionalisation	283
Appendix	288
Select bibliography	290
Index	292

PREFACE

In recent years regional integration has become an increasingly prominent feature of the politics of new states. From a time when Western Europe was the only area in which integration was being pursued, and the process could thus be considered a characteristic of the politics of older, developed states, it is now the case that most such groupings in the world are to be found amongst new states. It is the European experience which has come to appear isolated and exceptional. Yet, despite its obvious and growing importance, the phenomenon of regional integration amongst new states is still not particularly well understood by political scientists. Most of the academic work that has been done on the politics of regional integration has been concentrated on Europe, and the prevailing tendency has simply been to assume that much the same forces are at work in respect of the integration of new states.

The theoretical literature on integration has been dominated by the neofunctionalist school of thought, which was, in origin, an approach derived almost wholly from the growth of supranational institutions in Western Europe in the late 1950s and early 1960s. For all that, it was pressed into service as a comparative model, and exaggerated claims were made in respect of its universal validity as a tool for understanding regional integration. The reality was that as an explanatory theory neofunctionalism was utterly bound by its roots − appropriate only to the pluralist politics of industrialised states and dated by the 'end of ideology' image of consensus which was its intellectual underpinning. Critics were certainly swift to point out its irrelevance to the world of new states. In short, such theorising as there has been about the process of integration amongst new states has only taken place at second hand as an offshoot of a theory designed to explain events in Western Europe, and has by now been largely discredited. Thus political science presently lacks a valid theoretical model to guide the study of regional integration in this type of setting.

For this reason, any attempt to move towards an understanding of the politics of integration amongst new states has to be founded, for the moment, upon the case-study approach. This book is conceived in that mould: it is a study of the politics of the Caribbean Community, which is the name given to the structure of regional integration established in recent years between the various territories of the Commonwealth Caribbean. The particular choice of subject was determined by a number of factors. In the first place, the Caribbean Community can reasonably claim to be one of the more successful of the integration movements that have lately emerged in the Third World. This has the advantage of giving the analysis something to bite on and of enabling attention to be focused on the reasons why such movements survive when and where they do survive. Secondly, the states of the Commonwealth Caribbean are typical new states in many ways: it cannot easily be argued that the value of the discussion is vitiated by the exceptional character of the states involved. They have experienced a long history of colonialism and none has yet been independent for two decades. Some indeed have only just acquired independent status, whilst others are still moving in that direction. All, however, possess typically underdeveloped economies – heavily reliant on primary production, dependent on external markets and decisions and riven by high unemployment and severe disparities of income. In sum, the Caribbean Community is probably as good a case study to work from as is currently available.

The study begins with a review of the history of intra-regional relations in the Caribbean from the days of early British rule to the moment of the Federation's collapse in 1961 and thus establishes the framework in which the ensuing account of contemporary Caribbean integration is set. Part I traces the path by which the regional idea again came to the forefront of West Indian politics in the 1960s and the way in which it was institutionalised, first, within the Caribbean Free Trade Association and, latterly, within the Caribbean Community itself; Part II examines the various elements in the Community system – economic integration, functional co-operation and foreign policy co-ordination – and analyses the manner in which decisions have been taken within the integration movement, including the implications this has for the whole question of political integration. The study concludes with an assessment of

Preface

the overall experience of the Caribbean Community and a brief attempt to derive from it something of benefit in the search for a general understanding of the role of regional integration in the politics of new states.

The materials used in preparing this work have been both numerous and diverse. Primary sources include the various agreements and declarations pertaining to the integration movement itself, United Kingdom Government Papers, White Papers published by West Indian governments, proceedings of House of Assembly debates, reports of United Nations bodies and of the many institutions and associate institutions of the Caribbean Community itself, and several unpublished speeches and addresses by politicians and regional officials. Access has also been had to the press releases and communiqués issued by the Community Secretariat in Georgetown, which add up to a comprehensive picture of the public face of the integration movement. In addition, close attention has been paid to the contents of various itinerant West Indian periodicals and to the regional press, in particular the Jamaican *Daily Gleaner*, the *Trinidad Guardian*, the *Barbados Advocate-News* and the *Guyana Graphic*. Approximately twenty-five confidential interviews were also conducted with politicians, civil servants, regional officials, academics and businessmen in Antigua, Barbados, Guyana, Jamaica, St Lucia and Trinidad between May and July 1975, but it should be said that information obtained in this way has only been used when reinforced by other evidence. Finally, to supplement and sustain these various sources, the large and expanding secondary literature on Caribbean politics and society has been widely drawn upon.

The research has been supported financially by the Social Science Research Council, which granted me a studentship for two years in the Department of Government at the University of Manchester, and by the Inter-Universities Council for Higher Education Overseas, which arranged for me to be attached to the University of the West Indies during the academic year 1974-75 and covered the cost of my field-work in the region. To both institutions I am very grateful.

Many people have also helped me in the preparation of this work, both in England and the West Indies, inside and outside the academic world. They are too numerous to mention by name here, but I thank them all. There are some debts, however, that must be personally acknowledged. The first is to my typists, Jane Davies and Nancy Alexander, who have laboured with considerable skill over the various drafts of this work. The second is to Professor Dennis Austin, on whose shoulder I have leant throughout this study. Only he and I know the true wealth of the encouragement, advice and friendship that he has consistently given me. I can only hope that the finished work is some recompense for his efforts. The third is to my wife, Jill, who not only supported me financially during the greater part of the period in which this research was done but also herself acted as critic, typist, proof reader and valued adviser on countless other connected matters. It is to her that this book is dedicated.

Finally, I am grateful to the Secretariat of the Community for permission to reproduce the map, and the diagrams which appear in chapter nine.

A.J.P.
Huddersfield
December 1979

ABBREVIATIONS

ACP	African, Caribbean and Pacific Countries
ALP	Antigua Labour Party
AMP	Agricultural Marketing Protocol
BOAC	British Overseas Airways Corporation
BTN	Brussels Tariff Nomenclature
BWIA	British West Indian Airways
CACM	Central American Common Market

Abbreviations

CAIC	Caribbean Association of Industry and Commerce
CARICOM	Caribbean Community and Common Market
CARIFESTA	Caribbean Festival of Arts
CARIFTA	Caribbean Free Trade Association
CCC	Caribbean Consumers Council
CCL	Caribbean Congress of Labour
CDB	Caribbean Development Bank
CET	Common External Tariff
CFC	Caribbean Food Corporation
CIC	Caribbean Investment Corporation
ECCM	Eastern Caribbean Common Market
ECLA	Economic Commission for Latin America
EEC	European Economic Community
EIU	Economist Intelligence Unit
FAO	Food and Agricultural Organisation
f.o.b.	free on board
GDP	Gross domestic product
JLP	Jamaica Labour Party
LAFTA	Latin American Free Trade Association
LDC	Less developed country
LIAT	Leeward Islands Air Transport Company
MDC	More developed country
OAS	Organisation of American States
PNC	People's National Congress
PNM	People's National Movement
PNP	People's National Party
PPP	People's Progressive Party
QR	Quantitative restriction
REC	Regional Economic Committee
SITC	Standard International Tariff Classification
UN	United Nations
UNCTAD	United Nations Conference on Trade and Development
UNDP	United Nations Development Programme
UNESCO	United Nations Educational, Scientific and Cultural Organisation
UNIDO	United Nations Industrial Development Organisation
UWI	University of the West Indies
WISA	West Indies Associated States
WISCO	West Indies Shipping Corporation
WITASS	Association of West Indies Trans-Atlantic Steam Ship Lines
WMO	World Meteorological Organisation

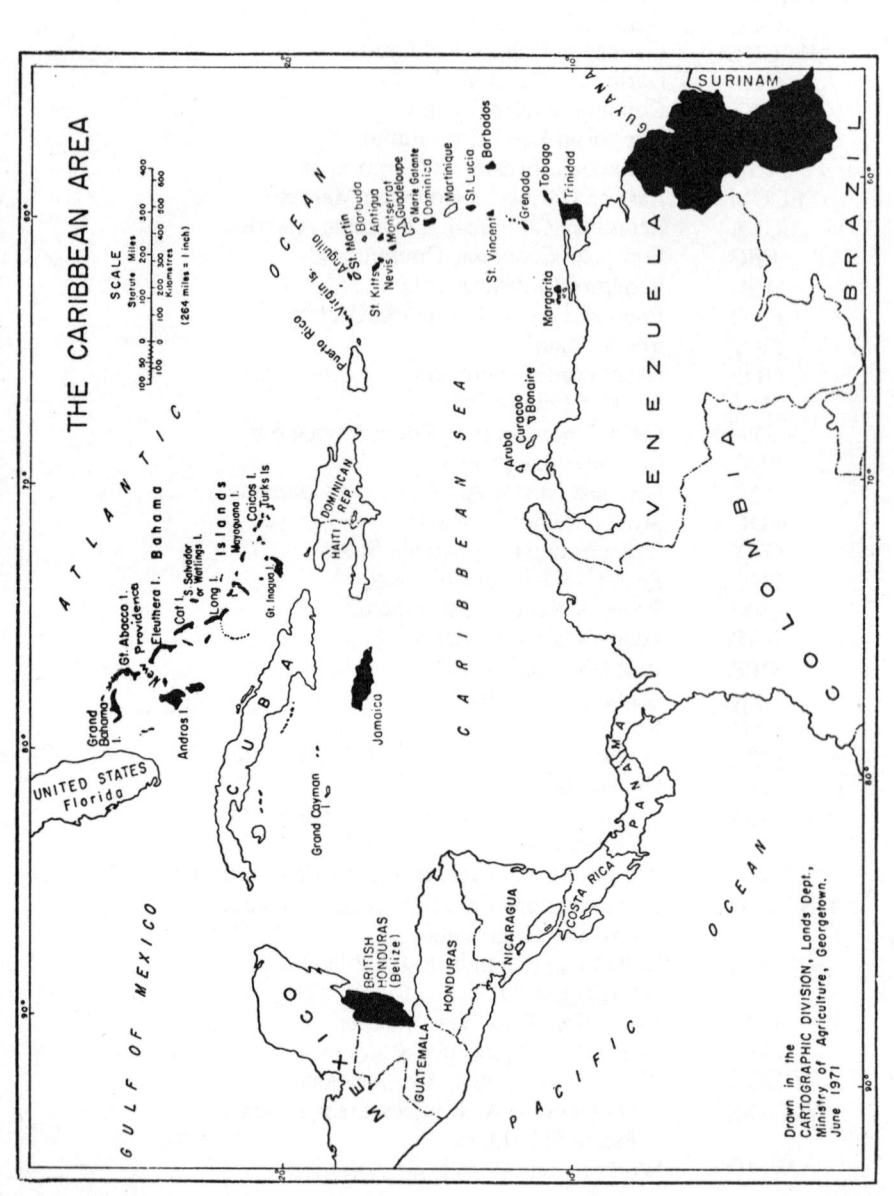

INTRODUCTION

The paradox of regional history in the Caribbean

Relations between the territories of the Commonwealth Caribbean are, and always have been, governed by the underlying paradox of the region's geography. One must never forget that the West Indies are a chain of islands. They stretch from Jamaica on the western tip of the northern Antillean range, through the Leeward and Windward Islands, to Barbados and Trinidad at the south-eastern point of the archipelago, and embrace at either end the two mainland territories of Belize (formerly British Honduras) and Guyana (formerly British Guiana). The distances involved are considerable – Jamaica is fully a thousand miles from the Eastern Caribbean and Belize some seven hundred miles west of Jamaica. Undeniably, too, water separates more effectively than land. As one writer on the Caribbean, a man with a professional background as a geographer, has testified, 'Polynesians and Melanesians, more at home with the ocean, make it a highway instead of a barrier, but the Caribbean Sea more often constrains and attenuates the social network'.[1] And yet the facts of geography do impose some sort of unity. Separated by sea though they may be, the territories of the West Indies clearly constitute a region in the geographic sense. They form an obvious group on the map and are broadly contiguous in location, the Leewards and Windwards, in fact, being close enough for them to be in sight of their nearest neighbours. In other words, the West Indian frame of reference is, at one and the same time, the island *and* the region. Historically, this dualism has been internalised within the minds of those native to or concerned with the area, and has engendered persistent doubt as to whether the island or the region is the appropriate unit for political and economic action. As a result, the history of intra-regional relations in the Commonwealth Caribbean has come to acquire a schizophrenic character, exhibiting simultaneously the stamp of integration and fragmentation. We need to begin by looking back over that history.

Early administrative links[2]

The idea of forging some sort of union between the territories of the West Indies dates back to the earliest days of British rule. In 1625 Thomas Warner, the man responsible for planting the first British settlement in the region, was appointed the royal lieutenant of St Kitts, Nevis, Barbados and Montserrat, whilst two years later the authority of the Earl of Carlisle was extended to cover all the 'Caribee Islands'. However, as British possessions in the West Indies grew in number, their joint administration became increasingly impracticable. In 1671 the Leeward Islands were given their own Governor, Sir William Stapleton, and they henceforth acquired a history of their own. Stapleton soon took it upon himself to gather for joint consultation representatives of the various island executive councils and legislative assemblies. This modest initiative gradually evolved into a sort of informal federal council and was officially ratified in 1765, only to fade quickly into inactivity thereafter. Nevertheless, the unity of the Leewards was preserved until 1816, when they were divided into two separate governorships. The estrangement was only temporary, and in 1833 all the Leeward Islands, together with Dominica, were again placed under one governor. He was their sole link until in 1869 the Colonial Office urged the then incumbent, Sir Benjamin Pine, to form these islands into one colony, with a single court, treasury and police corps. After eighteen months of difficult negotiations he was only able to persuade them to agree to a weakened form of federal union, which came into being with the Leeward Islands Act of 1871 and, in fact, lasted until 1957. It was not, however, a happy arrangement. The territories only acceded to it reluctantly and protested throughout its existence against the additional financial burdens it imposed upon them. The report of one outside observer, James Sanderson, in 1877 confirmed the complaints and concluded that 'the people of these islands have been most dreadfully deceived as to the results which were to accrue to them from the adoption of Federation'.[3]

Although they too developed a history of their own, the Windward Islands experienced much looser forms of association. For a number of years organised government was virtually ruled out by fluctuations in the military fortunes of the rival imperial powers, Britain and France. In 1764, however, at the end of the Seven Years War, the ceded islands of Grenada, St Vincent, Dominica and Tobago were placed under a single governor and executive council with plans for a federal legislature. The experiment proved short-lived, since Dominica withdrew in 1771 and St Vincent in 1776, and Tobago was returned to France by the Treaty of Versailles. When the Windwards were again declared British in 1814, after another period of war, they were allowed to go their separate ways till 1833, when Grenada, St Vincent and Tobago were grouped with Barbados under a single governor, to be joined three years later by St Lucia and, for a brief period till 1842, Trinidad. In 1869 the Colonial Office instructed the Governor of the Windwards to work towards a federation of the islands under his control, persisting with the proposal even in the face of his adverse recommendation. Vigorous objections were expressed by the House of Assembly in Barbados, and amidst violent disturbances the scheme was finally dropped in 1876 and Barbados subsequently given its own governor.[4] In 1869 Tobago was removed from the group and integrated with Trinidad. The idea of closer association lingered on amongst the Windwards but cannot be said to have received much local support. Even the innocuous plan to appoint a common chief justice for Grenada and St Vincent in 1891 led to such a threat to order in St Vincent that a British warship had to be displayed off the island to restore calm.[5]

In sum, the West Indies suffered from a bewildering and unsettling series of experiments in inter-colonial administration for a period which lasted for more than two and a half centuries. Only the relatively remote territories of Jamaica, British Guiana and British Honduras were excluded from the merry-go-round. In the seventeenth and early eighteenth centuries this process was warranted, in Britain's eyes at least, by the need to organise the defence of its prized possessions against rival imperialisms, but later in the eighteenth and nineteenth centuries it is not too much to say that the West Indian islands were treated entirely as creatures of Colonial Office convenience. The area was a regular victim of the constant demand for savings in the cost of governing the British Empire. It was as if a succession of tidy minds, brooding over a map of the West Indies on some wall in Whitehall, could not resist devising plans for amalgamating these irritatingly dispersed islands into neat and manageable groups.

Because the motive behind inter-island association in this period was no more than a desire to increase the ease and economy with which Britain might be able to administer its possessions in the Caribbean, the resulting unity was felt more in the Colonial Office than actually in the West Indies. At no stage did Britain consider it necessary to promote co-operation amongst her West Indian subjects. In consequence, there was little communication between the territories on the political level, and even less economically. In the aftermath of the gradual extinction of the region's indigenous Arawak inhabitants under early Spanish rule, and the abandonment of subsequent British attempts to create a settler type of economy, the introduction of sugar in the seventeenth century condemned the islands to evolve as appendages of the overseas economy of Britain in the classic form of the 'pure plantation economy'.[6] Each individual plantation was closely tied to a metropolitan merchant firm within the framework of a joint-stock trading company and had practically no dealings with other plantations even in the same island – let alone those in other neighbouring territories. Indeed, every plantation was in competition with the others, so much so, in fact, that sugar production in the West Indies has been said to have 'engendered and nurtured an inter-colonial rivalry, an isolationist outlook, a parochialism that is almost a disease'.[7] By comparison with the facts of economic life, the succession of inter-territorial administrative combinations which we have described made little or no impression upon the West Indian mind.

The 'closer union' debate

In spite of this, the idea of closer union continued to have attractions to those responsible for the formulation of British policy towards the region. Indeed, the Royal Commission dispatched to Dominica in 1894 went out of its way to urge the desirability of a federation embracing all the West Indian colonies, only to find the Colonial Office newly concerned that administrative changes should be acceptable to local opinion before they were implemented. The lesson that seemed to have been learnt from previous initiatives, especially, one may suppose, the confederation *débâcle* in Barbados in 1876, was that no union could be effective, and could perhaps not even be established, without the approval of responsible opinion within the region itself. From Britain's point of view, federation was an attractive proposal and might be regarded as the ultimate objective of policy, but it was definitely something which should not be forced upon the colonies. At the turn of the century the priority was, rather, the patient encouragement of forms of administrative co-operation which would have the effect of gradually drawing the islands together.

Advocacy of constitutional association *per se* was left to individuals, and a number of schemes were advanced. But on the whole the subject was not really discussed as if it was practical politics. This changed, however, with the general rise in the political temperature of the region after the First World War. Ordinary West Indians, radicalised by the experience of fighting in the allied armies, returned home to demand not only greater representation and a broader franchise, but also federation, because it was felt that the various political associations of the islands had to stand together in order to make any impression upon the Colonial Office. The call for unity was voiced in Marryshow's *West Indian*, in the *Georgetown Chronicle* of

A. R. F. Webber, in the speeches of Cipriani, and even by the Chambers of Commerce of Barbados and Trinidad. In 1920 Sir Edward Davson, President of the Associated Chambers, drew up a plan for a central conference of officials and unofficials, backed by a permanent secretariat, and circulated it around the region. Under growing pressure to investigate the questions of constitutional advance and regional association, and in spite of the Colonial Office's concern to act circumspectly and not be seen to be putting on pressure, the Secretary of State eventually decided to send his Under-Secretary, the Hon. E. F. L. Wood, to the Caribbean.

Wood's *Report* in 1922 was a landmark in the history of intra-regional relations in the West Indies. After a three-month tour that took him to all the British possessions except British Honduras and Montserrat, he concluded that 'however much it would be to the evident advantage of these colonies to secure machinery for greater unity and co-operation there are practical and political objections which, for the present at any rate, make this impossible'.[8] The absence of adequate transport facilities was one, Wood observing that he could never have carried out his mission if he had not had the services of a Royal Navy destroyer; but more important even than that consideration was what the *Report* took to be the neutral state of West Indian opinion, which made it 'both inopportune and impracticable'[9] to attempt any general federation. Nevertheless, Wood's *Report* was of the greatest significance in the long term because it tied the prospect of closer union to the test of widespread local acceptance just at a time when the advance of the elective principle in West Indian legislatures was bringing to the fore political leaders more representative of the West Indian population as a whole. After 1922 the movements for self-government and federation were inextricably bound together, whereas Wood had unquestioningly accepted that 'public opinion' was encompassed by the views of merchants and planters. They, not the spokesmen of the emerging Representative Government Associations, were the people to whom he talked and whose views he faithfully reported.

The inter-war depression began early in the West Indies. The price of sugar dropped consistently throughout the 1920s, accentuating the demand for change throughout the region and reinforcing, by the mutuality of suffering, the growing belief that unity in protest was the only way to influence the Colonial Office. The British government was forced again formally to reopen the question of federation, although only in a limited way. It thus announced the appointment of a Royal Commission, but asked it merely to examine 'the possibilities of closer union between Trinidad and the Windward Islands and the Leeward Islands or some of them'.[10] To prepare and coordinate their submissions to the Commission, radical political and labour leaders from all the territories concerned, plus Barbados, met in Roseau, Dominica, in October 1932, but in the event even the very limited demands they advanced could not be accommodated by the Commission when it reported in 1933. It concluded that the people whose opinions it valued in Trinidad – again the planters, merchants and officials – were so vehemently opposed to the idea of associating with the smaller islands, and possibly having to give them financial support, that it was wisest to leave Trinidad untouched, whilst even for the Leeward and Windward Islands it only advised a loose form of association under the figurehead of a single governor. Acknowledging that these suggestions would be seen as a retrograde step, the Commission justified them as a means of laying 'a sound foundation for a structure designed eventually to grow, if the communities concerned desire, into a West Indian Federation'.[11] Yet the price the Colonial Office was prepared to pay for such a sound foundation was not high: when estimates indicated that the scheme was likely to lead to an increase in administrative costs of some £6,000 p.a. it was quickly abandoned.

The complacency of British policy towards the region was rudely shaken by the disturbances of the 1930s, and a Royal Commission under Lord Moyne was quickly dispatched to investigate. It considered the federal question at length, and reported:

> although the question of closer union has remained officially in abeyance since [1933], there is evidence that a lively and growing interest has continued to be taken in it in many political circles in the West Indies ... we therefore put to most of the unofficial witnesses, who appeared before us in a representative

political capacity, the question whether they favoured the idea of the closer union of the West Indian colonies. Almost every witness thus questioned was in favour of closer union, but few of them were able or prepared to define the degree or nature of federation which they considered desirable. Our general impression ... is that while local opinion has made a considerable advance in the direction of political unity since 1932, it is doubtful whether time is yet ripe for the introduction of any large scheme of federation. ... There is room therefore for doubting the readiness of West Indian opinion to accept federation, in principle. Even if that doubt could be removed, practical difficulties appear still to be insuperable.[12]

Although it accepted that a West Indian federation was the 'ideal to which policy should be directed',[13] the Commission only felt able to propose a union of the Leeward and Windward Islands on the pattern of the Leewards Federation, with Barbados, British Guiana and Trinidad to be encouraged to amalgamate services with the federated colonies. In the light of the *Report's* admission that nearly all its witnesses favoured closer union, Moyne's hesitant approach stemmed from recognition of the fact that, although radical opinion in the area took federation for granted, conservative businessmen, officials and planters were still not ready for a move embracing all the territories of the region. And, as always, the key to British policy was the feeling that things should not be rushed in advance of the necessary 'urge from below'. Just what characterised the threshold of acceptability was never made clear by the Colonial Office, and in fact was probably never precisely known. In July 1944 Oliver Stanley, the Secretary of State, still considered that 'the one thing that might delay or even in the end entirely destroy that prospect of an all-island union would be to force a decision too early',[14] yet in March 1945, less than a year later, the time was thought to be at hand, and Stanley sent a dispatch to representatives of the various colonies inviting them to meet and discuss with him a positive advance towards federation.

Functional federalism

Before examining the consequence of that dispatch we must consider the other side to the general regional movement which grew up in the West Indies in the first half of this century, the emergence of what has come to be called 'functional federalism'.[15] In contrast to the overtly constitutional character of the 'closer union' debate, the notion of 'functional federalism' signified the common handling by the various governments of the region of specific problems of a generally economic and technical character. Regional collaboration of this kind was always supported by the British government, which hoped that regular promotion of such non-political activity would gradually, but not too conspicuously, educate the West Indian colonies in the habit of co-operation. Indeed, the initial impetus to the development of 'functional federalism' was given by a Royal Commission, that of 1897, which included amongst its few positive recommendations the proposal – implemented immediately – that an Imperial Department of Agriculture be set up, primarily for the Leeward and Windward Islands, but also to advise the other territories. In the same vein there followed the holding of a Quarantine Conference in Barbados in 1904, the creation of a West Indian Court of Appeal in 1919 and the establishment of the Imperial College of Tropical Agriculture in Trinidad in 1924. In addition, *ad hoc* conferences of officials were frequently convened.

In time, though, something more substantial was felt to be needed, and in 1926, following Davson's earlier suggestions, the Secretary of State summoned to London a preliminary conference of legislative nominees from all the British Caribbean territories. Its official aim was to equip the territories of the region 'with a flexible, well understood and eminently British piece of political machinery for adjusting their own internal and inter-colonial relations'.[16] The Colonial Office seemed well pleased with the experiment and promoted a second Standing Conference in 1929, which reached agreement on the desirability of unified action on a number of matters of common concern. Moreover, in some of these areas – as, for example, in the projected appointment of a joint West Indian Trade Commissioner to Canada and the establishment of a University College of the West Indies – this agreement was eventually translated into action (in 1934 and 1948 respectively). At the time, however, no attempt was made to strengthen the authority of the conference beyond its original advisory function, and when the 1931 meeting was postponed indefinitely, at the instigation of the regional governments themselves on the grounds that they had nothing urgent to discuss, the conference was never revived. Informal meetings of officials and representatives of commercial interests, who debated issues like Canadian–West Indian trade or customs regulations or interisland shipping, were left to carry on as before.

The Second World War occasioned a new round of West Indian conferences. The 1940 deal by which the British government allowed the United States to establish a number of military bases in the West Indies in exchange for the supply of a number of over-age, but badly needed, destroyers, unavoidably linked British and American interests in the Caribbean, the relationship being formally recognised in 1942 by the establishment of the Anglo-American Caribbean Commission. Even the admiring account of its operation by Herbert Corkran Jnr. concedes that the Commission would probably never have been created had it not been for the exigencies of war, which necessitated the maintenance of 'stability' in the area, as well as the preservation of supplies in the face of considerable enemy submarine activity.[17] Although at the end of the war the Commission's ambit was broadened to include France and the Netherlands, acting on behalf of their respective possessions in the Caribbean, its main achievement was probably only to consolidate American influence in the region. For all its promotion of a succession of West Indian conferences between the years 1944 and 1945, it certainly cannot be said to have made a very effective contribution to the solution of the social and economic problems of the region. Although its research wing did collect a massive amount of data, and some useful achievements – like the Schooner Pool and the Land-Water Highway – could be claimed, the Commission's many reports were, on the whole, conservative documents, advocating common West Indian action on numerous subjects, but 'failing completely to face up to the problem of the organisation of appropriate regional political institutions without which any joint action on those issues would revert to the control of the Commission itself, with its traditional disinterest in organising independent West Indian action for West Indian purposes'.[18] In short, too much of the activity of the Anglo-American Commission seemed to be divorced from, and even opposed to, the more political interests of the new nationalist leaders. Another layer of officialdom, even if conceived on a regional basis, was not the means to satisfy their aspirations.

More promising in this respect, and perhaps the most notable example of the functional approach to closer union, was the Regional Economic Committee (REC). The REC was a quasi-federal body, composed of leading West Indian public figures and conceived as the motor behind the region's economic development. In the event, the Committee was given control only of the Trade Commissioner Service and was never able to acquire the powers that would have enabled it to extend its effective sphere of operation to include the promotion of new industries. Indeed, this was just where its limitations were most apparent, and Braithwaite was later forced to conclude that the REC 'was unable to do anything to foster a regionally conceived industrialization programme'.[19]

Finally, in considering the role of 'functional federalism', we must not ignore the many pre-federal ' "federal" associations and institutions'.[20] Reference has already been made to the regional organisation of the business community in the form of the Associated Chambers of Commerce, first summoned in 1917, and of the labour movement, which culminated in the creation of the strongly federationist Caribbean Labour Congress in 1945. There were also professional bodies organised on a regional basis and accustomed, therefore, to viewing their particular problems from a wider perspective, chiefly the West Indian Bar Association, the Caribbean Union of Teachers and the Federation of Civil Servants of the West Indies, as well as regional associations of commodity producers, like the British West Indies Sugar Association. In their own way, all were evidence of the existence of *some* sort of regional feeling amongst West Indians.

The difficulty lies in taking the analysis a stage beyond this observation and attempting to specify precisely what 'functional federalism' added up to *in toto*. Much of it was developed around the conference habit, which was of obvious, if limited, use. Frequent regional meetings promoted an interchange of ideas and served as a forum in which regional leaders could meet and become acquainted. The REC was especially valuable in this regard because of the way it rotated its meetings between the various island capitals. It is necessary, therefore, to concede something to the Colonial Office argument that 'the growth of a regional approach to the solution of social and economic questions' was one of the crucial factors which encouraged it eventually to give a direct boost to the federal cause in the form of its 1945 dispatch.[21] And yet it can equally well be said that the early gatherings only involved senior civil servants, themselves often still expatriates, and the later ones included only a few of the newer political leaders. All of them suffered, in addition, from being convened under the external auspices of either the Colonial Office or the Anglo-American Caribbean Commission. The round of non-governmental organisations and conferences also lacked a sense of common purpose. The labour movement, for example, looked to a strong federal state, capable of executing democratic and progressive reforms; the business community, for their part, saw federation as the natural political embodiment of their own region-wide commercial interests and as an effective device for negotiating trade agreements with external buyers and investors; whilst the deliberations of the lawyers and civil servants were always underpinned by a keen anticipation of the sectional advantages they stood to gain from a federal administration, which would require their special skills in abundance.

All in all, then, 'functional federalism' played an ambivalent role in the evolution of the 'closer union' movement. To those already convinced of the advantages of federation the various functional achievements were seen as confirmation of their views and as evidence that all that was wrong with the regional principle was that it had not yet been pushed far enough. On the other hand, opponents of federation tended either to use the obvious limitations of the functional approach to discredit the whole notion of regional association, or, alternatively, also to stress the achievements and thus argue that federation was unnecessary because these subtler techniques were themselves sufficient to ensure the benefits of regional co-operation.[22] In the

The paradox of regional history

final analysis, whichever view was more widely held probably mattered less than any of the protagonists would have admitted at the time. In the half-century before 1958 the functional approach to closer union in the West Indies was no more than a sub-plot.

The Federation[23]

The major drama concerned the establishment of a federal constitution as a conscious act of political construction. On this front, Stanley's dispatch was the break-through, in that it led directly to the Montego Bay Conference in Jamaica in 1947 which took the decision to embark upon the detailed planning and preparation of a regional federation. In many ways his initiative was long overdue. As we have seen, the idea of federation had long been a familiar theme of political discussion in the region. It was taken for granted by the new generation of elected leaders in the eastern Caribbean, and even in Jamaica (where the federal notion was embraced at a much later stage and in a less emotional way) men like Norman Manley and Sangster had been impressed by their experience of the REC and other forms of inter-island functional co-operation. There also existed considerable common ground between the West Indian leadership and the British government. The official British view of the time held that it was 'clearly impossible in the modern world for the present separate communities, small and isolated as most of them are, to achieve and maintain full self-government on their own'[24] – the reasoning being that certain minimum criteria of size, measured in terms of economic resources, population and territorial area, which countries as small as Jamaica and Trinidad, much less Barbados, did not fulfil, were necessary for a colony to be 'viable' and thus able to claim and sustain sovereign status. Federation was, from this point of view, a means of increasing the effective size of the West Indian territories to a point where they became eligible for self-government as one unit. Within these limits, the attitude of the British government towards the West Indies was benevolent and well-meaning, and for the most part West Indian leaders endorsed without query the prevailing assessment of the implications of small size. Manley, for example, at Montego Bay argued in very similar terms to the British government that it was 'impossible to suppose that every single one of these territories, or perhaps even the largest of us, can achieve alone the basic services which it is the whole aim of politics to create and make possible for the common man'.[25] At times there seemed almost to be a unity of spirit between British policy and West Indian thinking. The Fabian background of Manley and other leading figures of the Federation period and their confidence in the British Labour Party prevented them from renouncing the 'values of empire' and, indeed, attracted them to the ideal of dominion status for the future West Indian Federation. There was certainly no need for them to bang on the door of the Colonial Office, demanding federation and independence from an intransigent British government. In short, Montego Bay marked by far the most promising stage yet in the development of the cause of West Indian federation.

The consequence, however, of this broad consensus of purpose was that the West Indian leaders found themselves engaged in negotiation, not with the Colonial Office over the *principle* of federation, but with each other over the *details* of the structure of the proposed federation. It was a task which proved to be much more problematic than anyone had anticipated, and it gradually took its toll of the participants. When the planning stage was, at last, completed – eleven long years later – in January 1958, the West Indian spirit, as Springer observed, 'was at a very low ebb and only momentum carried forward the unifying process'.[26] Since 1947 circumstances had changed radically in two essential respects.

In the first place, all the territories of the region had advanced constitutionally, thanks to the British policy of continuing to grant measures of self-government to individual islands throughout the very period in which they were supposed to be hammering out a common political fate within a federation. The seeds of dissension in this respect were sown at Montego Bay, when the delegates declared that the political development of the 'several units of the British Caribbean territories ... must be pursued as an aim in itself, without prejudice and *in no way subordinate* to progress towards the federation'.[27] Bustamante, the leader of the Jamaican delegation, gave the conference full warning that unless federation and self-government came together, those territories which were more advanced constitutionally would be unacceptably held back, whilst, on behalf of Trinidad, Gomes pointed out that to allow 'the system of graduating single isolated units in varying stages towards self-government' would encourage the already strong centrifugal tendencies in the region.[28] Neither, however, was heeded. Universal adult suffrage, which had already been granted to Jamaica in 1944 and Trinidad in 1946, was extended to Barbados in 1949 and to the Leeward and Windward Islands in 1951, and, as if that was not a sufficient indication of the prizes to come, ministerial government was established in Jamaica in 1952, then in Trinidad and Barbados, and was even granted to the Leewards and Windwards in 1956.

Secondly, the two leading West Indian territories, Jamaica and Trinidad, had experienced a vast improvement in economic well-being in the years after 1947, chiefly because both countries appeared to have successfully initiated policies of industrialisation. Following the publication in 1951 of a pamphlet by W. Arthur Lewis[29] which argued, in essence, that the West Indies could only escape from its traditional economic underdevelopment by devising a range of investment incentives that would encourage metropolitan industrialists, possessing technical skills and capital and already commanding markets for their products, actually to locate their plants in the region, both the Jamaican and Trinidadian governments quickly erected the institutional and legal apparatus attendant upon this policy of 'industrialisation by invitation', as it was soon accurately, if derisively, dubbed.[30] Foreign capital responded to the supine posture of the two governments and flowed into the region in massive quantities, bringing in its wake a number of highly visible manufacturing industries. Nor indeed was manufacturing the only growth sector in the economies of Jamaica and Trinidad in the 1950s. Sugar exports, although still susceptible to fluctuations of price in the world market, were once more sheltered from the harshest effects of this dependence by their preferential market in the United Kingdom under the terms of the Commonwealth Sugar Agreement. The newer commodity exports, like citrus and bananas, also had assured outlets in the British market. Moreover, bauxite production began in Jamaica in 1952 and grew swiftly in the boom conditions of the 1950s to an output of one million tons by 1953 and six million by 1958, adding enormously to the island's national income, whilst in Trinidad oil production, which since its discovery had come to dominate the country's economy, more than doubled in volume during 1947-58. Indeed, in terms of their overall gross domestic product Jamaica and Trinidad were amongst the fastest-growing economies in the world in the decade after 1947.[31]

The combined effect of these changing circumstances turned the politics of the Federation on end. As Sir John Mordecai put it, 'the desire for self-government now began to work against federation, instead of in its favour'.[32] It did so largely because the idea that federation was an indispensable prelude to the attainment of West Indian self-government gradually lost relevance as the region's leaders came to perceive that the worldwide process of decolonisation had drifted so far past its original conception of what constituted a feasible new state that it was beginning to incorporate territories as small as their own. They also increasingly realised that the planned Federation, so far from being in the vanguard of the region's march towards self-government, was, in actuality, a not very convincing vehicle in which to make the journey. Even a man as conservative as the Barbadian leader and future Federal Prime Minister, Grantley Adams, dismissed the federal constitution proposed by the Standing Closer Association Committee in 1949 as 'not much more than a glorified Crown Colony'[33] and, although advances on this position were undoubtedly won at the London conferences of 1953 and 1956, the final product still did not add up, in constitutional terms, to full internal self-government, a status which was granted to Jamaica just a year after the Federation had been inaugurated, and to Trinidad and Barbados before it was conceded to the Federation itself. In the economic sphere, too, the effect of the changes we have described was to raise doubts about the necessity for joint regional action in order to be able to secure economic development. Springer has testified that, whereas in 1947 the economic position of Jamaica had been such that it was natural to believe that union with the Eastern Caribbean territories, including oil-rich Trinidad, was the best if not the only avenue to economic improvement, by 1958, the position had changed; it was possible to hope with some confidence that Jamaica would achieve on her own the self-sustaining economic growth that would lead her eventually into the ranks of the 'modernised' and developed countries.[34]

Some Jamaican industrialists even felt that this could be facilitated by withdrawing altogether from the federal venture and openly seeking association with the United States and Canada.

These were important changes of perception. Just as the region's sense of common destiny declined under pressure from what Etzioni has called 'uneven internalisation',[35] so the governments of the larger territories grew in self-confidence. In Trinidad this new assertiveness was for a time channelled into a demand (eloquently voiced in *The Economics of Nationhood*[36]) for a strong, centrally directed federal system, capable of co-ordinating the economic development of *all* the constituent territories and thus of reducing the gap between the general living standards of the better-off and the poorer islands. In Jamaica, however, it developed into a virulent localism. Some have, with hindsight, seen the various inter-unit struggles of the federal period as evidence of a principled confrontation between a powerful Hamiltonian vision of federation, as advocated by Trinidad, and a looser Jeffersonian notion of confederation, as favoured by Jamaica. In reality the conflict was a much baser, less high-minded affair, more suited, in fact, to the billing 'Jamaica versus the Rest'.[37]

The history of the period between 1947 and 1962 is very much a story of the reduction and limitation of the planned and actual powers of the federal government − whether over taxation, customs duties or other matters − in successive attempts to make the resulting balance of responsibility between centre and units acceptable to Jamaican opinion, and its most sceptical voice, Bustamante. It was Bustamante's opportunistic opposition to the Federation which forced Manley, at a very early stage, to go on the defensive in his espousal of the federal cause, discouraged him subsequently from assuming the Prime

Ministership of the Federation, which was his for the taking in 1958, and finally turned this most convinced federalist into a narrowly insular negotiator in all his dealings with his regional colleagues. At the conclusion of the Inter-governmental Conference of 1961, it was clear that Jamaican pressure (which reached its apogee with the proposal to put the question of staying in or leaving whatever federal structure was finally decided upon by the conference to a binding referendum of the Jamaican people) had won a complete victory. The majority of Manley's demands had been conceded, including the exclusion of the federal government from any responsibility for the collection of income tax or the promotion of the region's industrial development. By this stage, too, Trinidad's earlier magnanimity had faded and had been replaced by a Jamaican-like determination not to allow its own entrenched economic interests (the prevention, for example, of the introduction of free movement of people between the islands and the consequent inflow of unemployed 'small islanders' into Trinidad which, it was assumed, would immediately result) to be prejudiced by handing over too much power to the federal centre. From the federalist point of view the unfortunate truth was that, in the last resort, neither the government of Jamaica nor the government of Trinidad was prepared to endanger in any way the economic growth which each was presiding over within the boundaries of its own territory. Indeed, as economic units, the members of the Federation competed more than they collaborated, a situation amply illustrated by Jamaica's attempt to set up its own oil refinery in direct conflict with Trinidad's position as the leading oil refiner in the Commonwealth Caribbean. In the face of these sorts of policies the federal government was unable to make any headway in the direction of the economic integration of the region, failing even to establish a customs union, without which, as every report on the question emphasised, a federation becomes an absurdity.[38] In the end, all that was left to represent the hopes and aspirations of federationists throughout the West Indies was a weak and powerless central Cabinet – in Eric Williams's dismissive phrase, 'just a lot of Federal Ministers running about Port-of-Spain spreading joy'.[39]

Much of the explanation of the failure and speedy demise of

the West Indies Federation can, then, be found in Millette's observation that 'politically' it was 'the least important event of its time'.[40] For the small islands of the Leewards and Windwards, and even Barbados, it seemed for a while to promise considerable political and economic advantages and, certainly, it was heavily weighed in their favour both in terms of membership of the Federal Parliament and representation in the Federal Cabinet. However, for the larger islands of Jamaica and Trinidad, political and economic development appeared to be taking place very satisfactorily at unit level. The fate of the Federation was conclusively settled by its inability to become anything more for them than a forum for the expression of regional rivalries. It had always been seen in the West Indies as a means to an end, latterly as the gateway to independence, and never, therefore, as an end and an ideal in its own right. When this argument was finally invalidated by Macleod's intimation to Manley in January 1960 that Jamaica was eligible for independence on its own, the little remaining substance left to the Federation was removed and only the formal structure remained. The negative vote of the Jamaican people in the referendum of September 1961 merely applied the *coup de grâce*.

Conclusion

The purpose of beginning this study with a review of the history of intra-regional relations in the West Indies has been to try to derive from it an appropriate framework in which to set the ensuing account of the post-federal period. It is not the easiest of tasks. There is undoubtedly a temptation to see the events described in this chapter as evidence of the existence in the West Indies of a deeply ingrained commitment to the principle and practice of regional integration. The subject has, after all, kept on cropping up – 'no people', it has been said, 'have entered a federal union with a longer history of experimentation in constitutional *inter-se* association'[41] – and if more or less continuous discussion of an idea for a period of three hundred years or more is a sufficient testament to its power, then indeed we might be justified in assuming that the notion of regional integration was the central theme around which any history of inter-territorial relations had perforce to be constructed. This is not, however, an assumption that the writer cares to make, for to draw such a conclusion would be to exaggerate, and in fact to misunderstand, the role that 'integrative activity' has played in West Indian history. As Gordon Lewis argues, 'an examination of the prolonged discussion preceding the Montego Bay meeting makes it painfully clear that the federation debate ... possessed no clear purpose, no central driving force to give it energy and direction'.[42]

In the first place, as Lewis went on to point out, there was a 'complete absence of agreement as to the scope of the proposed federation'[43] in terms of which territories to include. In addition, there were often conflicting motives at work behind the general espousal of the regional approach. There were also different visions of the end-product and different views as to the best means of attaining it. And, indeed, it ought not to be forgotten that in fact very little that was lasting or substantive was achieved in the way of regional integration, most of the ventures we have described either ending in total failure and dissolution or fading into irrelevance. It would also be erroneous to interpret every example of regional thinking – every proposal, every suggestion, every regional body – as proof of the existence of a vibrant and burgeoning sense of West Indianism in the population at large.

In fact, the history of integrative action in the region has been consistently characterised by the absence of any movement of popular enthusiasm behind it. For three centuries the regional idea was the plaything of a few British officials and parliamentarians, aided and abetted, on occasion, by white planters and merchants. Even when the issue of federation became intertwined with the movement towards self-government, it remained the preserve of the politicians; with the brief exception of the series of lectures on federation given by Eric Williams in Trinidad in 1955 and 1956,[44] none of them sought to bring the question before the mass of the people. The West Indies Federal Labour Party was primarily a coalition of expediency welded together to fight the federal elections of 1958; it was certainly not conceived with a propagandist role in mind.[45]

The regional press, for its part, failed to carry on the federal tradition of the old *West Indian* under Marryshow's editorship, whilst the University College of the West Indies was too wedded to its vision of itself as a colonial Oxbridge to take on the burden of popular education. In short, the whole federal debate was conducted in isolation from popular life. Small wonder that on the one occasion when the verdict of the people was required – in Jamaica in 1961 when the political elite was divided and in need of an arbiter – the resulting vote was finally opposed to any further participation in the federal venture.

For all their historical experience of regional organisation, most West Indians have, therefore, been left with a strong sense of their homeland. Indeed, one of the most striking features of the region's political culture is, and always has been, the intensity of insular self-regard. In psychological terms this is no doubt perfectly understandable, but it nevertheless creates at times its own theatre of the absurd. One finds, for example, that not only is Carriacou, one of the tiny island dependencies of tiny Grenada, typically conscious of its own individuality in relation to Grenada, but that, in turn, the people of its dependency, the even tinier island of Petit Martinique, identify scarcely at all with the people of Carriacou. Insularity of this fervour traditionally begets an ignorance and suspicion of the other islands, which is maintained by the existence of stereotyped images, like the traditional Jamaican contempt for 'small island' problems and the renowned self-esteem of Barbadians. Everyone in the Caribbean knows, for example, the characteristic, if apocryphal, story of the telegram pledging support for the British government at the beginning of the last – or, for that matter, any – war which read, 'Go on England, Barbados is behind you'. It was usually not until he went abroad (and that until recently was a privilege of the rich and educated) that the ordinary Jamaican or Trinidadian found himself treated as a West Indian, thanks largely (it must be said) to the ignorance of Europeans and Americans who very often could not distinguish between the various West Indian islands, let alone appreciate the subtleties of their respective self-images. For the rest, the island, in Selvon's phrase, was the world.[46]

The most notable feature of the history of intra-regional

relations in the West Indies is, then, the fact that the multifold nature of those relations has not led to the development of a strong, popular sense of community in the region. Both centripetal and centrifugal forces have been at work simultaneously; that much is virtually a truism, but it does not take the analysis very far at all. It seems, however, that their interaction has taken place in a particular way, which is obscured if all the emphasis is given to the notion of regional integration. The writer would argue that, on the contrary, the fundamental characteristics of regional international history in the Caribbean have always been fragmentation, isolation and insularity, and that the bouts of integrative activity have only reflected transient and passing reactions to the irrationality, impracticality or simply the inelegance of this underlying pattern. The point which needs to be made is that regional activity in the West Indies − eye-catching though it may have been − has been an essentially superficial phenomenon when set against a back-cloth on which has always been depicted severe political and economic fragmentation. In the political arena, the island has never been superseded as the main unit of action, from the point of view of both government and opposition, whilst in the economic sphere the same is true, except that, if anything, the islands have had even fewer and weaker links. Thus, in the context of this study, the significance of the Federation's dramatic collapse in September 1961 lies in the fact that, both politically and economically, it seemed to represent the triumph of regional fragmentation in the history of the West Indies.

Notes

1. D. Lowenthal, *West Indian Societies*, London, 1972, p. 8.
2. Much of the account of intra-regional relations which follows in the next two sections is drawn from the excellent survey by J. H. Proctor in 'The Development of the Idea of Federation of the British Caribbean Territories', *Caribbean Quarterly*, vol. 5, no. 1, 1957, pp. 5-33. All references are to this unless otherwise specified.
3. J. Sanderson, *A Report of the Working of the Federal System of Government in the Colony of the Leeward Islands*, Barbados, 1877, pp. 36-9, quoted in D. Lowenthal, 'Levels of West Indian Government', *Social and Economic Studies*, vol. 11, no. 4, 1962, p. 383.
4. For a fuller account, see B. Hamilton, *Barbados and the Confederation*

The paradox of regional history

Question, London, 1956.

5. C. Harris, 'The Constitutional History of the Windwards', *Caribbean Quarterly*, vol. 6, nos. 2 and 3, 1960, p. 172.

6. The original formulation of this notion is to be found in L. Best and K. Levitt *et al.*, *Externally Propelled Industrialization and Growth in the Caribbean*, Montreal, 1968.

7. E. Williams, *From Columbus to Castro: The History of the Caribbean, 1492-1969*, London, 1970, p. 116.

8. *Report by the Hon. E. F. L. Wood, M.P., on His Visit to the West Indies and British Guiana, December 1921 to February 1922*, Cmd. 1679, London, 1922, p. 29.

9. *Ibid.*, pp. 32-3.

10. *Report of the Closer Union Commission (Leeward Islands, Windward Islands, Trinidad and Tobago)*, Cmd. 4383, London, 1933, p. iv.

11. *Ibid.*, p. 33.

12. *Report of the West Indian Royal Commission 1938/9*, Cmd. 6607, London, 1945, Chapter XVIII, Sections 8-9.

13. *Ibid.*, Section 9.

14. 402 House of Commons Debates, 5s., c. 466, quoted in Proctor, *Caribbean Quarterly*, p. 26.

15 L. Braithwaite, 'Progress toward Federation, 1938-1956', *Social and Economic Studies*, vol. 6, no. 2, 1957, p. 162.

16 *Report of the West Indian Conference*, Cmd. 2672, London, 1926, paragraph 3.

17. H. Corkran Jr., *Patterns of International Cooperation in the Caribbean, 1942-69*, Dallas, 1970, Introduction.

18. G. K. Lewis, *The Growth of the Modern West Indies*, New York, 1968, p. 350.

19. Braithwaite, 'Progress towards Federation', *Social and Economic Studies*, p. 176.

20. See L. Braithwaite, ' "Federal" Associations and Institutions in the West Indies', *Social and Economic Studies*, vol. 6, no. 2, 1957, pp. 286-328.

21. *Report of the Conference on the Closer Association of the British West Indian Colonies, Montego Bay, Jamaica, 11-19 September 1947*, Cmd. 7291, London, 1948, Part I, p. 3.

22. These various points of view are well illustrated in J. H. Proctor, 'The Functional Approach to Political Union: Lessons from the Effort to Federate the British Caribbean Territories', *International Organisation*, vol. 10, no. 1, 1956, pp. 46-8.

23. The best account of the Federation is J. S. Mordecai, *The West Indies: The Federal Negotiations*, London, 1968.

24. *Memorandum on the Closer Association of the British West Indian Colonies*, Cmd. 7120, London, 1947, Part II, paragraph 11.

25. *Proceedings of the Conference on the Closer Association of the British West Indian Colonies, Montego Bay, Jamaica, 11-19 September 1947*, Col. no. 218, London, 1948, submission of Mr N. W. Manley (Caribbean Commission).

26. H. W. Springer, *Reflections on the Failure of the First West Indian Federation*, Harvard, 1962, p. 42.

27. *Report of Conference on Closer Association of British West Indian Colonies*, Cmd. 7291, Resolution 2. My emphasis.
28. *Proceedings of Conference on Closer Association of British West Indian Colonies*, Col. no. 218, submissions of Mr Alexander Bustamante (Jamaica) and Mr A. Gomes (Trinidad).
29. W. A. Lewis, *Industrial Development in the Caribbean*, Port of Spain, 1951. The pamphlet, published under the auspices of the Caribbean Commission, contained two articles by Lewis: 'Industrial Development in Puerto Rico', originally published in *The Caribbean Economic Review*, vol. 1, nos. 1 and 2, 1949, and 'The Industrialization of the British West Indies', originally in *The Caribbean Economic Review*, vol. 2, no. 1, 1950.
30. By the group of New World economists. See N. Girvan and O. Jefferson (eds.), *Readings in the Political Economy of the Caribbean*, Kingston, Jamaica, 1971, Introduction, p. 1.
31. For the source of the discussion above and for a fuller account of the economic history of Jamaica and Trinidad in these years, see O. Jefferson, *The Post-war Economic Development of Jamaica*, Kingston, Jamaica, 1972, and S. D. Ryan, *Race and Nationalism in Trinidad and Tobago: A Study of Decolonization in a Multiracial Society*, Toronto, 1972, pp. 384-428.
32. Mordecai, *op. cit.*, p. 33.
33. Quoted in *ibid.*, p. 41.
34 Springer, *op. cit.*, pp. 18-19.
35. A. Etzioni, *Political Unification: A Comparative Study of Leaders and Forces*, New York, 1965, p. 149.
36. Government of Trinidad and Tobago, Office of the Premier and Ministry of Finance, *The Economics of Nationhood*, Port of Spain, 1959.
37. For a discussion of these themes, see G. K. Lewis, *op. cit.*, pp. 377-83.
38. See *Report of the Commission on the Establishment of a Customs Union in the British Caribbean Area* (McLagan Commission), Col. no. 268, London, 1950; *The Plan for a British Caribbean Federation. Report of the Fiscal Commissioner* (Caine Report), Cmd. 9618, London, 1955; and *Report of the Trade and Tariffs Commission* (Croft Report), West Indies Federal Government, Port of Spain, 1958. For a commentary on these various reports and a discussion of the politics of a customs union during the Federation period, see Mordecai, *op. cit.*, especially pp. 42-3, 48-50, 55-6, 59-60, 163-4, 214-16, and 264-7.
39. E. Williams, 'Speech to PNM Special Convention, 27 January 1962', *The Nation*, vol. 4, no. 19, 2 February 1962.
40. J. Millette, 'Review Article – "The West Indies: The Federal Negotiations"', *Social and Economic Studies*, vol. 18, no. 4, 1969, p. 415.
41. S. S. Ramphal, 'Federalism in the West Indies', *Caribbean Quarterly*, vol. 6, nos. 3 and 4, 1960, p. 211.
42. G. K. Lewis, *op. cit.*, p. 344.
43. *Ibid.*
44. E. Williams, *The Pros and Cons of Federation*, Port of Spain, 1955.
45. See Mordecai, *op. cit.*, pp. 80-1, 86-9 and 171-2.
46. *An Island is a World* was the title of a novel written in 1955 by the eminent Trinidadian writer, Samuel Selvon.

PART I

Origins and establishment

CHAPTER ONE

The vision of an economic community

As the result of the Jamaican referendum gradually emerged in September 1961, the prevailing response amongst supporters of the regional idea throughout the West Indies was a mixture of despair and uncertainty. The economist Norman Girvan, who at the time was an undergraduate at the University of the West Indies, has talked of the 'sense of shock' he experienced upon hearing the news, 'the feeling that a whole world had collapsed'.[1] Others tried to conceal their disappointment as much as possible by a display of bombast and bravado. The Chief Minister of St Lucia, George Charles, prophesied at a public meeting in Castries that, one day, Jamaica would 'come crawling at the feet of the Big Little Eight, begging to be let into the Federation'.[2] Not many, though, can have found that a very realistic prospect as they read reports of bells being rung throughout Jamaica – 'from Negril Point to Morant Point'[3] – in celebration of the crushing defeat which the federal cause had clearly suffered. To most federalists, the referendum looked like the end of a long road.

There were, however, some hardened optimists, who professed to see the referendum result as a blessing in disguise, which offered an unexpected opportunity to rebuild a strongly centralised federation, unencumbered by the restraining influence of Jamaica. They immediately turned their attention to the exploitation of this possibility and, in particular, to the question of Trinidad's attitude, for Trinidad, easily the largest and wealthiest of the remaining units, would be required to sustain any new federation virtually single-handed. The chances of her agreeing to undertake this role were at best unpromising: during the previous year Williams had said on a number of occasions that, if Jamaica seceded from the Federation, Trinidad would have to seriously consider following suit.[4] There seemed, moreover, little chance that he would change his mind given that, during the latter part of the life of the Federation, verbal communication had virtually broken down between the region's leaders.

Nevertheless, on the night of the referendum Professor Arthur Lewis, then Principal of the University of the West Indies and an old friend of the Trinidad Premier, hurried to see Williams in the hope of persuading him to keep Trinidad within the federal fold. He later recalled the meeting:

> Dr Williams was in a very bad mood ... [and] ... was absolutely fed up with most of the principal characters. Fortunately he had already decided to lie low, and say nothing for the time being. It was clear that if forced to speak, he would simply announce that Trinidad too was coming out of the Federation and seeking its independence ... He would have nothing whatever to do with the Grantley Adams Federation; that must pack up and its leaders disappear.[5]

Williams, however, did affirm that he still stood by the principles of *The Economics of Nationhood*, and agreed that Lewis should embark upon a tour of the other West Indian islands to test out the ground for a continuation of the Federation on those lines. At Williams's bidding, the governing party in Trinidad, the People's National Movement (PNM), announced that no decision would be taken on the future of the Federation until after the general elections due in Trinidad that December: the question would not even be discussed during the forthcoming campaign.[6] Having thus neatly sidestepped the danger of losing votes from small islanders resident in Trinidad, Williams was prepared, for the moment, to leave the federal question in the air and to concentrate his efforts upon the task of defeating the electoral challenge of the opposition Democratic Labour Party.

Since all the other governments in the eastern Caribbean were extremely anxious not to precipitate Trinidad's secession whilst Lewis's rescue mission still had a chance of success, Williams's stance forced them to adopt a similar policy of silence. However, as Lewis later realised, his valiant attempt to retrieve the situation was doomed to failure from the outset:

> So I set off touring all the islands, selling 'The Economics of Nationhood'. This was a mistake. At that time 'The Economics of Nationhood' was already impossible. In that document Trinidad had offered to bear an enormous proportion of the cost of running the islands. The mood in which such generosity was possible had long since evaporated. I was in the position of a salesman taking orders for a product which the company had already discontinued.[7]

Orders, though, there definitely were: according to his report,[8] Lewis found that there was a good deal of interest in a federation of the remaining nine territories and that former objections to a strong federal constitution had been much reduced by the alternative prospect of there being no federation at all. Lewis felt able to propose in his report a central government with even stronger powers than that envisaged in *The Economics of Nationhood*.

In the meantime, Williams had advanced the notion – which was more than questionable legally – that the Federation would be dissolved automatically at the moment of Jamaica's withdrawal. In his view, therefore, there was no relevance to the debate about whether Trinidad should, or should not, remain in the Federation. That mess was finished, and the only issue worthy of consideration was what structure of association might replace it. At a press conference on 5 November 1961, Williams strove to keep his options open. A federation of the nine was not to be ruled out, but nor was the possibility of Trinidad proceeding alone to independence. 'I am quite open', he observed, 'anything is possible'.[9] His closest associates, however, in both the PNM and in the government were fiercely opposed to *any* arrangement involving the small islands and were urging him to lead Trinidad to independence,[10] a status Jamaica was clearly soon going to achieve. On 7 December the PNM executive established a committee to study the problem and report back to a special party convention, scheduled for 27–28

January 1962. 'Whether by design or not', it seemed that 'the committee contained several persons who were known to favour a federal solution'.[11]

It was at this juncture that Reginald Maudling, the new Secretary of State for the Colonies, announced his intention to visit Trinidad at the beginning of 1962. Williams presumably suspected that Maudling's motive was to press Trinidad to remain within the Federation, and in order to forestall this tactic he abandoned the committee procedure he had only just initiated and called an extraordinary meeting of the General Council of the party for Sunday, 14 January, which, ominously, was the day before Maudling was due to arrive. In the event, Maudling arrived on the very Sunday of the meeting and before the end of the day was brought news of a resolution passed by the General Council. It read as follows:

> BE IT THEREFORE RESOLVED, That Trinidad and Tobago reject unequivocally any participation in a Federation of the Eastern Caribbean, and proceed forthwith to National Independence, without prejudice to the future incorporation in the unitary state of Trinidad and Tobago of any Territory of the Eastern Caribbean whose people may so desire, and, on terms to be mutually agreed or to the future establishment of a Common Economic Community embracing the entire Caribbean area.[12]

Apart from a few, minor changes in phraseology, the resolution was subsequently endorsed by the party convention with a unanimity which, according to Williams, had 'never been exceeded in PNM's history.'[13] It was of critical importance in determining the future pattern of international relations in the Caribbean and, therefore, merits close attention.

Belying the haste with which the whole decision seemed to have been taken, the text of the resolution bore the hallmarks of diligent preparation. It was supported, for example, by sixteen tables of statistics and preceded by twenty-three 'Whereases', which carefully presented the economic case against federation and for independence. In the first place, the resolution noted that Trinidad's trade with the other eight territories which were still interested in federation only amounted to TT$16 million p.a. out of a total external trade of TT$897 million p.a., and it proceeded to question how valuable this market would be in the light of the 'injudicious duplication'[14] in Barbados and many of the other eastern Caribbean islands of a number of industries already established in Trinidad. Trinidad (it went on to argue) had already wasted a lot of time and money on the Federation and could not afford the many additional burdens which she would be bound to incur in any new federation. These, it was suggested, would include not only the revenue contribution (75 per cent of the total) envisaged in the Lewis scheme, but the cost of sustaining the administrative structures of all the units after grants-in-aid from the British Treasury had been suspended, the assumption of the net public debt of the union as a whole, the prospect of considerable population migration into Trinidad and, finally, the mass of complicated problems which would inevitably arise from the disparate levels of economic development prevailing amongst the various units. In sum, the little islands of the eastern Caribbean were portrayed as wholly unmitigated burdens, likely to sap the well-being and prosperity of Trinidad in any future federation, whilst, by comparison, the case against independence was largely ignored. Indeed, to combat charges that Trinidad was too small and poor to be able to sustain independence, statistics were adduced to show that she was better positioned to do so than many of the states in Africa and Asia that were already fully independent.

At any rate, the PNM convention was wholeheartedly convinced by the case made out in the resolution. In 'a long and effective speech'[15] (his own words), Williams argued that there was a further 'solid political factor'[16] to be considered were the party to opt for federation. That was the possibility that an opposition minority in Trinidad could come to control the Trinidad economy by virtue of participating in the federal government. Delegates were asked to consider whether they could be sure that this would not occur in any new federation. 'You could be sure of it', Williams told them, 'in a unitary state'.[17] Williams at this stage appeared to have a peculiar attachment to the unitary state idea, admitting to Arthur Lewis on the night of the Jamaican referendum that his mind was moving in that direction.[18] From a negative point of view, he clearly did not relish the prospect of embarking once again upon a round of seemingly endless negotiations with the other political leaders of the region over the detailed structure of a federation. But, in addition to that, the idea undoubtedly appealed to his egotistical temperament and, in a way, reflected his enduring anger with the leaders of the other eastern Caribbean islands. If they preferred to remain 'tupenny rulers' of tiny colonies, rather than be saved by the PNM, 'the undisputed intellectual leaders of the colonial nationalist movement in this part of the world',[19] then so be it. He had made his offer, viz, 'one single state ruled by one single party, the PNM, which lays down the blueprint for legislation and development'.[20] Although Mordecai reports that Williams apparently anticipated 'that both Grenada and St Vincent would accept it, and he hoped that St Lucia and Dominica might follow'[21] – 'he said so, privately, at the time'[22] – it does seem that the supporters of independence in the party and in the Cabinet only tolerated the offer of a unitary state because they were sure it was utterly impracticable and could never be realised.[23] After all, the economic arguments advanced against an Eastern Caribbean Federation in the resolution of January 1962 were even more powerful when applied to the concept of an Eastern Caribbean unitary state. On its own, for example, the cost of raising the general level of public salaries and services in the rest of the eastern Caribbean to that prevailing in Trinidad would have been prohibitive.

The General Council resolution must, therefore, be seen as a compromise between conflicting tendencies within the leadership of the PNM. In retrospect, however, we can see that the pro-federalists in Trinidad were decisively outmanoeuvred. A sub-committee of the party's policy committee, which had been appointed to study the question of migration within the eastern Caribbean, had come out in favour of federation, but its report was not circulated at the convention and the author was reportedly discouraged from defending it at the General Council meeting.[24] At the convention itself there was little support in the party for participation in an Eastern Caribbean Federation and an alternative motion, setting out this option, was withdrawn before it could be voted upon.[25] The 'independence' wing in the party was clearly in the ascendancy, and their victory was only tempered by Williams's own insistence that Trinidad's policy should have a regional dimension in some form or other. Both as an historian and as a politician he had long been one of the foremost apostles of West Indian federation, and as Research Officer of the erstwhile Caribbean Commission he had developed 'a truly Caribbean vision which, in 1932 in Trinidad, had been limited to Trinidad and Tobago, and in 1939 had expanded at Oxford to embrace the British West Indies'.[26] Indeed, in his autobiography he felt able to refer to himself as the 'intellectual spokesman of the Caribbean peoples ... a West Indian who had more direct and closer contact, historically and actually, with the Caribbean area as a whole than any other'.[27] It was from this background that there sprung the idea of an Eastern Caribbean unitary state, albeit dominated by Trinidad, and the concept of a wider Caribbean Economic Community. To convinced federalists, however, these two proposals looked 'suspiciously like an attempt to justify a crime against the present by a promise of adequate compensation in the dim, distant and remote future'.[28]

Nevertheless, most Trinidadians were content to follow the lead offered by the PNM – as equally they would have been if the nod had been given to another federation. During the early part of the federal period there had undoubtedly been a considerable degree of enthusiasm for 'West Indianism' in Trinidad, much of it inspired by the personality of Williams himself. But in a period of growing affluence for the majority of Trinidadians, it was a sentiment which Williams could dissipate as effectively as arouse. This he clearly realised, intimating as much in a speech in the election campaign at the end of 1961:

> We know that we enjoy the confidence of the population to such an extent that we merely have to explain the issues, the pros and cons, argue this and argue that, and the whole population, when it sees the issues ... would go along as one united nation on this issue. ... They tell me that 99 per cent of the people in the country would follow blindly whatever I say on Federation.[29]

And certainly it was true that most of the population of Trinidad was uninterested in, and unappreciative of, the subtle difference that existed between a federation, a unitary state and a Caribbean Economic Community.

Not so, of course, the leaders of the other eastern Caribbean

The vision of an economic community

islands, who were more than aware of all the implications of each proposal. As a result, the initial impact of the PNM resolution upon the regional future of the Caribbean was disruptive.[30] When they heard the text of the resolution, the leaders of the eight remaining territories, who were all in Trinidad to consult with Maudling, agreed between themselves to form a new federation and (Gairy, the Premier of Grenada, briefly excepted)[31] to ignore Trinidad's unitary state offer. Maudling appeared dubious, questioning the practicality of their plan, but was persuaded in the end that a merger with Trinidad – which in the view of the Colonial Office was the neatest solution – was indeed impossible. In his own talks with Maudling, Williams made no attempt to pursue the unitary state idea, whilst, for their part, the leaders of the other eastern Caribbean islands privately made it clear that they had no intention of bowing to the terms offered by Trinidad, terms which they took to be the portent of a new local imperialism which would require their small island units to abandon their individuality and become wards of Trinidad after the example of Tobago. The new Premier of Barbados, Errol Barrow, who had flown to see Williams the previous December to offer his co-operation in building an Eastern Caribbean federation, articulated their views when some months later he referred to the PNM offer as 'the most gratuitous insult that could ever have been extended to any group of people'.[32] Faced with this response, Maudling had no alternative but to give his encouragement to a new federation of the Eight and proceed with the formal winding up of the old ten-member Federation. He announced these decisions to the Federal Cabinet on 25 January 1962, explaining that an enabling Act would be passed in the British House of Commons in March so that the Federation could subsequently be dissolved by an Order in Council. The meeting was a desultory affair, as Mordecai's account makes clear:

> the odour of failure hung heavy in the room. There was no discussion or protest. Two junior Ministers started to remonstrate but their voices soon trailed off. The Prime Minister [Adams] slumped forward staring dejectedly at one spot on the table before him, at the end stirring himself to mutter thanks to the Secretary of State'.[33]

Yet, from the federalist point of view, even worse was still to come. The leaders of the 'Little Eight' met in Barbados at the end of February 1962 and speedily agreed upon a federal constitution. Another conference in London in May also proceeded smoothly, and the proposals arising out of the Barbados meeting were substantially accepted. In Lewis's judgement, they constituted 'an excellent foundation for a new federation'.[34] However, while the British government temporised over the amount of financial aid the federation would require, the unitary state idea again raised its head. In elections in Grenada in August 1962, the opposition party campaigned strongly in favour of unitary statehood. As Lewis put it, 'the pro-Trinidad party offered access to the riches of Trinidad's oil wells. The pro-Federation party offered nothing, since the treasury would not talk'.[35] This tactic enabled it to win an easy victory, and the new government of Grenada accordingly broke away from the 'Little Eight' effort and opened negotiations with Trinidad. Confronted with this test of the sincerity of its policy, the Trinidad government stalled, while the East Indian opposition in Trinidad, upon whose support the scheme depended since it involved a change in the constitution, began to voice its dissent more loudly. Not unnaturally, East Indians viewed the idea of a unitary state as a shady plot to provide the PNM (which was overwhelmingly African-supported) with sufficient imported black votes to establish a one-party dictatorship over the Indian community. At any rate as far as the attempt to build another federation was concerned, the Eight had become the Seven, and they were being forced to await the appearance of reports prepared by the endless number of commissions which the Colonial Office had insisted on appointing to survey the economic needs and problems of the area. It was obvious, even to participants in the negotiations, that much of the early momentum behind the projected Eastern Caribbean federation had already been lost.

In the meantime, there were decisions to be taken about the future of the common services which between 1958 and 1962 had been administered on a regional basis by the federal government. For the sake of these at least some sort of *modus vivendi* had to be worked out between the ex-members of the

Federation. The Interim Commissioner appointed by the British government, Sir Stephen Luke (an ironic choice, since he had been Comptroller for Development and Welfare and Pre-federal Commissioner in the West Indies in the 1950s) accordingly called an inter-governmental conference in Port of Spain in July 1962 to deal with such matters. Euphemistically called the 'Common Services Conference', it had all the characteristics of the wake at which members of the deceased's family gather to dispose of his few pieces of bric-à-brac. Nevertheless, the business was conducted relatively efficiently and there proved to be limits to the 'spill-back' involved in the dissolution of the Federation. Even those who had been opposed to the concept of federation realised that shared services would be less costly and more effective than similar services operated at the local territorial level. The attitude of the Jamaican government was, as it said itself, 'to ensure that any service which it would be in Jamaica's interest to continue on a regional basis would be supported'.[36] Such a view did not contain much room for regional sentiment, but it did prove conducive to hard, if somewhat sour, bargaining.

In the result it was decided to maintain the Federal Shipping Service (two ships, gifts from Canada) and establish a Ministerial Council to supervise its management; to continue certain research schemes funded by the Colonial Development and Welfare Organisation; to accept a Trinidad government offer for many of the physical assets of the Federation; to preserve the Regional Labour Board office in Washington with all previous members, except Trinidad; and to carry on with the Meteorological Service, although the 'Little Eight' territories, who spoke with more or less one voice throughout, indicated that they would withdraw in September 1963. Most important of all, the delegates agreed to support the University of the West Indies on its existing regional basis for at least three further triennia. Some months earlier, British Guiana had declared its intention of withdrawing and establishing its own College of Arts and Sciences as the nucleus of a future university; but further tentative moves at the Common Services Conference, suggesting that Trinidad (whose St Augustine campus possessed the agriculture and the engineering faculties) might also cease to support the University, were sharply reversed when the Trinidad delegation heard on the local radio station the contents of a speech given by Williams to West Indian students in London in which he pledged his unreserved support for a single first-class university in the region.

Not all the outstanding issues could be settled, however. Both Jamaica and Trinidad were reluctant actually to pay the contributions which they had promised to the federal government when it undertook to expand the West India regiment, whilst no agreement could be reached on the precise conditions under which the Federal Development Loan and Guarantee Fund should continue to operate. Finally, the conference could not reach unanimity on the proposal to establish a permanent organisation to supervise the limited regional infrastructure which still remained in existence. This was significant: it demonstrated more clearly than any other factor that the conference saw itself only as the final act of a long and protracted drama, rather than as the prologue to a new era.

The immediate aftermath of the referendum vote in Jamaica in September 1961 was thus 'a time of dismantling and of falling apart in the Caribbean'.[37] The Federation was legally dissolved on 1 June 1962, and Jamaica and Trinidad became independent on 6 and 31 August respectively. As we have seen, only a nucleus remained of the common services administered under the direction of the Federation. British Guiana, which took no part in the Federation, had moved even further away from her regional neighbours by withdrawing from the University of the West Indies; Grenada had opted to dangle at the end of a string unwillingly held by Trinidad; whilst the energy with which the remaining seven territories had initially embarked on the construction of a new federation was slowly evaporating. Many, indeed, thought that the parting of the ways was permanent and that the prospect of a united West Indies had disappeared for ever. In retrospect, though, this same period can also be seen to contain the very tentative beginnings of a process of rebuilding the regional community in a less formal and structured manner. The first sign of this had been the reference in the PNM resolution of January 1962 to the creation of a Caribbean

Economic Community. At the time, the air was filled with dramatic denunciations of Trinidad's betrayal of Caribbean history by refusing to participate in another federation, and little attention was paid to this particular aspect of the statement. To his credit, however, Williams was the first to perceive that federation was but *one* manifestation of the regional idea and that, in other words, it was only a mechanism and not necessarily the best available at that. In his speech to the PNM convention in January 1962 he portrayed the proposal for a Caribbean Economic Community, embracing not just the British West Indies but the wider Caribbean as a whole, as 'nothing short of a revolution in Caribbean society with its history of disunity and separation, metropolitan domination and outward looking.'[38] Pan-Caribbeanism, it seemed, had always been his real goal, since, as he pointed out, Trinidad's best customers in terms of export sales were not the states which had been in the Federation at all, but other Caribbean territories like Curaçao, British Guiana, Surinam and Guadeloupe.[39]

Williams's immediate preoccupation in the first half of 1962 was, of course, the negotiation of Trinidad's independence, and it was not until this was finalised that he began to concentrate his attention upon the specific manner in which he planned to implement the commitment he had given to create a Caribbean Economic Community. It seems, though, that the key to his thinking at this early stage was the British application to join the European Economic Community, submitted at the end of 1961. Williams undoubtedly realised a good deal sooner than other West Indian leaders that this move would seriously prejudice Britain's ability to continue absorbing on preferential terms the bulk of the West Indies' exports of primary products and that, since West Indian agricultural production was widely thought to be higher-cost than that of competing countries, this would gravely threaten the viability of the entire regional economy.[40] In this light, he saw a number of tangible advantages in Trinidad seeking Associate Status with the EEC: not only would it safeguard Trinidad's economic connection with Britain, but it might open up the possibility of there being forged a Caribbean Economic Community of states similarly associated. Williams had already held trade talks in March 1962 with the Prime Minister of Surinam, whose application for EEC association was then being processed in Brussels, and he did so again in August of that year. In June he held discussions with the French government in Paris on the possibility of opening negotiations with Martinique and Guadeloupe, which, as Overseas Departments of France, were already embraced by the Treaty of Rome, and in October he was in Holland, discussing his plans with the Dutch government.

Even critics of Williams's strategy had to admit that there was a certain rationale behind it,[41] deriving, in large part, from the way in which it was proposed to utilise the root cause of the segmentation of the Caribbean region, namely, its division by rival European imperialisms, as the basis for a new sort of regional integration. The strategy's basic defect, on the other hand, was its misconception of the nature of 'independence', commentators rightly arguing that the 'real independence of the Caribbean as well as integration cannot take place under conditions in which so much initiative is left in European hands'.[42] There was no time, though, and perhaps not much inclination, to initiate a debate on such fundamental issues: at the Commonwealth Prime Ministers' Conference in September, 1962 – the first attended by Jamaica and Trinidad – Bustamante, who had been elected the first Prime Minister of Jamaica, expressed open disagreement with the Trinidad government's thinking on the question of Associate Status, and, reflecting a general Jamaican caution about Williams's ideas on the subject of a Caribbean Economic Community, went on to assert that he could see no way in which the Treaty of Rome could be of benefit to either the Commonwealth or the Caribbean.[43] Before this breach could be healed, however, British negotiations with the EEC broke down and the prospect of a Caribbean association of Associates receded into the distance.

Williams was forced, therefore, to rethink the whole conception of a Caribbean Economic Community. He may for a while have hoped that the United Nations could be induced to take over as sponsor of the economic integration of the West Indies, and said as much when opening a meeting of the Food and Agriculture Organisation Cocoa Study Group in Port of Spain in March 1963.[44] This idea seemed, though, to be just a passing thought and was not heard of again. Williams turned instead to a somewhat more realistic attempt to repair Trinidad's standing with her neighbours and ex-partners in the Commonwealth Caribbean. A visit to Jamaica in February 1963, which led to an agreement to exchange High Commissions and establish a joint working party of officials to examine trade matters, was followed a month later by talks in Georgetown. These ranged over a number of areas of collaboration, but Williams, in particular, extorted a promise from the British Guiana government to reconsider its decision to develop colleges of engineering, agriculture and medicine under the regime of its own national university in exchange for Trinidadian agreement to pay more for the rice it purchased from British Guiana. In April 1963 Williams was in Barbados, and it emerged that an ulterior purpose of his extensive travelling had been to arrange a summit meeting of the region's heads of government.

The hope was that a series of such conferences would lead to the creation of a loose, informal association of Caribbean states. Williams has himself given this explanation of Trinidad's diplomacy:

> Our next move towards the achievement of a Caribbean Economic Community... was to organise what has come to be called the Conference of Heads of Government of Commonwealth Caribbean countries. I cleared the way personally for this private and informal discussion with the Prime Minister of Jamaica and the Premiers of Barbados and British Guiana... I took as my model the Organisation of African Unity, and proposed the limitation of our meetings to Heads of independent and self-governing countries, so as not to be involved in consideration of Britain's responsibility for the non-self-governing countries of the Caribbean.
>
> I was particularly careful to check this point with Errol Barrow, and he was insistent that the smaller countries should be left out, and that if there was to be any contact with these smaller countries... Barbados would undertake to be the intermediary through the Regional Council of Ministers.
>
> Both Jamaica and British Guiana also felt that the

Conference should be limited to fully-governing and independent countries.

Our own view in Trinidad and Tobago was from the start that the Conference should be extended as soon as possible to include the non-British Caribbean countries in the area which were not colonies in the strict sense of the word or whose semi-colonial status would be ignored for present purposes. We were not prepared, however, to extend this concept to the Caribbean republics of Cuba, Haiti and Santo Domingo – not at that stage – because of the obvious difficulty of associating with regimes which were hostile to the democratic processes developed and practised in Jamaica, Trinidad and Tobago, British Guiana and Barbados. But our colleagues would not go along with this thought, and preferred to limit our Conference to Commonwealth countries in the Caribbean.[45]

Thus it was that the First Heads of Government Conference met in Port of Spain at the end of July 1963 and was attended by high-level delegations from Trinidad, Jamaica, Barbados and British Guiana – the 'Big Four' of the Commonwealth Caribbean. Mindful of the short lapse of time since the dissolution of the Federation, it was something that the meeting took place at all. In his opening speech Bustamante infused the proceedings with a cold douche of realism by making it clear 'that this is not a conference to revive federation – that is stone cold dead'.[46] Otherwise the discussions were conducted in a friendly manner, and, in the view of Donald Sangster, the Jamaican Deputy Prime Minister, the conference served at least 'to stabilise and improve the image of the Caribbean ... in the eyes of the world',[47] something which was very necessary in the light of the bad publicity aroused internationally by the federal saga. It cannot be said, though, that the decisions taken were memorable. The record shows that the heads of government prepared a long statement setting out the region's requirements in terms of economic and technical aid, agreed to protest to Venezuela about the 30 per cent surtax placed on her imports from the West Indies and to concert their representations to Britain on the subject of the Commonwealth Immigration Act, and, finally, promised to examine together the issues arising in respect of the forthcoming World Trade Conference. Many of the presentations were also over-hastily prepared and a

The vision of an economic community 41

projected British Guiana paper on a regional customs union was not even submitted owing to a civil servants' strike in Georgetown just before the conference began. In short, the conference failed to face up to the fundamental issues of Caribbean economic underdevelopment. For the most part the issues discussed could have been handled by normal government-to-government contact, many of them probably at civil servant level. In an interesting newspaper article, published during the conference, the Trinidadian economist, Lloyd Best, set out what he thought *should* have been the agenda for the meeting. It was as follows:

AGENDA. Exploratory Talks on Basic Issues

I. Objectives of Economic Planning

i) Diversification of the productive base of the Caribbean economies.

ii) Population and employment policy against a background of rapid population expansion.

iii) Meeting the demands of the population for social welfare with special reference to health and housing facilities.

iv) An institutional framework for intra-regional trade and transport.

v) Establishment of a regional framework of financial institutions.

vi) Development of a regional system of Higher Education.

II. Objectives of Foreign Policy

i) Definition of an ideological position compatible with the independence of separate national systems and permissive of international collaboration.

ii) Articulation of an ideological basis for the granting and accepting of aid.

iii) Enunciation of a scheme for changing the terms of international trade in favour of a more democratic distribution of world income with special reference to the pricing of oil, bauxite, sugar, bananas, citrus, cocoa and coffee.

iv) A programme for the movement of peoples from less developed to more developed areas. Immigration to North America, Oceania and Western Europe including the Soviet Union.

III. Immediate Collaboration on Urgent Problems

    i) Financing the next series of Territorial Five-Year development plans.
    ii) World Trade Conference, 1964.
    iii) The Venezuelan Surtax.
    iv) The maintenance and development of British West Indian Airways as a regional carrier.
    v) Regionalisation of the approach to tourist promotion.
    vi) North American and British tax arrangements as a factor in regional investment.
    vii) Co-ordination of incentive legislation.
    viii) Dissolution of the Eastern Caribbean Currency Board.
    ix) Appraisal of the University of the West Indies.
    x) Problems of West Indian immigration to Britain (Legal Aid and the Commonwealth Bill).
    xi) A solution to the problem of British Guiana.
    xii) A Caribbean approach to the Cuban question.[48]

In tacit recognition that Best's criticism of the conference's preoccupation with trivia was justified, Williams subsequently admitted that 'what was important was not altogether what we achieved ... but the fact that we were meeting in order to try and find common ground and in order to lay the foundations for some more comprehensive understanding'.[49] In that perspective the most important achievement of the conference was the decision to meet again in Jamaica in January 1964.

At this Second Heads of Government Conference the discussion was again dominated by technical and functional matters with only a limited political dimension — the setting of secondary school exams, for example, the provision of a social centre for West Indian immigrants in London, mutual disaster assistance, the Commonwealth Sugar Agreement and world trade developments. The leaders also signed a declaration on foreign policy which, although bland and unremarkable for the most part, merely recording their commitment to peace and friendship, disarmament and other universalistic principles, did demand 'recognition of the view that differences between the economic and social systems of countries should not prevent developing countries from taking advantage of expanding markets for trade'.[50] Promising, too, was the acceptance of a proposal to establish 'a permanent agency' to keep under observation the region's economic problems, but this was only done, it seemed, with a view to facilitating the acquisition of foreign economic aid on a basis that was both more generous *in toto* and more suited to the particular needs of the Caribbean. It remains doubtful that such decisions could have been reached only amidst the pomp and circumstance of a summit conference.

The one real test faced by the heads of government at their second meeting – and it was, in a sense, a test also of the whole conference strategy – was the position they would adopt over the crisis in British Guiana. The transfer of power in this Caribbean territory had had a troubled history.[51] Once the vision of a smooth transition to eventual independence had been blurred by the British government's suspension of the colony's constitution in 1953, the dominant People's Progressive Party (PPP) coalition of expediency collapsed. It split on racial lines into two parties, neither of which showed any signs of consensus on the broad issue of a constitution for a future independent Guyana. By the end of 1962 violent disturbances and killing in Georgetown and the Marxist terminology used by the East Indian Premier and PPP leader, Cheddi Jagan, had combined to make the colony a focus of international attention and a source of great worry to the other West Indian leaders. Fully understanding the way in which all the territories in the West Indies were perceived as a single unit by the outside world, Williams sent a telegram to Bustamante and Barrow in April 1963, expressing his concern 'about the possible repercussions on all of us ... if we make no effort to mediate in the British Guiana difficulty',[52] by which he meant, in particular, the general strike then gripping the territory. But, despite the fact that a number of overtures were made along these lines, including a blunt offer from Bustamante during a private session of the First Heads of Government Conference in July 1963 proposing that he initiate regional talks on a constitution for British Guiana,[53] Williams's expression of concern had still not been translated into a regional peace-keeping initiative by the end of the year.

Indeed, when the Second Heads of Government Conference opened at the beginning of 1964, the political future of British Guiana was as uncertain as ever. The three warring party leaders, Jagan, Burnham and D'Aguiar, having asked the

Secretary of State for the Colonies to resolve their inability to agree upon an independence constitution for the territory by imposing one upon them, were again at loggerheads over the solution he had proposed, which was a system of direct elections by proportional representation. As Jagan immediately realised, this opened up the possibility that he could be ousted by a coalition of the other two parties, and he denounced the scheme as a manoeuvre to prevent British Guiana moving to independence under his Marxist leadership. If it wanted to be taken seriously the Heads of Government Conference had, therefore, to take some sort of collective stand on the controversy – it was, after all, at the centre of the process of decolonisation of one of its participant territories. However, the item on the agenda which commentators presumed to have been conceived specifically to accommodate a discussion of the British Guiana question, a topic labelled 'Political and Constitutional Development', was withdrawn at the last minute at Jagan's instigation. As a sop, the four leaders met to discuss the controversy privately, away from the formalities of the conference, but they failed to achieve a meeting of minds, being unable even to agree on a proposal to continue talks on the subject the following weekend in Tobago. It is impossible to know precisely what took place, but from their own statements it seems that Williams and Jagan, in particular, fell foul of each other. The Trinidad government later released the draft of a declaration of principles drawn up by Williams and allegedly rejected by Jagan. It observed that the 'overriding principle of Caribbean survival' made it mandatory that British Guiana should achieve independence and stated that the 'imposition of a settlement by the United Kingdom, whatever its explanations, and for however temporary a period, is inconsistent with the achievement of this fundamental objective'.[54] 'Whatever the particular variations of constitutional forms or economic practices which they may adopt', it continued, those factors which the Commonwealth Caribbean had in common were 'more important than the incidental differences of emphasis or temperament which may occasionally divide them'.[55] As might be expected from a document of Williams's authorship, the draft represented a skilful blend of the different perspectives of the

The vision of an economic community

participants in the talks – Bustamante's fierce anti-Communism, Jagan's desire for support in his call for independence, and Williams's own domestic need in the light of the ethnic composition of the Trinidadian population to be seen to be assisting the leader of the East Indians in British Guiana. One might perhaps have expected Jagan to have signed, but he apparently took exception to a suggestion in the statement that the leaders had considered his 'representations' that they should use their good offices to achieve a settlement – presumably because he wanted the declaration to appear as an expression of solidarity more or less voluntarily given.[56]

Although, admittedly, this was primarily a semantic dispute, it did reflect the existence of more fundamental differences of outlook between Jagan and the other West Indian leaders which had been concealed by the uncontroversial subject matter of the first two Heads of Government Conferences. The difficulty was that Jagan's politics had a very pronounced ideological dimension, a characteristic which was lacking, for the most part, in Bustamante, Barrow and even Williams. His opening speeches at both conferences had a restless, almost revolutionary flavour not at all in keeping with the outlook of his colleagues. In Port of Spain in July 1963 he had exhorted them to 'join forces with all our brothers, wherever they may be, who are engaged in the same battle for human progress',[57] whilst in Kingston six months later he was urging them to 'stand up and be counted' on matters involving the pursuit of freedom.[58] In Jagan's view, Williams's draft statement on the British Guiana problem failed these tests by only tamely protesting against what he saw as a 'rape of democracy'. The other three heads of government, all of whom in their way were concerned to develop a consensus of opinion on the issues facing the Commonwealth Caribbean, certainly found his presence in the regional leadership more than a little unsettling.

Williams, as we know, felt that in any case membership of the Heads of Government Conference should be extended to include the leaders of a number of neighbouring non-Commonwealth Caribbean territories. Despite his West Indian colleagues' initial lack of enthusiasm for this idea, he was determined not to allow the coolness of their reaction to force him to abandon his aim of building a wider Caribbean Economic Community. He decided, therefore, once again to try a different approach. The alternative strategy he evolved was to concentrate discussion upon ways of improving the state of sea and air communications in the area of the Caribbean sea – something which, he argued, was the essential foundation of any increase in intra-regional trade. His own suggestions were twofold: in the realm of shipping, to extend the route plied by the two 'Federal ships' to include Puerto Rico, the Netherlands Antilles and Surinam, and in regard to air transport, to transform the Trinidad national airline, British West Indian Airways (BWIA), into a regional carrier in return for financial assistance from other territories, not excluding the purchase of shares.[59] With these aims in mind, Williams embarked upon another round of intensive diplomacy – receiving Dr Lastra, the Secretary of Commerce of Puerto Rico, in May 1964 and himself visiting San Juan in July of that year; holding talks with the French Foreign Minister also in July, and entertaining Jonckheer, the Prime Minister of the Netherlands Antilles, in August 1964 and Pengel, the Prime Minister of Surinam, in January 1965. These various talks produced the usual formal activity – a plethora of joint working parties – but nothing of substance. Problems arose because of the diverse constitutional links that bound the non-Commonwealth territories to their metropolitan overlords: Martinique and Guadeloupe were Overseas Departments of France, the Netherlands Antilles and Surinam were members of the Tripartite Kingdom of the Netherlands, and the 'Commonwealth' of Puerto Rico was a part of the political and economic system of the United States of America. In the final analysis, Williams's vision of a Caribbean Economic Community must be accounted a victim of the political divisions wrought upon the whole Caribbean region by its history of exploitation at the hands of various imperial powers. As Williams reported to his 'students' in the 'University' of Woodford Square in April 1965:

> We talked to Surinam, Surinam said 'we don't want any association with Puerto Rico, that's an American colony'; we talked to the French and the French said 'we are not willing to get into any association because Puerto Rico means the

American State Department'; and we talked to Puerto Rico and they said 'we don't want to get into any arrangement with Martinique because that means President de Gaulle'. That is the sort of thing that is going on.[60]

By this time, too, even the *entente* which he had hoped to build up between the leading states of the Commonwealth Caribbean seemed to be in the throes of disintegration. In May 1964, after letting it be known that his services as a mediator were once more available, Williams was formally asked to try and resolve the continuing impasse in British Guiana. His report to Jagan on the results of his mission was written in his loftiest and most scathing vein, concluding that 'there was no readiness on any side to subordinate sectional interests or personal antagonisms or ideological vagaries to the overriding national interest' and that there existed, therefore, 'no basis or reasonable hope for any accommodation between the political parties'.[61] These observations, although valid enough from an impartial point of view, nevertheless provoked an angry personal attack on 'Little Eric', as Williams was disparagingly called, in the columns of *The Mirror*, the PPP paper.[62] With the bit now firmly between his teeth, Williams used the Commonwealth Prime Ministers' Conference in London in July 1964 to put forward his personal solution to the problem, which was that the government of British Guiana should be vested in a Commissioner selected by and responsible to the United Nations.[63] It was, by any standards, an unpractical and naive suggestion, and it was completely ignored by the conference. The point was that, at the very same gathering in London, African and Asian Prime Ministers had been fighting to establish that Rhodesia was Britain's constitutional responsibility. To have agreed that British Guiana, on the other hand, could be passed off into UN hands would have undermined their whole argument and was something they were obviously not prepared to countenance.

From the local Caribbean point of view, the most important feature of the Commonwealth Conference was the way Sangster on behalf of the Jamaican government joined in pouring cold water on Williams's proposed scheme. His unsympathetic response further reinforced the coolness which, during the course of 1964 had begun to develop in relations between Trinidad and Jamaica – the axis upon which the post-Federation revival of regional contact had been based. At the beginning of the year, with Bustamante ill and out of the country, the Jamaican government had obstructed a request from the other three leading West Indian territories that the projected date of the Third Heads of Government Conference be advanced from late July to June. The Trinidad government was the prime mover behind this, because, as Williams later revealed, it felt there was an urgent need to discuss three issues of key importance to the region: British Guiana (obviously); the agreement reached by Williams and the Canadian government to hold a joint Canada–West Indies conference in Trinidad in September 1964; and the failure of the Jamaican government to put into practice a previous agreement on joint Jamaica–Trinidad diplomatic representation in Africa.[64] The disagreement at the Commonwealth Prime Ministers' Conference in London was then followed by a brief diplomatic flurry and exchange of telegrams over a criminal attack on the Jamaican High Commissioner in Port of Spain and, more seriously, by the absence of the Jamaican minister from a Regional Shipping Council meeting in December 1964, on the grounds, ostensibly, that the invitation was received too late for a representative to be sent. This was the precursor of what was to become a familiar Jamaican diplomatic tactic and, in fact, reflected a major disagreement over regional shipping policy. It had been decided at the previous Council meeting in April that, owing to the high cost of running the federal ships, permission should be sought from Canada to replace them with more economical vessels.[65] In the meantime, Williams's unwillingness to risk offending the Canadian government in the light of the projected trade and aid conference and his plans to extend the service to Puerto Rico and the Netherlands Antilles had led him to change his mind about replacing the ships, a reversal of positions with which the Jamaican government, paying 26 per cent of the subsidy the ships needed, was not in sympathy. At the end of 1964, therefore, relations between Jamaica and Trinidad had reached probably their lowest point since the referendum vote in 1961.

Indeed, it looked for a while as if a Third Heads of

The vision of an economic community

Government Conference, planned for Barbados and already postponed for a number of months, would never take place. Williams was reluctant to press again for it to meet, Barrow was preoccupied throughout 1964 preparing a new Draft Federal Scheme for the Little Seven federation,[66] and Bustamante was again taken ill early in 1965. However, after new elections had been held in British Guiana in December 1964 under proportional representation, Forbes Burnham emerged as head of a coalition government and quickly offered to hold the next summit meeting in Georgetown. Burnham was a sincere believer in Caribbean regional collaboration — one may readily admit that — but the domestic political advantage afforded by this opportunity to demonstrate to the people of British Guiana, so soon after his election to office, that the leaders of the other three major West Indian states recognised his regime, was also very obvious. It was known that Britain and the USA supported Burnham's government, and there were undoubtedly sighs of relief in the region's capitals at Jagan's loss of office. Accordingly, the conference was summoned to meet in Georgetown on 8-10 March 1965. Just before it was due to commence, however, Williams announced that he would not attend and that the Trinidadian delegation would be led by Dr Solomon, the deputy Prime Minister. The PNM organ, *The Nation*, in its most recent edition had carried an open letter to Williams on the front page, entitled 'Please Stay, Don't Go', in which the Trinidad Prime Minister was fervently implored not to go to Georgetown. His presence, it was argued, would be used 'to bolster a government nurtured in the very bosom and tradition of colonialism'.[67] The party had not been enamoured of his previous efforts to intervene in British Guiana and did not now want him providing a solution 'in the interest of any one side'.[68] Williams's influence on *The Nation* was considerable, and it is possible that the letter was inspired by sources not too far from the Prime Minister's office. The exhortation contained within it certainly coincided with the strategy dictated by the domestic political situation in Trinidad at the time, the fulcrum of which was a major strike in the sugar belt in the southern part of the island. To have further angered the East Indian sugar workers by so obviously throwing his prestige behind

Burnham's African-supported government would have been highly injudicious: hence Williams's decision to stay at home. Since Sangster also had to deputise for Bustamante, who was still sick, the third Summit opened in an atmosphere of anticlimax, attended by neither of the Prime Ministers of the two independent states of the grouping. The delegates reached few firm decisions, remaining content for the most part to exchange views on topical issues, such as the decline in the sale of West Indian rums in Canada and the whole Canada—West Indies conference (which had not taken place, as Trinidad had wanted, the previous September), membership of the Organisation of American States, British immigration policy, the Regional Shipping Service and the employment conditions of UWI personnel resident in Jamaica.[69] On this last, at least, some action resulted. Shortly after his return to Jamaica, Sangster, who, as a former member of the Regional Economic Committee during the 1950s, was perhaps the most regionally-minded of the Jamaican leaders, announced − in the face of considerable opposition, even within his Cabinet[70] − that his government had agreed to the request of the other regional governments that it exempt Commonwealth members of the UWI staff from requiring work permits. That apart, the only other achievement of the conference was to demonstrate the strength of British Guiana's new commitment to a Caribbean, rather than a continental, destiny. Burnham presented a paper to the conference, calling for the establishment of a permanent conference secretariat − nothing ever having come of the earlier proposal to set up a standing regional economic agency − and arguing, in support of the proposal, that such a body was essential if the series of Heads of Government meetings was to develop any teeth. In the event, the idea was rejected out of deference to the Jamaican delegates, for whom any mention of a secretariat, even with limited functions, somehow raised the spectre of federation,[71] but it was a portent of the vanguard role in regional affairs which British Guiana under Burnham's leadership was to assume in the next decade.

At the end of the conference, however, the prospect of a revival of regional collaboration must have seemed bleak indeed. The heads of governments' unwillingness to take up Burnham's proposal demonstrated the extent to which the summit idea – *per se* – had run out of steam. The initiator of the programme of summits had seen fit to absent himself from only the third meeting in the series, whilst the Georgetown conference not only achieved very little by way of policy co-ordination but, in its refusal to underwrite its own proceedings by establishing a permanent secretariat, showed that it did not even take itself seriously. Williams's wider strategy of linking the Commonwealth and non-Commonwealth territories in some form of regional association was equally in the doldrums. As he himself conceded in March 1965 in an article in *The Nation*, 'more than three years after the enunciation of our goal of the Caribbean Economic Community, PNM's policy has been conspicuous by its lack of success'.[72]

In addition to these failures, the mythical prospect of Grenada's absorption into the state of Trinidad which had been kept alive, if only formally, by the establishment of investigatory commissions, finally evaporated at the end of January 1965, when the crucial economic report was published.[73] It calculated that some 6,800 Grenadians were likely to emigrate to Trinidad if, as seemed unavoidable in a unitary state, there was free movement of persons and advised that this number of arrivals could not be accommodated by the Trinidadian economy without risk of dislocation. To complete the picture, the Little Seven effort, which had been marked by indecision, disagreement and waning enthusiasm for some time, collapsed just a couple of months later. In March 1965, at the behest of the newly elected government of John Compton, the Legislative Council of St Lucia voted to reject the draft federal scheme.[74] At the end of the same month, on hearing that the Secretary of State was reluctant to accept a proposal that unit services could only be transferred to the central authority of the proposed federation with the unanimous consent of all concerned, the Antiguan government also withdrew, to be quickly followed by Montserrat. The tenth meeting of the Regional Council of Ministers convened, as a result, in an atmosphere of intense gloom and was adjourned *sine die* on 29 April 1965. Its adjournment can be said to mark the end of the immediate post-Federation phase of regional international relations in the

Caribbean.

What place, then, do these three and a half years occupy in the history of intra-regional relations? They were, above all, transitional years and for that reason they can be looked at in two ways. Both the unitary state proposal and the continuing preoccupation of the Little Seven with federation were essentially hang-overs from the previous era – necessary attempts to clear away the psychological and practical debris left behind by the abrupt manner of the Federation's demise, but nevertheless doomed from the outset. In one sense, therefore, it is possible to argue that the period was only an epilogue to the stirring events of the preceding decade.

There did exist, however, a more positive side to the period on which, from the perspective of this study, we have seen fit to concentrate, viz. the transfer of 'the regional idea' away from a predominant concern with constitutional formulae into the area of economic and functional co-operation. From this point of view, the most important feature of the period was undoubtedly Eric Williams's advancement of the notion of a Caribbean Economic Community. It was perhaps a vision more grandiose than grand, for a Pan-Caribbean union was never a practical possibility in the context of the region's fragmentation into a number of metropolitan spheres of interest. The idea drew strength largely from Williams's own picture of himself as the undisputed leader of the whole Caribbean, and inevitably, in the end, there was a reaction against his arrogant personal and political style. By the spring of 1965 Trinidad was not on close terms with any of the leading states in the West Indian community.

Yet this did not mean that everything was lost. The period of reappraisal in regard to regional relationships that was required after the federal *débâcle* had taken place. Old models of associations went out of favour as the thinking that lay behind Williams's advocacy of a Caribbean Economic Community became more familiar and more acceptable. By mid-1965 the focus of intergovernmental co-operation had, without doubt, been shifted perceptibly towards the economic arena.

Notes

1. N. Girvan, 'West Indian Unity', *New World Fortnightly*, no. 45, 8 August 1966, p. 11.
2. Quoted in J. S. Mordecai, *The West Indies: The Federal Negotiations*, London, 1968, p. 418.
3. *Daily Gleaner*, 20 September 1961.
4. See Mordecai, *op. cit.*, pp. 297-8, 335 and 341.
5. W. A. Lewis, *The Agony of the Eight*, Bridgetown, 1965, p. 9.
6. See S. D. Ryan, *Race and Nationalism in Trinidad and Tobago: A Study of Decolonization in a Multiracial Society*, Toronto, 1972, p. 270.
7. Lewis, *Agony of the Eight*, p. 12.
8. W. A. Lewis, *Eastern Caribbean Federation: Report to the Prime Minister*, Port of Spain, 1961.
9. Quoted in Mordecai, *op. cit.*, p. 434.
10. See Ryan, *op. cit.*, p. 302.
11. *Ibid.*
12. *The Nation*, vol. 4, no. 16, 15 January 1962. Resolution's emphasis.
13. E. Williams, *Reflections on the Caribbean Economic Community*, Port of Spain, 1965, p. 28.
14. *The Nation*, 15 January 1962.
15. E. Williams, *Inward Hunger: The Education of a Prime Minister*, London, 1969, p. 279.
16. E. Williams, 'Speech to PNM Special Convention, 27 January 1962', *The Nation*, vol. 4, no. 19, 2 February 1962.
17. *Ibid.*
18. See Lewis, *Agony of the Eight*, pp. 9-10.
19. Williams, *The Nation*, 2 February 1962.
20. *Ibid.*
21. Mordecai, *op. cit.*, p. 444.
22. *Ibid.*
23. See *ibid.*
24. See Ryan, *op. cit.*, p. 308, note 41.
25. The full text of the motion is quoted in *ibid.*, p. 309.
26. Williams, *Inward Hunger*, p. 68.
27. *Ibid.*
28. A. Gomes, *Trinidad Guardian*, 28 January 1962.
29. E. Williams, Speech at Fifth Street, Barataria, undated tape, 1961, quoted in Ryan, *op. cit.*, p. 271, note 26.
30. For a fuller discussion of the reaction to the PNM resolution and the demise of the Federation, see Mordecai, *op. cit.*, pp. 441-52.
31. K. Bahadoorsingh, 'The Eastern Caribbean Federation Attempt', in R. Preiswerk (ed.), *Regionalism and the Commonwealth Caribbean*, Port of Spain, 1969, pp. 157-8.
32. *Trinidad Guardian*, 23 June 1962.
33. Mordecai, *op. cit.*, p. 448.
34. Lewis, *Agony of the Eight*, p. 23.
35. *Ibid.*, p. 24.

36. Government of Jamaica, *Ministry Paper No. 34. Common Services Conference*, Kingston, 1962, p. 1.
37. S. S. Ramphal, *The Prospect for Community in the Caribbean*, Georgetown, 1973, p. 4.
38. Williams, *The Nation*, 2 February 1962.
39. *Ibid.*
40. See A. McIntyre, 'Some Issues of Trade Policy in the West Indies', in N. Girvan and O. Jefferson (eds.), *Readings in the Political Economy of the Caribbean*, Kingston, Jamaica, 1971, pp. 173-5.
41. See, for example, C. Y. Thomas, 'The Dynamics of Caribbean Integration', *New World Fortnightly*, no. 1, 30 October 1964, pp. 22-34.
42. *Ibid.*, p. 33.
43. *Daily Gleaner*, 13 September 1962.
44. *Trinidad Guardian*, 26 March 1963.
45. Williams, *Reflections on the Caribbean Economic Community*, pp. 30–1.
46. *Daily Gleaner*, 23 July 1963.
47. *Ibid.*, 30 July 1963.
48. L. Best, 'Little Summit Plan Hastily Prepared', *Trinidad Guardian*, 25 July 1963.
49. Williams, *Reflections on the Caribbean Economic Community*, p. 31.
50. *Daily Gleaner*, 18 January 1964. This aspect of the declaration was a concession to Jagan, who was keen to promote British Guiana's trade with Communist states.
51. For a discussion of the decolonisation process in British Guiana, see, amongst much else, R. T. Smith, *British Guiana*, London, 1962; P. Newman, *British Guiana: Problems of Cohesion in an Immigrant Society*, London, 1962; and P. Reno, *The Ordeal of British Guiana*, New York, 1964.
52. E. Williams, *Trinidad and Tobago and the British Guiana Question*, Port of Spain, 1963, p. 7. This pamphlet, which is a reproduction of a speech given by Williams to the Trinidad House of Representatives in November 1963, contains a full account of the diplomatic activity undertaken in connection with the British Guiana question in that year.
53. Williams reported that 'Bustamante said something like this: 'Look here, Jagan, I do not want to get in any discussions on this matter; I do not want any argument. What we are asking for is this: that Williams, Barrow and Bustamante should meet in the same room with Burnham, D'Aguiar and Jagan and that we would try to work out a constitution in that atmosphere'. *Ibid.*, p. 11.
54. *Daily Gleaner*, 7 February 1964.
55. *Ibid.*
56. See *ibid.*, 9 February 1964.
57. *Trinidad Guardian*, 23 July 1963.
58. *Daily Gleaner*, 14 January 1964.
59. E. Williams, 'Speech at Woodford Square, Port of Spain, 22 April 1965', *The Nation*, vol. 7, no. 32, 30 April 1965.
60. *Ibid.*
61. Williams, *Inward Hunger*, p. 298.

The vision of an economic community 55

62. *The Mirror*, 5 July 1964.
63. See Williams, *Inward Hunger*, pp. 299-300.
64. Williams, *Reflections on the Caribbean Economic Community*, p. 31.
65. According to figures released by the Regional Shipping Council, only about 20 per cent of the cargo-carrying capacity of the ships was being used, which had resulted in an annual deficit of some TT$800,000. See *Trinidad Guardian*, 3 May 1964.
66. For an account of the attempt to establish a federation of the remaining seven Eastern Caribbean territories, see Bahadoorsingh in Preiswerk (ed.), *op. cit.*, pp. 161-6.
67. *The Nation*, vol. 7, no. 24, 5 March 1965.
68. *Ibid.*
69. See *Final Communiqué of the Third Heads of Government Conference*, Georgetown, 1965.
70. See *Daily Gleaner*, 17 March 1965. Senator Wilton Hill, Minister without Portfolio, resigned over the issue, and other ministers reportedly threatened to do likewise.
71. See B. Collins, 'The Caribbean Regional Secretariat', in Preiswerk (ed.), *op. cit.*, pp. 109-10.
72. *The Nation*, vol. 7, no. 25, 12 March 1965.
73. *Report of the Economic Commission appointed to examine Proposals for Association within the framework of a Unitary State of Grenada and Trinidad and Tobago*, Port of Spain, 1965.
74. The rejection of the scheme by the new government of St Lucia has been described as the consequence of 'the arrival of a newcomer' on the regional stage. Lewis, *Agony of the Eight*, p. 31.

CHAPTER TWO

Free trade v. production integration

Not until the second half of the 1960s did advocates of a West Indian economic community turn their attention to the more serious business of regional economic *integration*. The immediate cause of this development was the publication in 1965 of an important new analysis of the economic underdevelopment of the Commonwealth Caribbean. The work was entitled *The Economics of Development in Small Countries with Special Reference to the Caribbean* and its author was William Demas.[1] Demas is in every way the central figure of our story. In 1965 he was the Head of the Economic Planning Division of the Trinidad government and thus a senior civil servant, but for five months from January to June 1964 he had been a guest fellow of the Centre for Developing Area Studies at McGill University in Montreal. The outcome of this sabbatical was the appearance of the slim, but influential, study of the West Indian economy which we have just mentioned.

The book's significance derived from the fact that Demas realised earlier than most that the post-war pattern of economic growth in the West Indies – for which so many extravagant claims had been made by the various governments concerned – had not been accompanied by any genuine development of the regional economy and was indeed beset by a number of fundamental weaknesses. In the passage of time these shortcomings can be seen to be many, but by 1965 two already stood out.[2] Firstly, the level of unemployment and underemployment in the region was still high and, so far from decreasing over the previous decade, was thought actually to have grown – and not only in absolute numbers but also as a percentage of total population. The high wage rates paid in the new mineral and manufacturing sectors had the perverse effect of raising the reserve price of labour and thus of encouraging people to sacrifice low-paid agricultural employment in order to join the ranks of the urban unemployed. At the same time, most of the imported technology used in these sectors was highly capital-intensive and unsuited to the special needs of the labour surplus economies into which it had been introduced. For example, the 146 industries which, by the end of 1965, had been established in Jamaica under the incentive legislation programme had provided a mere 9,000 jobs[3], whilst in Trinidad the employment potential of industrialisation had been equally disappointing: only 4,666 jobs were made available by ninety-nine new industries between 1950 and 1963.[4] Many more were needed, in view of the steady year-by-year rise in the size of the total population of the region,[5] just to prevent the unemployment level from worsening. Secondly, the use made of local West Indian resources in the process of growth had been negligible. Foreign investors in the manufacturing sector had preferred, on the whole, to locate within the Caribbean no more of the production process than was necessary to be awarded the tax incentives. The industries that grew up were usually, therefore, only 'screwdriver' final-assembly operations, producing shoes, cosmetics, household chemicals, stoves, refrigerators and other similar consumer goods. In the mineral sector, too, the value added locally to the region's major raw material exports was very small; for example, the bulk of the bauxite mined in Jamaica and Guyana was shipped away in its original form as an ore and its processing into alumina and aluminium – the stages which contribute most to the final price – was undertaken outside the region. Even the tourist industry was characterised by its failure to create a web of linkages with local agriculture and was thus partly responsible for the area's growing imports of foodstuffs.

Demas argued that the resulting failure of the West Indian

states to transform their economies during this period was no accident, but rather that their capacity to achieve economic development was constrained in a crucial manner by their small size, defined in terms of both land area and population number.[6] Here was the core of his analysis. The smallness of the domestic market, he reasoned, imposed sharp limits on the process of import-substitution industrialisation and thus removed the option of balanced growth, incorporating a roughly equal mixture of export stimulation and import substitution, a goal which could only really be attained by large continental countries. In order to secure the benefits of economies of scale, small economies had, therefore, of necessity, to place special emphasis upon the production of a small number of manufactures for export to world markets. The obstacles in the way of capturing the necessary markets were, however, formidable:

> the most prominent being restrictions against so-called 'cheap labour' imports into the markets of the industrial countries; wage rates in the under-developed countries which do not reflect the true cost of labour as determined by relative factor supplies; the low income-elasticity of demand in the advanced countries for the simpler, labour-intensive products; the fear of creating excess capacity in the face of the uncertainties of the world market; all the numerous factors inhibiting incursions into export markets; and, finally, the fact that nearly all under-developed countries are protecting the simpler labour-intensive final consumer goods.[7]

In view of the difficulties thereby involved in the pursuit of both import substitution and export stimulation, Demas turned his attention to two alternative strategies. One was near or full economic integration with a large country or large trading bloc on the lines of Puerto Rico's relationship with the United States or Luxembourg's with the Benelux countries, but that could be objected to on the grounds that it was a form of 'neo-colonialism' unlikely to provide development in the smaller, poorer partner of the alliance; the other was economic integration with neighbouring underdeveloped countries. This was the direction, Demas opined, 'in which it appears more likely that many countries will move',[8] and which he was himself inclined to favour.

What in detail were the arguments which Demas marshalled behind the case for regional economic integration? Let us start with a negative point. They were not those of neo-classical customs union theory, for, as he had already argued in an article on a West Indies customs union written during the days of the Federation,[9] the conventions of this theory suggested that a customs union between underdeveloped countries like those in the Caribbean would bring no overall economic benefit whatsoever. Customs union theory refers to a fairly recent body of writing associated primarily with the name of Jacob Viner.[10] It assumes, first of all, that inputs of factors of production, the state of technical knowledge, taxes and economic organisation are all constant, that trade within each country is perfectly competitive, and that there is full employment in all parts of the union. It then purports to analyse the circumstances under which the removal of customs barriers between countries living in the real world leads to advantageous or disadvantageous static shifts in the pattern of production, consumption and trade within the union as a whole. The so-called 'production effects', which are generally held to be the most important, can be either trade-creating or trade-diverting. Trade creation occurs if a union causes a member to replace its own high-cost production of particular commodities with imports from other members of the union which have lower costs. It is most likely to be seen when the union is between countries producing much the same range of products but with differences in the comparative advantage with which they do so – a union, in other words, in which the member economies are actually competitive but potentially complementary. After the formation of the union, competition will lead, it is suggested, to a pattern of specialisation, in which high-cost industries in each country will tend to be displaced by their low-cost competitors in neighbouring states and each member will consequently be supplied by the lowest-cost source within the union. On the other hand, trade diversion is said to occur when the effect of the union is to cause members to switch their purchases from low-cost sources external to the union to high-cost sources within the union. The union will not, in these terms, have been beneficial because it will have caused a shift of resources into less efficient uses and thus brought about a deterioration in specialisation on a world scale.

Analysed in these terms, a customs union seemed to have little to offer the Caribbean. Trade creation (the beneficial effect) is likely to predominate in unions between countries where only a small proportion of total expenditure is on external trade, and where a high proportion of that external trade takes place between the countries of the union. The less important the external trade with non-union countries, the smaller will be the effect of the union in diverting imports to higher-cost internal sources, and the more important domestic trade is in total expenditure, then the more the union is likely to create intra-union trade by displacing high-cost domestic production with low-cost imports from the other countries within the union. The Caribbean economies were competitive in the sense that they produced the same range of primary products, but they could hardly have been said to be potentially complementary. The removal of barriers between them would not have had a great redistributive effect on the pattern of production within the union (i.e. replacing high-cost domestic production by lower-cost supplies from partner countries) because the level of industrialisation in the region was generally too low. Moreover, external trade was huge compared with domestic trade, so one would have had to anticipate an excessive trade-diverting effect and, therefore, a net loss in terms of the efficiency with which resources would be utilised within the area covered by the union. Hence conventional customs union theory was bound to conclude that the economic integration of the Caribbean would be irrelevant at best and harmful at worst.

Demas, however, questioned the appropriateness of this whole argument when applied to economic integration schemes between *underdeveloped* countries. Even in static terms – the theory's home ground, as it were – Demas argued that it had to be turned on its head to produce any real bite. Was trade creation – to the limited extent, that is, to which it might be expected to occur – really a benefit at all? Competition between recently established industries in underdeveloped countries surely had its hazards. As Demas put it, 'it does not make sense for a stronger infant to kill a weaker infant!'[11] He also took issue with the alleged disadvantages of trade diversion in economies where the neo-classical assumption of full employment was inapplicable and, making direct use of the economic arguments for the protection of 'infant' industries, suggested that:

> where the alternative for the Caribbean worker who gets new or higher-productivity employment by this act of trade diversion is unemployment, underemployment or low-productivity employment ... there will be some clear-cut addition to the social product. In under-developed countries such as the West Indies, it cannot be too often emphasised that while the money cost of the new trade-diverting product may be quite high, its real social opportunity cost may be very low, or even possibly zero.[12]

Nevertheless, these modifications, valuable as they were, did not constitute the kernel of the theory of economic integration as argued by Demas. In his view the main advantage lay in the so-called 'dynamic' benefits which participant states could be expected to gain. It is here that the prescription relates directly to the diagnosis. For, in the light of an analysis which pinpointed small size as the crucial limiting factor upon economic development in the Caribbean, the real gain brought about by regional economic integration was the wider market it created and the chance of capturing economies of scale and external economies thus offered to small states otherwise constrained by the hand of nature. Demas anticipated that integration would not only promote industrial growth by making possible the elimination of excess capacity in existing manufacturing industry, but also – and more important – by stimulating investment in new industries which would become economically feasible for the first time in the Caribbean on the basis of the expanded market. He was keen to point out that the long-term objective was balanced growth and that 'integration may often not remove the necessity to seek export markets outside the region', merely assisting 'in building up an industrial structure which must still be largely geared to outside markets'.[13] No one was in any doubt, though, that, in Demas's mind, the key to the strategy of economic integration was the pursuit of import substitution on a regional basis. As he himself put it, 'the creation of an economic region can mean that the development pattern for the region *as a whole* can approximate more to import-substitution – although from the point of view of individual member countries there will still be a large volume of "exports" to and "imports" from other countries'.[14] In a sense, therefore, the aim was to secure the very production effect condemned by traditional customs union theory, viz. the diversion of trade from extra-union sources to higher-cost intra-union sources, which is, after all, the essence of import substitution.

One point we must make clear. Although we have chosen to present these views in the way they were argued by Demas with reference to the Caribbean, they were not in any way exclusive to the region. By the mid-1960s market integration along these lines had become the new conventional wisdom in development economics.[15] Moreover, integration groupings were actually beginning to spring up in different parts of the underdeveloped world – notably in Latin America, where there had been established the Latin American Free Trade Area (LAFTA) and the Central American Common Market (CACM). In the Caribbean, where, as we have seen, economic matters had moved to the forefront of intra-regional activity as a result, largely, of Williams's espousal of the notion of a Caribbean Economic Community, there undoubtedly began to develop a feeling that the region should not miss the boat, as it were, and that perhaps the easiest point at which to commence the economic integration process was the creation of a free trade area.

Yet when a positive initiative was made in this direction it took the Caribbean wholly by surprise. On 6 July 1965, after secret talks, Premiers Barrow and Burnham announced that a free trade area would be established between Barbados and British Guiana not later than January 1966. It was stated that participation by other territories in this proleptically named 'Caribbean Free Trade Association' (CARIFTA) would be welcomed and that the ultimate objective was the creation of a viable economic community and common market – within the context of early independence – for all the Caribbean territories who desired it. Reactions were mixed. The leaders of the Little

Free trade v. production integration   63

Seven, with whom Barbados was still *formally* negotiating the creation of an Eastern Caribbean Federation, and who had not been consulted before the pact was announced, felt that they had been given 'a slap in the face'.[16] The Trinidad government was undeniably piqued, particularly since most commentators immediately declared that the Premiers' pronouncement was a real step towards the achievement of Caribbean economic integration. Dr Williams's government was placed in the awkward position, therefore, of having to endorse an initiative, which, in effect, represented the supersession of its own policy on regional collaboration. Yet, for all the doubters, there were certainly many who felt that the 'news that Mr Barrow and Mr Burnham have taken the bull of free trade by the horns was like a breath of fresh air through the fog of Caribbean economic community chatter'.[17] Scant interest, however, was aroused in Jamaica.

By any standards, the announcement of the free trade area was a considerable diplomatic *coup d'éclat*. What was the thinking that lay behind it? In view of all the attention we have just given to the theoretical case for economic integration, this may seem an unnecessary question; but it is nevertheless true that the motivation behind the initiative was not solely, or even primarily, economic. Since the available market would not have been widened sufficiently in either territory to promote much new industrial investment, the only economic benefits lay in reallocating trade in the products which each had obtained, till then, from Trinidad. Barbados may well have looked to this to advance the development of its embryonic light manufacturing sector, and British Guiana may have hoped thus to increase the size of its exports of rice and timber. There was no great advantage, however, to be had from either of these developments, and obviously nobody thought that a free trade association, embracing just two states, both still colonies, had much 'transformative' potential in economic terms. On the other hand, the announcement of CARIFTA did have a very pronounced *political* impact, which suggests that it may have been conceived with this, rather than the limited economic gains, in mind.

It was certainly seen at the time as a primarily political move, regarded by many as being, at heart, 'an anti-Trinidad maneuver'[18] designed to snub Williams, rather than a genuine effort to advance Caribbean integration. This interpretation held that 'the whole idea was dreamed up by Burnham and Barrow over drinks in Barbados' and mischievously enquired: 'were they talking about little Eric at the time?'[19] There is, moreover, a certain amount of circumstantial evidence to support the implied allegation. Relations between Trinidad and the Burnham regime had been bad for some months before the free trade area was announced. In addition to the rancour aroused by Williams's continuing condemnation of the proportional representation system which had brought Burnham to office in British Guiana, trading arrangements between the two territories − normally uncontroversial − had lately become a bone of contention. The Trinidad government was particularly annoyed by the threat to its traditional markets implicitly contained within the trade pact signed between Jamaica and British Guiana during the Third Heads of Governments Conference in March 1965, by which British Guiana agreed to buy the bulk of its requirements of cement and concentrated fruit juice from Jamaican manufacturers,[20] and by the similar arrangement Burnham's government had reached with Puerto Rico with regard to asphalt. It had responded by letting it be known that it was considering finding a new supplier of rice when its current contract with British Guiana expired, and then in June 1965 it announced a ban on the import of plantains from British Guiana in full knowledge that the mainland colony was faced with a glut of that particular commodity and was having to dump much of its crop. Unglamorous issues, maybe, but often the stuff of which political decisions are made in underdeveloped countries. For his part, Burnham was said to be angry at the way Williams was inclined to strut the Caribbean stage, and much the same was thought to hold for Barrow as well. Immediately after coming to power in Barbados in December 1961 he had, as mentioned earlier, flown to see Williams to offer to work with him in an attempt to save the Federation, but had been politely rebuffed. Many suspected, therefore, that CARIFTA was conceived primarily as a ploy to wrest the leadership of the West Indies out of Williams's hands.

Free trade v. production integration 65

The suggestion is not so much wrong as less than the whole truth. It ignores, for example, the effect of Barrow's exasperation with 'the interminable indecision'[21] of the leaders of the Little Seven states and their failure to appreciate what he saw as the generous sense of responsibility displayed by Barbados in even discussing with them the possibility of an Eastern Caribbean Federation when, alone, Barbados had long possessed all the adjuncts of nationhood.[22] Above all, the anti-Williams theory of CARIFTA fails to recognise the extent to which the agreement was designed – as the original announcement made clear – to prepare the way for the economic integration of the whole of the West Indies. It was principally an enabling act, an attempt to set the ball rolling politically. Burnham, in particular, frequently pointed out that the agreement was 'not intended to be exclusive'[23] and that new members to the club would be welcome, although invitations would not be issued. In response to these entreaties, Antigua quickly joined. Its Premier, Vere Bird, was by then thoroughly out of sympathy with the federal movement in the eastern Caribbean and was undoubtedly attracted by the prospect of CARIFTA establishing a protected market for the petroleum products of a new oil refinery which his government had just succeeded in attracting to Antigua. St Vincent toyed with the idea of joining for a while, before finally rejecting it; and that was all.

It was, nevertheless, with a feeling that a new start was being made in the history of regional collaboration in the West Indies – this time by West Indians for West Indians – that the Caribbean Free Trade Association Agreement was signed by Bird, Barrow and Burnham at Dickenson Bay, Antigua, on 15 December 1965. The Preamble described the governments of Antigua, Barbados and British Guiana as:

> SHARING a common determination to fulfil within the shortest possible time the hopes and aspirations of their peoples and of the people of other Caribbean territories for full employment and improved living standards;
> CONSCIOUS that these goals can most rapidly be attained by the optimum use of available human and other resources and by accelerated and sustained economic development;
> AWARE that the broadening of domestic markets through the

elimination of barriers to trade between the territories is a prerequisite to such development;
[and] CONVINCED that such elimination of barriers to trade can best be achieved by the immediate establishment of a Free Trade Area and the ultimate creation of a Customs Union and a viable Economic Community for all the Caribbean territories who so desire.'[24]

The agreement itself was a straightforward document, setting out simply 'to foster the harmonious development of Caribbean trade and its liberalisation by the removal of barriers to it'.[25] The major provisions were found in Articles 4, 5, 13 and 17. Article 4 decreed that, subject to a small number of items reserved for protective or revenue reasons, 'Member Territories shall not apply any import duties on goods which are eligible for Area tariff treatment in accordance with Article 5'.[26] Article 5, in turn, specified that goods should be eligible for free trade if they met one of three conditions:

(a) that they were wholly produced within the area;
(b) that they fell within a description of goods listed in a 'Process List' to be drawn up by the intergovernmental ministerial Council, which was set up to supervise the application of the whole CARIFTA agreement;
(c) that they were goods with 50 per cent of their export value added within the region, subject to the provision that certain materials not extensively produced in the area (if at all) and listed in a 'Basic Materials List',[27] should be decreed to be of area origin.

Article 13 declared that member territories should not apply any quantitative restrictions on imports of goods from any other part of the area, and Article 17 prohibited the introduction of any form of regional export aids, 'the main purpose or effect of which is to frustrate the benefits expected from such removal or absence of duties and quantitative restrictions as is required by this Agreement'.[28] The remaining articles served to complete the typical apparatus of a free trade area. They included the establishment of arrangements to safeguard the dislocation caused by urgent cases of 'trade deflection' (which is said to occur when one territory's sales of a particular commodity suffer unfairly because another territory with lower tariffs on imported materials and semi-finished products pre-empts regional trade in that commodity) and the specification of steps to prevent dumping and to control restrictive business practices. Indeed, CARIFTA, in the words of one West Indian economist, was 'literally a transcription of the European Free Trade Association Treaty'.[29] It seemed, then, that, as a supplement to the popular policy of 'industrialisation by invitation', the Caribbean was about to embark upon the path of 'integration by imitation'.

Yet, once the agreement was signed, a hiatus occurred. The pace of events slackened markedly. Six months later CARIFTA had still not been implemented, even in its limited three-territory form. However, the subject of economic integration had begun to interest a number of scholars at the University of the West Indies (UWI). Alister McIntyre, the Director of the University's Institute of Social and Economic Research, had already attracted considerable attention – not least in government circles – with a paper deliverd to the second Caribbean Scholars' Conference in 1964, in which, after a gloomy but realistic review of the trading options open to the region, he had called for the development of a suitable theoretical framework for effecting the economic integration of the Caribbean.[30] The University's standing in the region was very high in the mid-1960s, and the Jamaican and Trinidadian governments decided to jointly commission a series of studies on economic integration from a team of UWI economists. They did not, however, make any move to join CARIFTA. In fact, in Trinidad government ministers began to talk of the need to develop closer relations with the country's Latin American neighbours, who constituted, as was pointedly mentioned on more than one occasion, a not inconsiderable market of some 200 million people,[31] in comparison to which the Commonwealth Caribbean market was minuscule. In the autumn of 1966 Williams's disgruntlement with the CARIFTA initiative, and the failure of his own Caribbean Economic Community policy, spilled out into the open. Trinidad, he declared,

> has adopted a deliberate policy on this matter of Caribbean

unity. Whatever Trinidad and Tobago said has been objected to by a policy of envy by the other territories. Trinidad has adopted a particular policy. It says nothing, and leaves it to the others to speak and just says yes to anything which involves Caribbean unity.[32]

International relations within the West Indies, as we have noted, have long been conducted in an atmosphere of intense inter-island competitiveness, even when relations have generally been friendly. Personalities who are dominant figures in their domestic political environment have naturally tended to recoil from the prospect of entreating favours from regional colleagues. Since this was what was seen to be involved in Article 32 of the CARIFTA agreement, which affirmed that any territory could participate in the free trade area 'subject to prior approval of the Council . . . on terms and conditions decided by the Council',[33] no one, least of all Williams, was eager to step forward and apply.

The impasse was eventually broken by the Incorporated Commonwealth Chambers of Industry and Commerce of the Caribbean. This businessmen's organisation had first been formed in 1917, but had long lain dormant.[34] In 1964 it had been revitalised and, in keeping with the economic fashion of the times, it soon appointed a special committee to consider 'the phased freeing of trade' within the region. In June 1966 the Hunte Committee, so named after its chairman, Senator Kenneth Hunte, one of the leading businessmen of Barbados, appointed a six-man delegation of prominent local industrialists, several of whom had investments in more than one West Indian territory, and directed them to tour the region, interviewing 'all Heads of Government of the Commonwealth Caribbean for the purpose of urging joint action to bring about a Free Trade Area between their respective countries'.[35] It was decided that the delegation should not itself put forward a set of detailed proposals for the implementation of regional free trade, which enabled it at least to deflect, although not allay, the anxieties of the smaller territories of the region that they were being asked to open up their markets to the manufacturing interests of the more industrialised countries, like Jamaica and Trinidad, without themselves receiving any tangible benefits at all. The delegation felt that before these specific problems could even be broached a measure of agreement in principle had necessarily to be reached. Its main aim, therefore, was simply 'to seek agreement from individual Governments to sit with their counterparts to examine the problems which exist and which they alone have the authority to remove'.[36]

To this end the delegation advanced, in each of the countries visited, much the same case for regional import substitution as had been articulated by Demas in his book. The need for free trade was urgent, it was suggested,

> because in the face of a rapidly growing population and working force, and a relatively high incidence of unemployment in most territories, it was necessary to enlarge the several markets by removing barriers to trade so that ultimately there would be one market sufficiently large as to warrant a greater measure of industrialization and to provide wider trade facilities thus creating more employment opportunities.[37]

Special emphasis was given to 'the problem of population explosion' and to the prediction that 'unless new jobs are created in the area at a faster rate than is presently the case, there will be approximately 900,000 more people enter the labour force, between 1960 and 1976, than leave it',[38] and to the consequent worsening of unemployment levels in the region which this would inevitably bring about. Indeed, the delegation's entire analysis was imbued with the fear of a future 'in which present trends continue, the pressure of population on the land increases ... industrial and agricultural development does not take place fast enough to accommodate the increase, unemployment rises ... internal tensions and civil strife lead to convulsions ... and ... destitution prevails'.[39] One should point out, too, that for all their altruistic advocacy of the phased freeing of trade as the only means by which the Caribbean could escape the doom they described, the members of the Incorporated Chambers – especially those in the larger industrialising states – also had a direct interest in the benefits such a strategy could offer. The majority of the industries established in the region under the incentive legislation programme of the 1950s had been geared not to world export markets, as Arthur Lewis had originally hoped, but merely to the amount of demand in their domestic territorial markets.[40] The businessmen represented by the Incorporated Chambers were therefore experiencing at first hand – which is to say in respect of their profit margins – the constraints imposed by small size on the process of insular import substitution.

The mission's forceful espousal of the merits of regional free trade during the course of its thirty-day tour in September and October 1966 had a catalytic effect upon the various governments. With the exception of only Barbados and Jamaica, they all indicated their willingness to attend a special intergovernmental meeting to consider the phased freeing of trade in the Commonwealth Caribbean. For his part, Barrow expressed a desire to consult first with his two CARIFTA colleagues, but since he repeated his commitment to the concept of the widest possible grouping of states within a Caribbean free trade area there seemed to be no real obstacle there.[41] In Jamaica the acting Prime Minister, Sangster, declared it to be his preference that the whole subject be routinely discussed at the next meeting in the series of regular Heads of Government Conferences, rather than at a special meeting. He reaffirmed, however, that Jamaica was already on record as supporting the principle of Caribbean free trade and had partially financed the UWI studies, to which the Cabinet would in due course give the most careful consideration.[42] It was a more cautious response, certainly: but raising no real problem. In short, the delegation had been 'knocking on an open door',[43] as Williams had told them at the outset of their mission in Trinidad. Everybody was waiting for somebody else to make the first move. During the tour it emerged that Burnham was the most widely acceptable leader to act as convenor of the special Summit conference, and that the consensus of opinion favoured the holding of a preliminary gathering of economic advisers to consider the available options and prepare recommendations. Burnham accepted the role thereby thrust upon him and undertook to call both meetings as soon as possible.[44]

In the autumn of 1966, then, there appeared to be virtual unanimity amongst the region's governments that the future of the Caribbean lay in some form of regional economic integration. It was a situation which, we have argued, had not existed in, say, March 1965. How had the change come about? Some of the reasons have already been mentioned – the failure of industrialisation to reduce drastically the numbers of unemployed, the 'bandwagon effect' induced by the prolific expansion and ostensible success of integration groupings around the world, and the example of CARIFTA itself – but two other factors remain to be considered. The first was the effect of renewed anxiety about the future market prospects of the region's vital exports of primary products which, in mid-1966, was being provoked by the seeming imminence of a second British application to join the EEC. Many thinking West Indians feared that Britain's gradual withdrawal from colonial responsibility for the area, coupled with the declining share of the West Indian market captured by British exports, would make her less concerned to withstand increasing international (mainly EEC) pressure to abandon or fundamentally modify the Commonwealth preference policy.[45] All of which, from the West Indian point of view, added considerably to the importance of preserving good trading relations with Canada, the region's other traditional preferential market. The Canada–Commonwealth Caribbean Conference, which Eric Williams had long been trying to convene and which eventually met in Ottawa in July 1966, was therefore invested with crucial significance in determining the future pattern of their relationship. Indeed, several editorials in the Jamaican *Daily Gleaner* expressed the view that the conference came at a time when the West Indies were 'looking for new leadership',[46] and raised the possibility that Canada, with no imperial past and no 'great power' complex but with, it was thought, a special affinity for the region, might become to the West Indies 'just what the United States has been to Puerto Rico'.[47]

The Canadians, however, were not in the least interested in fulfilling such a role. Since the middle of the nineteenth century they had favoured the creation of an economic trading system among the countries of the British Empire as a means of escaping from what they saw as undue American influence upon the Canadian economy, and had naturally seen the West Indian territories as useful partners in this enterprise. The economies of the West Indies were considered to be complementary to Canada's and capable of absorbing massive exports of Canadian salted fish and vegetables (and later manufactures) in return for the granting of preferential terms of access to the Canadian market for West Indian primary exports, like sugar. But in the period since the end of the Second World War, during which the Canadian economy inexorably slipped into greater dependence upon the United States for its main export markets and some of the West Indian economies became more competitive with the Canadian economy as a result of their import-substitution industrialisation policies, Canada's interest in its preferential ties with the West Indies diminished considerably.[48] Accordingly, at the 1966 Ottawa conference – the first Canadian–Commonwealth Caribbean gathering since the signing of the original trade agreement in 1925 – Canadian ministers talked sweet but acted tough. The only concrete benefits to be won by the West Indies were an increased aid programme and the abolition of the direct shipping requirements, by which preferences were only granted on goods shipped direct to Canadian ports. The removal of Canadian duty on West Indian sugar (which was subject, in any case, to the agreement of other Commonwealth suppliers) amounted to a price advantage of only £2 a ton and was meaningless in relation to the overall costs of production; whilst the agreement of the Canadian authorities to look at the restoration of shipping facilities between Canada and the Caribbean, which would particularly have benefited the banana industry, was no more than a promise to investigate the situation.[49] The message was simple – Canada was not prepared to become the West Indies' new fairy godmother – and despite ritual claims that the conference had been the most successful ever, the message undoubtedly went home.

The second and final factor concerned the question of migration, which throughout the 1950s had contributed not inconsiderably to reducing, or at least mitigating, the region's overpopulation. Here again, though, the world seemed to be closing in on the West Indies in a very literal sense. Following the passage of the Commonwealth Immigration Act in 1962, entry into the United Kingdom was tightly controlled, and the situation was no more favourable in respect of immigration to the United States and Canada. At the Ottawa conference, for example, although making token gestures towards easing this problem by agreeing to expand the seasonal 'farm labour scheme' with Jamaica and the 'special household worker service', the Canadian government reiterated its basic policy of keeping the door open only to 'qualified', which meant skilled, West Indians.[50] In this context, part of the lure of regional economic integration lay in the possibility that it might also open up new avenues for migration. During 1966 Burnham made a number of speeches in various different forums, emphasising his government's willingness to recruit immigrants from the other West Indian territories in order better to exploit the large expanses of savannah in the Guyanese interior. To take only one instance, the official communiqué of the Ottawa conference recorded that:

> The Government of Guyana explained that with accelerated development of Guyana's resources it would be possible for Guyana to absorb migrants from the Caribbean countries, and announced its willingness to make available immediately for settlement by Guyanese and other West Indians selected areas of known potential.[51]

The idea of West Indian migration to Guyana, the mythical 'El Dorado', was not new,[52] but many assumed that Burnham's vigorous promotion of the issue derived primarily from his awareness that the next elections in Guyana were only two years away. The suspicion was that, in order to circumvent the well established fact that the number of Indians of voting age in Guyana had increased since the last election, he wanted to import sufficient West Indians of African stock — who, it was thought, would be bound to give their votes to his African-backed People's National Congress (PNC) — to ensure his continued tenure of office. The opposition PPP certainly thought that this was the motivation behind CARIFTA, although the agreement itself contained no provision for the free movement of peoples between the signatory territories. As one contributor to the PPP party organ, *Thunder*, put it, 'the aim seems to be to flood Guyana with a mass of politically backward West Indians so as to retard the development of the progressive movement here'.[53] Economic integration was simply 'another attempt to defeat the People's Progressive Party'.[54] Whether we interpret his intentions charitably or uncharitably, there is no doubt that, in 1966, Burnham's vision of economic integration was inclusive of some scheme for organising the migration to Guyana of a certain proportion of the surplus population of the West Indies. One may feel, on reflection, that it was never very likely that the ordinary unemployed West Indian, wandering the streets of Kingston or Port of Spain, could be persuaded to opt for the hard, pioneering life in the Guyanese interior, but nevertheless, when it was first mooted, the idea had sufficient plausibility to attract itself to the leaders of what were, without exception, very crowded islands.

With its implicit message of salvation by means of regional self-help, the case for economic integration fell, therefore, on fertile ground. The favour in which the idea was held throughout the West Indies at the end of 1966 undoubtedly stemmed, in the main, from the feeling of vulnerability, neglect and isolation which had lately come to dominate the outlook of practically all the governments of the region. In fact, it could be said that, for the first time, the Commonwealth Caribbean was beginning to feel the cold draught of self-government. British Guiana (as Guyana) and Barbados had joined Jamaica and Trinidad as fully independent states in May and November 1966 respectively, and the Leeward and Windward Islands were shortly to be granted Associated Status, an arrangement which conceded full internal self-government but, for the moment, kept responsibility for defence and foreign affairs in the hands of the British government.[55] As Williams pithily observed, the main problem of the West Indies was 'that nobody wants them – the United States does not, Canada does not, and Britain wants them least of all'.[56] Furthermore, it increasingly seemed that the international community would only talk to them on a regional basis. During the preparations for the Ottawa conference Canada, for example, had left no one in doubt of her reluctance to deal with the various territories separately. In the circumstances, unity in adversity seemed to most West Indian governments to be a slogan worth hanging on to.

This sense of beleaguerment was heightened in May 1967

when Britain formally tabled its anticipated second application to join the EEC. Once more the prospect of the Commonwealth preference system being terminated without adequate safeguards served to hasten the slow advance towards regional economic integration. In order to ascertain whether it would be 'profitable to each and all of us if we could find a common approach in dealing with this problem',[57] the Jamaican government quickly summoned a meeting of the region's trade ministers, who, before the end of June, were in London receiving pledges from the British government that the trading interests of the Commonwealth Caribbean would not be sacrificed by the terms of British entry into the EEC. The British application also spurred the Trinidad government to emerge from the shell into which it had retreated as far as regional diplomacy was concerned. Indeed, it was Williams's appointee to a new Ministry of West Indian Affairs, Kamaluddin Mohammed, who made the running in regional affairs in 1967, pressing hard for a firm date to be set for the promised meeting of government officials to discuss the actual implementation of economic integration in the region. His efforts were successful, and the officials conference eventually met in Georgetown, Guyana, on 14 August 1967. For the sake of those who had yet to realise the imperatives of the time, Burnham used his opening speech to draw attention to the extent to which the embrace of economic integration in the West Indies had necessarily to be conceived defensively, stressing that it should be viewed as nothing less than a technique of survival. His message was undeniably dramatic:

> Either we weld ourselves into a regional grouping serving primarily Caribbean needs, or lacking a common positive policy, have our various territories and nations drawn hither and thither into, and by, other large groupings where the peculiar problems of the Caribbean are lost and where we become the objects of neo-colonialist exploitation, and achieve the pitiable status of international mendicants ... This is the naked truth. Either *we integrate*, or *we perish*, unwept, unhonoured.[58]

It might seem, then, that the officials had been left with little to decide – to integrate or perish – and were simply required, as Burnham said, to move the integration question 'from the theoretical to the practical'.[59] The matter was not quite that simple, however, for contained within the wealth of theoretical material laid before the conference were two contrasting prospectuses of economic integration, between which the delegates had to choose. On the one hand, there was the CARIFTA agreement. It had still not been implemented, partly because discussions between representatives of the new oil refinery in Antigua and the petroleum marketing company in Guyana about switching the source of Guyana's supply of lighter oils from Trinidad to Antigua had yet to be concluded, and partly because the Guyana government, in particular, was inclined to fish for a bigger catch, namely the participation in CARIFTA of the entire Commonwealth Caribbean. On the other hand, there were the much-heralded UWI studies, which had at last been made available, having been considerably delayed by the Jamaican government's seizure of the passport of one member of the team, George Beckford, as he embarked on a field-work trip to Cuba as part of the project. In protest against this breach of liberty, the six economists had suspended their use of the government funds which they had been granted and had undertaken to complete the research in their own time, with the result that the majority of the studies in the series were not published until mid-1967. Instead, however, of preparing a standard feasibility study on the question of free trade as applied to the Caribbean, the UWI team advanced a novel theory of regional economic integration, conceived not merely as an adjunct to the conventional tenets of customs union theory but as the central feature of a radical theory of social and economic transformation. There was, therefore, a considerable and very crucial choice lying before the officials. In it lay the key to the future pattern of Caribbean economic integration.

In a moment we shall look closely at the contents of the UWI studies, but first we need to consider the wider interpretation of West Indian economic underdevelopment, on which the UWI approach to economic integration was based.[60] In contrast to Demas's analysis, which located the impasse to the region's development in the factor of size, the UWI interpretation was constructed around the concept of 'economic dependence', defined not just as a reliance upon overseas demand for domestic economic activity but, in structural terms, as 'a lack of capacity to manipulate the operative elements of an economic system'.[61] Emphasis was laid on the dependence of the West Indian economies on the outside world for vital elements in the process of economic development, notably the supply of investment capital, technical knowledge and even decision-making by virtue of the widespread foreign ownership of the key natural resources of Caribbean economies. The theme, in short, was the region's structural integration into the international economy. Particular attention was paid to the operation of what were seen as the leading mechanisms of economic dependence, the subsidiaries of multinational corporations which dominated the principal export sectors and financial systems of all the region's economies. It was argued that, in consequence, much of the wealth seemingly created by the high growth rates of the 1950s had been drained away again in profit repatriation, interest and royalty payments, licence fees and management charges paid to these foreign companies – that, in fact, some West Indian countries had, over the period, exported more capital than they had attracted by incentive legislation. This, it was suggested, was simply the nature of economic dependence.

Turning to the integration studies themselves, the *magnum opus* of the series was without doubt *The Dynamics of West Indian Economic Integration* by Havelock Brewster and Clive Thomas.[62] Their main thesis was that, on their own, a free trade area and customs union did not constitute an adequate structure for procuring the gains from integration. Sufficient conditions were only established when this approach was combined with

> a functional and sectoral approach which explicitly allows for the introduction of planning techniques in an effort to ensure the positive development of certain agreed areas of economic activity in the region. In other words integration in the West Indies should not be limited to those conditions which govern the exchange of goods, but should also include in its perspective the integrated production of goods.[63]

The emphasis of the study was therefore on the possibilities of production integration, 'taking place from the basic resource inputs of the particular sector to the disposition and sale of final output yielded by the sector'.[64] The authors sought to identify 'integration areas' with a high degree of dynamic development potential and, at the end of their research, were able to conclude that, by following their recommendations, the West Indies could look forward to the establishment by 1975 of one steel mill based on imported scrap, one plant producing paper other than newsprint, one synthetic nylon factory, one sheet and plate glass factory, one caustic soda plant, one factory producing general-purpose rubber, one car factory (building vehicles with 60 per cent value added from regional components) and, in the agricultural sphere, a meat complex and a regional fishing industry.

It would, however, be an error to assume that these proposals merely represented a more advanced stage along the path of economic integration outlined by Demas. Brewster and Thomas were saying much more than that, for, in their view, economic integration was fully capable of acting as an instrument, not just of economic change, but of social change too. At one point they suggested that:

> This expansion of the productive base and the services which go with it, in differentiating human activity and the alternatives available to individuals can create a new dimension in the quality of West Indian life. One painful inheritance of slavery is the claustrophobia of size and our response to it; size not in the sense of measurable phenomena but in the sense of the degrees of psychological freedom which man has without endangering his creative survival.[65]

This philosophical perspective clearly added an extra dimension to their more technical economic arguments. Even when they appeared to talk the same language as Demas, in stating that the immediate purpose of economic integration was to promote regional import substitution, they usually meant different things – in this instance, interpreting regional import substitution not just as a means of reducing the level of imports but as a prime feature of economic development signifying the growth and structural transformation of regional productive capacity. Economic integration was not to be judged primarily by the extent to which items previously imported were subsequently manufactured within the region, but by the extent to which it reduced the wide disparity between the structure of domestic demand and the structure of domestic resource use forced upon the West Indian economy by the fact of its economic dependence. In short, Brewster and Thomas's priority was to see the West Indies consuming more of what it could produce, rather than producing more of what it wanted to consume – a fine but important distinction.

Achievement of this end, in their view, demanded a number of fundamental breaks with the economic policy pursued throughout the West Indies in the recent past and present. They argued, firstly, that 'final touch' manufacturing could never lead to the economic transformation of the region, and that widespread emphasis on this sort of 'horizontal' industrialisation should be replaced by a greater concern for 'vertical' industrialisation of the type they proposed; secondly, that there was 'a very strong case for the public ownership and development'[66] of integration industries in order to prevent their monopoly of the regional market being put to private advantage; and thirdly, that there was an urgent need to reorganise those areas of the economy in which the basic resources of the region, such as bauxite, bananas and sugar, were integrated into the operations of companies based in metropolitan areas. The preparation of detailed recommendations for the rationalisation of these areas was, however, left to the studies in Volume II of the UWI series.

Three of these were available in August 1967, but unlike Brewster and Thomas's mammoth study they were only of pamphlet size. Beckford and Guscott[67] concluded from their examination of intra-Caribbean agricultural trade that there was a need for a Regional Agricultural Trade Commission, which would – inter alia – establish formal trading arrangements between the marketing agencies of the various territories, work out regional commodity agreements designed to encourage the specialisation of production, and provide regional shipping and storage facilities. Beckford's individual study of the West Indian banana industry[68] set out proposals for the reorganisation of production according to acreage efficiency and made the case for the establishment of a regional shipping service as a means of reducing dependence on foreign-owned vessels. Finally, Girvan's examination of the Caribbean bauxite industry[69] contained a number of detailed suggestions for development in the direction of more smelting and refining of the basic ore within the Caribbean. He envisaged the establishment of a Caribbean Bauxite Commission (embracing Guyana, Jamaica, Surinam, Haiti and the Dominican Republic) to plan the gradual phasing out of the international corporations which dominated the business and to then undertake the radical revision of the industry under majority Caribbean shareholding.

The stage seemed to be set, therefore, for the economic officials who assembled in Georgetown in August 1967 to conduct a 'great debate' on the whole question of economic integration, assessing the strengths and weaknesses of each of the two strategies which lay before them. Yet, in the event, no such debate materialised. The truth of the matter was that the UWI studies were simply not taken seriously by the officials. They were not even given a proper hearing. On the opening day of the conference Brewster made a long presentation to a meeting of the heads of delegations, in which he forcefully reiterated his and Thomas's central point that measures to extend the market frontiers of the region should be 'followed by an integrated approach to production, particularly as regards large-scale industries'.[70] When, however, the guidelines for the critical sub-committee, which was to decide the manner of integration undertaken, were finalised, it was obvious where the interests of the delegates chiefly lay. Its agenda was as follows:

(i) Feasibility of freeing trade immediately with statement of reserved commodities.
(ii) Measures to deal with consequential revenue problems.
(iii) Measures for an equitable spread to all participating territories of the benefits of free trade.
(iv) Other trade and production measures.
    (a) integration of production.
    (b) common external trade policy.
    (c) harmonisation of fiscal incentives.
(v) Time Table for implementing (i) to (iv).[71]

In other words, the UWI concept of production integration was included, but only in token form as an item of secondary importance – point (iv) (a) on the agenda.

Why was this? A number of explanations have been offered,

Free trade v. production integration

none of them wholly satisfactory. From one point of view, the choice of priorities expressed in the agenda can be attributed to the naivety of the UWI economists in the world of affairs. They neglected the role of opinion-forming, it is said, and did not lobby the governments or even seek to mobilise support for their views outside government circles. This was certainly the case – the UWI team were intellectually contemptuous of politics – but, even so, does this interpretation say anything more than that they acted like the academics they were and not like the civil servants they were not? From another point of view, the explanation lay in the character of Brewster and Thomas's book: a turgid tome written in complicated, technical language and not at all easy for a layman to understand. Government economic advisers are not, however, expected to be laymen in matters of economics. Most often of all, commentators discussing the diffidence with which the officials reacted to the idea of production integration have pointed to the lack of a political dimension in the UWI studies as the main reason[72] – despite Brewster and Thomas's admission at one point that 'the main obstacle to integration of the West Indies is the low level of political "commitment" for the idea of integration'.[73]

This last observation is fair comment – up to a point. In deference to 'the dynamics of the internal political situation in Trinidad-Tobago and Guyana',[74] Brewster and Thomas did concede that the movement of people on a mass scale was neither politically feasible nor desirable, and they agreed that their projected Regional Commission on the Movement of Persons should do no more than study the possibility. For the most part, though, it is true to say that they tended to assume away the political problems of implementation. For example, for the other six regional institutions whose immediate establishment they urged – a Regional Commission for the Economic Integration of the Caribbean, a Monetary and Payments Union, a Regional Development Bank, a Transport and Allied Services Commission, a Committee on Price Stabilisation and Co-ordination and a Regional Monopolies Commission[75] – wide-ranging, almost federal powers were advocated, the granting of which would have been fiercely resisted by more than one government in the region. Moreover, scant attention was paid in any of the UWI studies to perhaps the most political question of all, the problem of the probable distribution of benefits. For all their research, Brewster and Thomas made no attempt to suggest, on objective criteria, where the industries should actually be sited. Most, they seemed to assume, would in practice have had to be located in either Jamaica or Trinidad, because of the presence there of particular resources and the need to harness the available external economies. Even the proposed regional fishing industry would have to have been based in Trinidad or Guyana, because of their proximity to the rich fishing deposits on the South American continental shelf. The benefits which Barbados and the smaller islands might have been expected to receive were left unspecified, although it was admitted that a strong case 'exists for designing part of the agricultural programme in such a way as to ensure that the distribution of the gains from integration is equitable to the various territories of the area'.[76] It is, in short, extremely unlikely, as many have noted, that the UWI proposals could have been 'sold' in practical terms in the political climate of 1967. To this, of course, the UWI economists can justly reply – as, indeed, Brewster has done[77] – that an elucidation of the economic possibilities inherent in the concept of integration was a task logically prior to the discussion of appropriate political formulae for translating it into practice, and that, anyway, the latter was no part of their brief. Both positions are quite tenable. It depends on whether one is talking the economics or the politics of development.

Either way, however, the argument, like the others, misses the most important point. The UWI proposals were *not* rejected by the officials on account of their political impracticability (although they might well have been), since, as noted earlier, discussion of the production integration strategy was stifled before it reached the stage of detailed debate. The primary reason for its rejection and the consequent adoption of free trade as the model for Caribbean economic integration is much less complicated. It was simply this: free trade was entirely consistent, in economic terms, with the view which West Indian politicians and businessmen held of themselves and their interests in 1967. As must by now be clear, the economic integration strategy propounded by Demas was essentially a neat extension of the economic policies being pursued by governments all round the region. It did not question the principles behind the strategy of 'industrialisation by invitation' or doubt the development potential of final-touch manufacturing, but asserted that the effectiveness of these policies had been muted by the small size of the market in which they had been promoted thus far and could, therefore, be substantially increased by breaking down regional tariff barriers and extending the size of the available 'home' market. The theme was very much 'more of the same'. By contrast, the UWI strategy demanded the overthrow of many of the policy shibboleths of the past decade, and at best would have necessitated tolerance of an uncomfortable era during which the region's subordinate and exploited position in the international economy was challenged. The business sector was naturally alarmed at the emphasis placed on the public ownership of integration industries, and the Incorporated Chambers' representatives at the officials' conference missed no opportunity to propagate the merits of private investment in engineering economic development.[78] The view developed in governmental circles that the UWI economists were over-zealous, inexperienced and immature – even Communist. It is not so difficult, then, to see why it was a foregone conclusion, from the first moment of the officials' conference, that the novel possibilities contained within the UWI strategy would not be risked and that the policy eventually adopted would be based, in principle, on regional free trade. The orthodox was always likely to be preferred to the unorthodox.

The only real question to engage the conference concerned the tactical approach to be adopted – in particular, whether the original Dickenson Bay agreement was to be 'adopted, scrapped or amended'.[79] In his opening speech Burnham declared that Guyana did not 'consider its membership of CARIFTA, as constituted at the moment, an impediment to economic integration on a wider scale',[80] but the Barbados delegation took a somewhat harder line, rejecting the possibility of the agreement just being set aside.[81] It was Demas, however, as head of the Trinidadian delegation who was the dominant figure of the conference, proposing adjournments to overcome procedural wrangles, intervening regularly in the discussion, and making the decisive speech in which he proposed the acceptance of the CARIFTA document 'subject to some modification'.[82] The other delegates followed this lead, and the officials accordingly recommended to their respective governments that all import duties and quantitative restrictions should be removed on the vast majority of products traded between the Commonwealth Caribbean countries with effect from 1 May 1968, using CARIFTA as a basis; that steps including consideration of a common external tariff and a common regime of quantitative restrictions towards third countries should be taken shortly after; that the principle of closer and more effective co-operation in agricultural marketing be accepted; and that a study should be carried out with a view to making recommendations regarding the harmonisation of fiscal incentives.[83] All this, of course, was encompassed within the ambit of the conventional theory of market integration.

Item (v) of the concluding resolution passed by the conference *appeared*, however, to offer something more. It urged:

> (a) That the principle of regional integrated industries, the products of which would from the date of commencement of production enjoy internal free trade and a common external policy, be accepted.
> (b) That the Economic Commission for Latin America ... be requested to initiate a study, using as one of the bases the University reports, of feasible regional industries including agriculture, fishing and livestock.[84]

The commitment, in fact, meant very little. Assertions to the contrary — to the effect that it had been possible to 'salvage' something from the UWI approach[85] — can only have been a manoeuvre or a misunderstanding of what the UWI studies were really proposing. Unless it was conceived as part of a total programme of economic transformation, as advocated by Brewster and Thomas and the other UWI economists, the concept of 'regional integration industries' offered little more than the conventional advantages of inter-territorial resource combination. The justice of the regional governments' frequent claims that free trade was only a beginning did not conceal the fact that the end product was only intended to be market integration, as outlined by Demas, and not production integration, as expounded by the UWI team.

Notes

1. W. G. Demas, *The Economics of Development in Small Countries with Special Reference to the Caribbean*, Montreal, 1965.
2. See *ibid.*, pp. 95-118.
3. O. Jefferson, 'Some Aspects of the Post-war Economic Development of Jamaica', in N. Girvan and O. Jefferson (eds.), *Readings in the Political Economy of the Caribbean*, Kingston, Jamaica, 1971, p. 112.
4. E. Carrington, 'Industrialization in Trinidad and Tobago since 1950', in Girvan and Jefferson (eds.), *op. cit.*, p. 144.
5. See A. Segal, with K. C. Earnhardt, *Politics and Population in the Caribbean*, Rio Piedras, 1969.
6. Demas, *The Economics of Development*, pp. 21-2. Demas himself inclined to the view that a small country is one with less than 5 million people and 10,000-20,000 square miles of usable land.
7. *Ibid.*, pp. 83-4.
8. *Ibid.*, p. 85.
9. W. G. Demas, 'The Economics of West Indies Customs Union', *Social and Economic Studies*, vol. 9, no. 1, 1960, pp. 13-28.
10. The classic statement is J. Viner, *The Customs Union Issue*, New York, 1950. Since the publication of this work a considerable theoretical literature has developed, refining Viner's initial formulation. See M. B. Krauss (ed.), *The Economics of Integration*, London, 1973, a book of readings which contains many of the most important contributions.
11. Demas, *The Economics of Development*, p. 88.
12. Demas, *Social and Economic Studies*, pp.15-16.
13. Demas, *The Economics of Development*, p. 89.
14. *Ibid.* Demas's emphasis.
15. See, for example, C. A. Cooper and B. Massell, 'Toward a General Theory of Customs Unions for Developing Countries', *The Journal of Political Economy*, no. 73, 1965, pp. 461-76; R. F. Mikesell, 'The Theory of Common Markets as Applied to Regional Arrangements among Developing Countries', in R. Harrod and D. Hague (eds.), *International Trade Theory in a Developing World*, New York, 1963, pp. 205-209; S. B. Linder, *Trade and Trade Policy for Development*, New York, 1967; and S. Dell, *Trade Blocs and Common Markets*, London, 1963.
16. J. Compton, Chief Minister of St Lucia, *Barbados Advocate-News*, 9 July 1965.
17. Editorial, *The Daily News* (Barbados), 7 July 1965.
18. T. Mathews, 'Problems and Leaders in the Caribbean', in A. C. Wilgus (ed.), *The Caribbean: its Hemispheric Role*, Gainesville, 1967, p. 37.
19. *New World Fortnightly*, no. 26, 29 October 1965.
20. See Government of Jamaica, *Ministry Paper No. 7. Trade with British Guiana*, Kingston, 1965.

21. Government of Barbados, *The Federal Negotiations 1962-1965 and Constitutional Proposals for Barbados*, Bridgetown, 1965, paragraph 97.
22. *Ibid.*, paragraph 99.
23. F. Burnham, 'Report to the Nation', in Burnham, *A Destiny to Mould: Selected Discourses by the Prime Minister of Guyana*, London, 1970, pp. 56-7.
24. *Agreement establishing the Caribbean Free Trade Association*, Dickenson Bay, Antigua, 15 December 1965, Preamble. Agreement's emphasis.
25. *Ibid.*, Article 2(d).
26. *Ibid.*, Article 4(1).
27. *Ibid.*, Schedule to Annex B – Rules regarding area origin for tariff purposes. The list contained some seventy-one materials.
28. *Ibid.*, Article 17 (1) (b).
29. H. Brewster, 'Caribbean Economic Integration – Problems and Perspectives', *Journal of Common Market Studies*, vol. 9, no. 4, 1971, p. 285.
30. A. McIntyre, 'Some Issues of Trade Policy in the West Indies', in Girvan and Jefferson (eds.), *op. cit.*, pp. 165-83.
31. See *Trinidad Guardian*, 6 December 1965, 26 February 1966 and 10 May 1966.
32. *Ibid.*, 3 September 1966.
33. *Agreement establishing CARIFTA*, Dickenson Bay, 1965, Article 32(1).
34. For the early history of the organisation, see L. Braithwaite, ' "Federal" Associations and Institutions in the West Indies', *Social and Economic Studies*, vol. 6, no. 2, 1957, pp. 286-93.
35. Incorporated Commonwealth Chambers of Industry and Commerce of the Caribbean, *Report of the Phased Freeing of Trade Delegation*, Port of Spain, 1966, p. 2.
36. *Ibid.*, p. 3.
37. *Ibid.*, p. 4.
38. *Ibid.*, p. 5.
39. *Ibid.*, p. 9.
40. For a discussion of this point, see S. De Castro, *Tax Holidays for Industry. Why We have to Abolish them and How to Do it*, New World Pamphlet No. 8, Kingston, Jamaica, 1973, pp. 1-8.
41. Incorporated Commonwealth Chambers, *op. cit.*, pp. 18-19.
42. *Ibid.*, pp. 36-7.
43. *Ibid.*, p. 13.
44. *Ibid.*, pp. 41-3.
45. See McIntyre, in Girvan and Jefferson (eds.), *op. cit.*, pp. 166-7 and 170-3.
46. *Daily Gleaner*, 8 July 1966.
47. *Ibid.*, 1 July 1966.
48. For an elaboration of this point, see McIntyre, in Girvan and Jefferson (eds.), *op. cit.*, pp. 168-70.
49. For full details, see *Final Communiqué, Commonwealth Caribbean –*

Canada Conference, Ottawa, 1966.
50. *Ibid.*, paragraph 15.
51. *Ibid.*, paragraph 16.
52. See *New World Fortnightly*, no. 43, 11 July 1966.
53. H. J. M. Hubbard, 'CARIFTA: what is it?', *Thunder*, vol. 18, no. 1, 1967, p. 3.
54. *Ibid.*
55. On Associated Statehood, see U. Forbes, 'The West Indies Associated States: Some Aspects of the Constitutional Arrangements', *Social and Economic Studies*, vol. 19, no. 1, 1970, pp. 57-88.
56. E. Williams, *Reflections on the Caribbean Economic Community*, Port of Spain, 1965, pp. 38-9.
57. *Daily Gleaner*, 20 May 1967.
58. Burnham, 'We must Integrate or Perish', in Burnham, *op. cit.*, pp. 246-7. Burnham's emphasis.
59. *Ibid.*, p. 250.
60. See, in addition to the articles in Girvan and Jefferson (eds.), *op. cit.*, G. L. Beckford, *Persistent Poverty: Underdevelopment in Plantation Economies of the Third World*, New York, 1972; N. Girvan, *Foreign Capital and Economic Underdevelopment in Jamaica*, Kingston, Jamaica, 1971; A. McIntyre and B. Watson, *Studies in Foreign Investment in the Commonwealth Caribbean*, vol. 1, *Trinidad and Tobago*, Kingston, Jamaica, 1970; and C. Y. Thomas, *Monetary and Financial Arrangements in a Dependent Monetary Economy*, Kingston, Jamaica, 1965, and *The Structure, Performance and Prospects of Central Banking in the Caribbean*, Kingston, Jamaica, 1972.
61. H. Brewster, 'Economic Dependence: a Quantitative Interpretation', *Social and Economic Studies*, vol. 22, no. 1, 1973, p. 91.
62. H. Brewster and C. Y. Thomas, *The Dynamics of West Indian Economic Integration*, Kingston, Jamaica, 1967.
63. *Ibid.*, p. 19.
64. *Ibid.*, p. 25.
65. *Ibid.*, p. 333.
66. *Ibid.*, p. 33.
67. G. L. Beckford and M. H. Guscott, *Intra-Caribbean Agricultural Trade*, Kingston, Jamaica, 1967.
68. G. L. Beckford, *The West Indian Banana Industry*, Kingston, Jamaica, 1967.
69. N. Girvan, *The Caribbean Bauxite Industry*, Kingston, Jamaica, 1967.
70. *Documents Relating to the Caribbean Officials' Conference on Integration, 14-18 August 1967, Georgetown*, Notes of a Meeting of Heads of Delegations to formulate an Agenda, paragraph 3.
71. *Ibid.*, Guidelines for Committee Discussion, Committee A.
72. See, for example, A. Segal, *The Politics of Caribbean Economic Integration*, Rio Piedras, 1968.
73. Brewster and Thomas, *op. cit.*, p. 27.
74. *Ibid.*, p. 33.

75. *Ibid.*, pp. 29-33.
76. *Ibid.*, p. 319.
77. Brewster, *Journal of Common Market Studies*, p. 288.
78. *Documents Relating to the Officials' Conference*, Report of J. Jardim, Head of Incorporated Commonwealth Chambers Delegation, pp. 3-4.
79. *Ibid.*, Notes of the 2nd Plenary Session, paragraph 21.
80. Burnham, 'We must Integrate or Perish', in Burnham, *op. cit.*, p. 250.
81. *Documents Relating to the Officials' Conference*, Notes of the 2nd Plenary Session, paragraph 24.
82. *Ibid.*, Notes of the Meeting of Committee A. Views expressed by W. G. Demas, Head of the Trinidad and Tobago Delegation.
83. *Ibid.*, Resolution Representing Item A on the Agenda, items (i)-(ix).
84. *Ibid.*, Resolution Representing Item A on the Agenda, item (v).
85. W. G. Demas, 'CARIFTA and the University Studies', *The Nation*, vol. 12, no. 40, 27 June 1969.

CHAPTER THREE

The establishment of CARIFTA

The only weakness which advocates of a *laissez-faire* strategy of Caribbean economic integration were prepared to admit concerned the manner of the distribution of the gains and losses to be derived from integration. Already, by the mid-1960s, it was a recognised feature of the doctrine that where an economic union is formed between countries at different stages of development economically, and where market forces are left to operate without restraint, the result is to increase the advantage that the more developed states have over their poorer partners.[1] Not only do they already possess industries better capable of taking immediate advantage of the enlarged market but, because they have various, important 'external economies' (including such factors as a wide range of public utility services, a skilled or semi-skilled labour force and the presence of banks and finance houses) they also prove more attractive to the location of new investment. In Myrdal's terms, 'backwash' effects, representing a self-reinforcing agglomeration of the gains in the more developed territories, tend to prevail over 'spread' effects, by which the benefits of the growth in the real income of the dynamic areas filter through the union as a whole via an increase in demand for the products of the less developed territories.[2] As a result, 'poles of growth' develop, which drain the development potential of the more backward countries of the union, thereby creating, in turn, 'poles of stagnation'. In the normal course of trade diversion the less developed countries have to suffer both the costs of paying higher prices for goods produced by regional industries, which are rarely competitive in world market terms, and the loss of customs revenue involved whenever goods are bought in the tariff-free regional market rather than from extra-regional sources. Far from receiving benefits from an increase in intra-regional trade, as the more developed countries are likely to do, it seems that they are more likely to retrogress in terms of industrialisation.

The problem of polarisation, therefore, is not simply one of unequal growth, where benefits may be accuring to the union as a whole and to each of the member units, albeit at an unequal rate, but rather the possibility that, without effective compensatory measures, some members will actually incur a net loss as a result of economic integration. Well might Demas observe that it was the 'fly in the ointment'[3] as far as the market theory of integration was concerned. As he fully realised, polarisation was the main obstacle to be overcome in the planning of a free trade area or customs union in the West Indies. From the outset it served to politicise the issue of comparative gains and losses from integration and reduced the debate about regional economic integration to the question of whether or not appropriate positive mechanisms designed to make the concept acceptable to the poorer territories could be negotiated between the various governments. The next phase of the integration movement, during which attention turned to the practical problem of implementing the broad strategy agreed upon by their officials in Georgetown, has therefore to be explained more by reference to the politics than the economics of integration. For in the period following the Georgetown conference the central actors in the integration drama were no longer the civil servants, the businessmen or the academics, but the politicians themselves.

The task of forging an intergovernmental coalition which would make economic integration politically viable began at the Fourth Heads of Government conference, held in Bridgetown, Barbados, in October 1967, the first in the series to be attended by the leaders of all the Commonwealth Caribbean territories. It was, in consequence, the largest and most prestigious gathering of West Indian leaders since the days of the Federation, and was taken with great seriousness by all the participant governments. Their deliberations centred on three main themes. The first was naturally the question of free trade. Barbados, according to reports, still favoured the initial implementation of CARIFTA on a three-territory basis,[4] other territories being left to join as they pleased and having thus to suffer the indignity of making a formal application for membership. The expected objections to this plan were eventually overcome by a neat formula whereby Antigua, Barbados and Guyana signed a supplementary agreement, incorporating a long resolution (passed by the conference) which set out the economic integration programme to be followed by the region as a whole. Any Commonwealth Caribbean government which deposited with the Antiguan government an instrument signifying its endorsement of the resolution was from that moment decreed to be a signatory territory of the CARIFTA treaty itself. The resolution, therefore, became the crucial text and read as follows:

> Free trade should be introduced with respect to all intra-Commonwealth Caribbean trade by 1st May 1968, subject to a list of reserved commodities which would be freed within a ten-year period for the less-developed countries; subject to special provisions for appeal by a less-developed Territory to the governing body of the Free Trade Area for further extension in any case where serious injury may be done to a territorial industry.
> 2. The Governors should approach the task of freeing of trade, by using the CARIFTA Agreement as a basis with suitable modifications.
> 3. The Commonwealth Caribbean countries shall immediately take steps to initiate studies to determine whether the objectives of achieving trade expansion to the mutual benefit of the member states can be facilitated by the establishment of a common external tariff in whole or in part.
> 4. The principle should be accepted that certain industries may require for their economic operation the whole or a large part of the entire regional market protected by a common external tariff or other suitable instrument. The location of such industries and the criteria to be applied in respect thereof, as well as the implementation of the principle accepted above, should be the subject of immediate study – such study to have special

regard to the situation of the relatively less-developed countries.

5. Subject to existing commitments a regional policy of incentives to industry should be adopted as early as possible on the basis of studies mentioned in Resolution 7 below, bearing in mind the special needs of the less-developed countries for preferential treatement, such as soft loans.

6. Marketing agreements for an agreed list of agricultural commodities should be sought to come into effect at the same time as the commencement of free trade and the territories in the region should examine the possibility of restricting imports from extra-regional sources of agricultural products that are produced within the region and are available for satisfying regional demand.

7. The principle of seeking to establish more industries in the less-developed countries should be accepted and the ECLA [Economic Commission for Latin America] Secretariat should be asked to undertake feasibility studies immediately with a view to identifying industries which should be located in the less-developed countries and to devising special measures for securing the establishment of such industries in these countries. These studies should be submitted to governments no later than one year after the commencement of free trade.

8. The Commonwealth Caribbean Countries should endeavour to maintain and improve regional carriers to facilitate the movement of goods and services within the region.

9. The Commonwealth Caribbean Countries should agree to negotiate with the Shipping Conference the rationalization of freight rates on extra-regional traffic.

10. The ECLA Secretariat for the Caribbean should be asked to undertake a number of studies, for example, studies on the harmonizing of incentives and the feasibility of establishing certain regional industries.

11. A Committee of Ministers should be set up immediately, functioning as a sub-committee of the Heads of Government Conference, with general responsibility for the establishment of the Free Trade Area.[5]

As can be seen, it followed closely the recommendations of the officials' conference, even down to the token bow in the direction of production integration, but it did, significantly, include a number of distinct concessions designed to relieve the position of those territories which seemed likely to suffer from polarisation. The smaller territories were, in fact, granted formal recognition as less developed countries in implied contrast to the more developed countries of Jamaica, Trinidad, Barbados and Guyana, and the terms 'LDC' and 'MDC' soon became part of the language of Caribbean integration.

Secondly, the conference turned its attention to the regional institutions which were felt to be necessary to reinforce the overall effect of economic integration. It accepted in principle, for example, the need for a regional news service and a regional bureau of standards, and agreed to establish a working party to consider the creation of a regional airline. The question of a regional secretariat also came up in the form of a paper from Guyana, which suggested that the progress achieved by the Central American Common Market – in comparison, at least, with the Latin American Free Trade Association – was in large part attributable to the former's possession of effective secretariat services.[6] As had been the case on previous occasions when a secretariat had been proposed, the Jamaican delegation was highly sceptical, challenging almost every clause of the draft agreement prepared by Guyana and proposing that a simpler and more economical Trade and Integration Committee was sufficient to deal with CARIFTA matters.[7] The other delegates, however, received with acclamation a speech by Williams, who argued that, in so far as Guyana had taken the lead in the matter of Caribbean free trade and had in every way demonstrated its re-entry into the family of West Indian nations, it was appropriate that the South American territory should be selected as the site of the Commonwealth Caribbean Regional Secretariat. The Jamaican government insisted on reserving its position to the last and was supported on the question of location and budget by Barbados, out of the latter's disappointment, perhaps, at not being considered itself for the site of the Secretariat.[8]

The last issue to concern the conference was the establishment of a regional development bank. Undoubtedly the Caribbean was poorly served from the point of view of international banking facilities. Not only was it effectively excluded from the World Bank's sphere of interest, because its territories were either not independent and therefore ineligible, or were too small to warrant even the minimum size of loan the Bank granted, or had *per capita* incomes just above the level required to qualify for soft loans, but it was also one of the few developing areas of the world not yet served by a regional development bank of its own. The idea, though, had been broached a number of times. In 1963, for example, Rafael Pico, President of the Government Development Bank of Puerto Rico, called for a Caribbean Development Bank to operate in conjunction with the Caribbean Organisation.[9] Three years later Demas proposed that a bank should be established, 'charged with implementing a regional investment policy designed to prevent polarization and to permit co-ordinated development',[10] and in April of the same year the *Report of the Tripartite Economic Survey of the Eastern Caribbean* urged the creation of a Regional Development Agency, incorporating a Development Bank Division.[11] The question came up too at the Canada–West Indies Conference in Ottawa in July 1966 and was once more favourably received.

It was, however, the Tripartite Report which eventually prompted some action. A conference in Antigua in November 1966 between the governments that had sponsored the report – Canada, the United Kingdom and the United States – and the governments of the territories to which it applied – Barbados and the Leeward and Windward Islands – led to the appointment of a United Nations Development Programme (UNDP) mission to study the region's banking requirements. After conducting discussions in all the territories concerned, it recommended that a Caribbean Development Bank (CDB) be established with a total capital of US$50 million and including as full members all the Commonwealth Caribbean states, the United States, Britain and Canada. The report was accepted, according to one of its authors, 'without even so much as five minutes discussion'[12] at the Georgetown officials' conference in 1967, and was adopted as a suitable basis for formulating definite proposals by the heads of government in Barbados shortly afterwards in just as perfunctory a manner. The only major amendment was forced by the statement of the United States representative that, owing to the constraints of the Congressional timetable, his country would be unable to contribute to the bank's equity, for which legislation was required, but would instead increase the special soft loan fund by an amount equivalent to its planned equity subscription. For their part, the heads of government were content to delegate the detailed planning of the Bank, and in particular the preparation of a draft charter, to an intergovernmental committee of officials advised by the UNDP, although they did briefly discuss the question of its location. The Jamaican representative stressed the importance of a businesslike approach to this problem and some preliminary consideration of possible sites took place,[13] but that was all.

The one crucial decision taken by the Heads of Government Conference with regard to the Bank concerned the date set for its inauguration − 1 May 1968, the same as that set for the commencement of regional free trade. This coincidence of timing was quite deliberate and was a factor of the utmost significance politically. In keeping with its brief, the UNDP report had recommended that the main objective of the Bank should be 'to provide economic growth and co-operation in the Caribbean, utilizing the resources at its disposal for financing regional and national projects and programmes which will contribute most effectively to the *harmonious* economic growth of the region and pay *special regard to the needs of the smaller areas*'.[14] As the report made clear, the underdevelopment of the LDCs in the region was aggravated by 'the relative absence of even the incomplete range of specialised finance institutions to be found in the larger territories'.[15] Despite the activities of the Commonwealth Development Corporation, there was a dearth of long-term development finance available to the smaller territories, and they were thus prevented from embarking upon their long backlog of infrastructural and other development projects. In this situation a Caribbean Development Bank, financed chiefly by contributions from metropolitan countries and the larger Caribbean states but geared especially to their needs, was a manifestly attractive bait to hold before the LDCs. This was, of course, the intention and the reason why the Heads of Government Conference elected to make a political link between the two issues of free trade and development banking by setting the same target date for the commencement of both. As far as the LDCs were concerned, the undoubted *quid pro quo* for CARIFTA was the CDB.

And so the deal was clinched – trading benefits for the more industrialised states, the Secretariat for Guyana, concessions on free trade and industrial allocation and the promise of development finance for the LDCs. It did not, however, hold for very long in the face of the hard-nosed attitude of the government of Jamaica. Jamaica's relationship with the eastern Caribbean has been distant and aloof throughout her history. Jamaicans have been widely viewed by other West Indians as aggressive and forceful, whilst the prevailing Jamaican image of the 'small' islands of the eastern Caribbean was of poverty, parochialism and a desire to exploit Jamaica's greater prosperity. The experience of the Federation, as we have seen, served only to reinforce these stereotyped attitudes and to widen the psychological gulf between the two ends of the Caribbean. A distinguished Jamaican caught the national mood of his country in late 1961 after the referendum when he wrote: 'now that this nonsense of Federation is finally disposed of, we can at last get to work on our problems'.[16] In the intervening years such feelings had been submerged beneath the formal politeness of intergovernmental diplomacy, but they had never been extinguished, least of all within the ranks of the Jamaica Labour Party, the party that had led the fight against federation and had since formed the government of Jamaica. Jamaica played her part in the gradual regional embrace of economic integration during the mid-1960s and she was obviously one of the territories with the most to gain from the freeing of trade. Yet she had done so with an obvious emotional reluctance and, although her delegation went along with the broad sweep of the decisions made at the October 1967 Heads of Government Conference, the Jamaican government's commitment to the integration movement was demonstrably less wholehearted than that of her eastern Caribbean partners. By the same token, its interest in extra-regional economic links with North America and with the European Economic Community (including the possibility of being granted Associated Overseas Territory status by the latter) was somewhat greater than that of its neighbours. In consequence, in all its dealings with the other governments of the region, the Jamaican government was calculating and cautious in outlook, alert to the balance of advantage and constantly looking for signs that the eastern Caribbean states were really striving to revitalise the idea of federation. In a sense, of course, the domestic political environment in Jamaica gave it no alternative. The response the government delegation received, for example, on returning from the Barbados conference was far removed from the warm congratulations proffered in the other capitals of the region. It was summed up by two pieces in the *Gleaner*: an editorial intimating that Jamaica would, as a result of the conference decisions, have to forgo some industrialisation,[17] and an article by the influential 'Political Reporter', questioning whether, in the light of the events of September 1961, 'any Government in Jamaica has the moral or constitutional right to place us in any relationship with the rest of the West Indies whatsoever which would to any great extent affect our sovereignty without putting the matter for decision by a Referendum to the voters of Jamaica'.[18] In implicit response to this, the government's Ministry Paper, reporting on the conference, drew special attention to Jamaica's willingness to co-operate with the other countries of the Caribbean, 'so long as it is clearly understood that the operative words are "economic cooperation" and *NOT* "political integration" '.[19]

The issue on which the Jamaican government decided to demonstrate its independence of the eastern Caribbean governments was the location of the Caribbean Development Bank. Although nothing had been decided in Barbados, the suggestion had been made that the Bank should be sited in St Vincent[20] in order to symbolise its standing as a pro-LDC instrument of integration. The Jamaican delegation had argued at the time that the decision should be taken not on sentimental grounds but on sound banking criteria. When this theme was developed further at the follow-up meeting of officials, held in Jamaica in December 1967, the MDC–LDC bargain struck so successfully in Barbados began to disintegrate. For the criteria for location settled upon by the officials did not point to St Vincent or any of the LDCs, but emphasised instead the possession of good communications with the rest of the area and the outside world, the widespread availability of social facilities like schools, housing and hospitals, and the prior existence of a developed financial and commercial environment[21] – all factors which distinguished the MDCs from their smaller island partners.

Meanwhile the plans for implementing CARIFTA were proceeding apace. The officials' meeting in Jamaica in December 1967 also pursued the task of preparing the reserve list and drafting the text of the supplementary agreement to the original CARIFTA document, whilst another officials' meeting held in Trinidad in January 1968 dealt with agricultural marketing arrangements, the regional airline and the regional secretariat. The final political decisions were scheduled to be taken at a meeting of Trade Ministers in Guyana in February 1968. It was at this point that Jamaica's disaffection with the arrangements for the location of the Bank and growing suspicion of the motives of the eastern Caribbean states seemed to spill over into the preparations for the establishment of CARIFTA. Using the familiar (and, over the passage of time, increasingly implausible) excuse that it had received the relevant documents too late, the Jamaican government sent no ministerial representative to the Guyana meeting, thereby provoking the rumour that it was about to renege on its commitment to CARIFTA. These doubts were in no way assuaged by the explanatory statement issued by Jamaica's High Commissioner to Trinidad, one of the only two Jamaican officials to make an appearance at the conference. 'Jamaica,' he declared,

> does not believe in the principle of marrying in haste and repenting at leisure. The suggestion has been made that other Commonwealth Caribbean countries contemplate going beyond a Free Trade Area and are looking towards the establishment of a common market with a common external tariff. The decisions of the recent Barbados Heads of Government Conference contain no commitment by the Caribbean countries to this immediate end. Certainly the CARIFTA document which was accepted as the basis of our economic co-operation does not contemplate a common market at this stage.[22]

Despite this reiteration of interest in free trade, a major difference of approach was revealed in the statement. The Jamaican government conceived of regional free trade merely as an exercise in economic *co-operation*, and declined to talk of economic *integration*, the term always used by the other West Indian territories. The distinction was much more than semantic, although it revealed itself less in the immediate preoccupation with planning free trade than in regard to the subsequent stages of a strategy of market integration. The Jamaican government genuinely feared that questions like the uniformity of external tariffs and the free movement of persons and capital, apart from sheering just a shade too close to the great taboo of political integration, might prejudice the negotiation of an Association agreement with the EEC, which it considered to be the more important goal. Jamaica's policy towards the Caribbean region, therefore, took the form of participation in the economic integration movement, tempered by a concern to restrain it at all costs from reaching a point where it closed off other economic policy options.

Moreover, with regard to the establishment of CARIFTA itself, there is no doubt that, in addition to the reservations induced by the dispute over the siting of the Bank, the Jamaican government was also being urged to think again by its own manufacturing interests. Their argument was that, unless they were allowed to import raw materials duty-free, as was generally the case in the rest of the region, they would, in a situation of free trade, be placed at a competitive disadvantage with their eastern Caribbean rivals[23] and would be rendered unable to compete effectively, not just in the enlarged regional market, but in the domestic Jamaican market itself, with obvious and damaging consequences for existing industries and the prevailing level of employment within the island. The Jamaican government perhaps thought – as many commentators certainly did[24] – that the apprehension of the business sector was due as much to loss of nerve after so many years of shelter behind the protection of high tariff barriers, but, given the structure of the Jamaican economy, it could not afford to ignore their views.

Faced with this situation, the Cabinet was far from united. Pro- and anti-CARIFTA factions emerged behind the respective figures of the Trade Minister, Robert Lightbourne, and the Finance Minister, Edward Seaga. Their particular offices naturally gave them a different perspective on regional integration – the one seeing the trade advantages at first hand, the other having to handle the Bank negotiations – but, more then this, the two were engaged in a personal battle for ascendancy within the Cabinet, a struggle in which the integration issue became inextricably entangled. In late February and early March 1968 it was probably true to say that the Jamaican government was still genuinely undecided about whether or not to join CARIFTA.

The ostensible reaction of the other West Indian governments was simply to ignore Jamaica's hesitant and prevaricating stance and to proceed, as planned, with the 1 May deadline. The Trade Ministers' conference had agreed on the final amendments to the CARIFTA supplementary agreement, and the Finance Ministers were due to meet shortly afterwards to conclude arrangements for the CDB. With the assistance of a team of Guyanese civil servants, acting as an unofficial secretariat, a considerable momentum built up briefly behind the integration movement and seemed, temporarily, to carry Jamaica with it. Having acceded to the demands of the Jamaica Manufacturers' Association on the question of import tariffs, Shearer, the new Jamaican Prime Minister, cabled all his fellow heads of government just before the Finance Ministers' meeting to affirm his country's readiness to participate fully in CARIFTA as from the agreed date.[25]

This move did not, however, presage any softening of the Jamaican position on the location of the Bank. Far from resolving the issue and fashioning an institution which, as Burnham put it, would be 'more lasting than bronze',[26] the Finance Ministers' meeting saw the row break out into the open. The cause was the continued advancement of St Vincent as the most suitable site by a number of eastern Caribbean delegations. On behalf of the Jamaican government, Seaga reminded everyone of the criteria agreed to, and witheringly demonstrated that St Vincent failed to meet them in every respect. He was also at pains to point out

> that the Caribbean region does not consist of the eastern region alone. Regional members extend from Belize in the west to Barbados in the east to the Bahamas in the north to Guyana in the south. The region is not the eastern Caribbean, the region

The establishment of CARIFTA

extends from Belize to Barbados and from Bahamas to Guyana, and when I look at my map which might be different from the maps of others, I see St Vincent located in the eastern Caribbean well distant from a section of it and, at the same time, if I am to look at Jamaica, I see it lying on an east to west axis almost midway between Belize and the eastern Caribbean and a north to south axis almost midway between the Bahamas and Guyana.[27]

In addition, Seaga's speech gave full voice to Jamaica's disregard and contempt for the eastern Caribbean and dramatically exemplified a favourite Jamaican thesis that the rest of the region depended upon the relative strength of its economy. Jamaica, he observed, was to be the largest subscriber of equity to the Bank, its contribution being 43 per cent of the regional total; he therefore felt justified in rejecting Guyana's proposal, which was that the headquarters of the Bank be located in St Vincent and a branch in Jamaica. Jamaica would support the motion if it was put the other way round, but would otherwise have no alternative but to 'withdraw from membership in the Bank'.[28]

One has to admit that, objectively, the Jamaican case was a powerful one. The Bank's initial capitalisation was such that it needed, from the outset, to attract investment from commercial and governmental sources outside the Caribbean, a task in which perhaps the greater wealth of Jamaican contacts with the international economic system would have proved useful; it did also require the presence of a central bank in which to deposit its funds. However, to give undue emphasis to the rationality of the Jamaican argument would be to misunderstand the highly charged atmosphere in which the negotiations took place. Much of this was revealed in the angry and bitter speech Errol Barrow made to the Finance Ministers' conference. Referring to the Bank as 'being born in sin and conceived in wickedness', he declared that, even before the Heads of Government Conference was convened in October 1967, 'a block decision' had been taken to put forward St Vincent for the site.[29] He went on:

It was very embarrassing to most of us, therefore, outside of the Associated States when the suggestion was made. But there appears to have been some political desideratum on the part of the Government of Guyana which constrained them to jump into the area and say: 'Oh, yes, we will support St Vincent for the Bank!' We were not satisfied ... that this was based on any more than political expediency. It is very bad to have to talk about your hosts in this manner, but the *quid pro quo* ... was soon disclosed when another illogical decision was made ... certainly we were not satisfied that the selection of Guyana as the location of the Regional Secretariat was one which was made from the point of the best interest of the region or from geographical centrality.[30]

Barrow's charge of 'horse-trading' and 'playing politics' rang true, and applied no less to the posturing of the Jamaican government, which was as keen as all the other governments to acquire its share of the pickings of regional integration. The CDB, of course, was the prize it particularly wanted, Jamaica being exceptional among the MDCs in having no special access to soft loans. Trinidad and Barbados, for example, as members of the Organisation of American States, were able to tap the resources of the Inter-American Development Bank, whilst in this sense Burnham's government in Guyana had a 'soft cushion' in Washington because of the US State Department's desire to prevent Jagan's return to power. Jamaica's many objections to the siting of the Bank in St Vincent derived, therefore, from a wider opposition to its putative role as an institution established primarily to serve the LDCs. The Jamaican government was thinking, above all, of its own interests: it undoubtedly hoped that having the Bank in Kingston would mean that its own loan applications, as host government, would receive an especially warm response. It could thus acquire – courtesy of the integration movement – the preferential source of soft loan finance which it had hitherto lacked.

In the aftermath of the speeches delivered by Seaga and Barrow the Finance Ministers were unable to come to any decision on the location issue and resolved only to meet again a month later, by which time the 1 May deadline would be a matter of days away. When the Jamaican delegation arrived in Antigua at the end of April 1968 for the resumption of this meeting, it discovered that a new arrangement had been forged between the leading states of the eastern Caribbean and that it faced a *fait accompli*. The favoured candidate for the siting of the Bank was not to be St Vincent, nor Jamaica, but Barbados. As the *Gleaner's* 'Political Reporter' commented suspiciously, there had been 'much feasting on curried goat and rum on the eve of the meeting'.[31] Seaga nevertheless reiterated the arguments in favour of Kingston and again threatened to withdraw. There does not, however, seem to have been any consideration of the possibility of conceding to Jamaica, even though it meant that she was being completely excluded from the allocation of the various spoils of the integration movement. Jamaica, it was said, had been chosen as the site of the main campus of UWI; but that was in 1948 and that had been a decision, not of the eastern Caribbean governments, but of the government of Britain. Because of Jamaica's 'minimalist' commitment to the integration movement, and her general reluctance to associate herself fully with the West Indian region, the leading territories of the eastern Caribbean were in no mood to see a prime part of the integration deal falling into Jamaican clutches. Angered by the aggressive tactics employed by the Jamaican government in its attempt to have the Bank located in Kingston, they preferred, on balance, to risk Jamaica's complete withdrawal. Put to the vote, the contest was easily won by Barbados, only four countries – thought to be Jamaica itself, the Bahamas, British Honduras and St Lucia[32] – voting for Jamaica. Thereupon the Jamaican delegation walked out and flew home. The clash obviously revived doubts about Jamaica's participation, not only in the Bank but in CARIFTA, the agreement of which was due to be signed in Antigua two days later. The enabling motion, although laid in the Jamaican House of Representatives, had not yet been called and debated and, in the aftermath of Jamaica's angry withdrawal from further discussions on the Bank, no attempt was made to do so before 1 May.

In the event, CARIFTA was inaugurated with only one additional state, Trinidad. At the last moment the Associated States, rather than actually signing the document there and then, laid a declaration of intent to join by 1 July 1968. Their last-minute hesitation needs explaining too. Were not the MDCs wont to assert that the great merit of the Caribbean economic integration movement, in comparison, say, to LAFTA, was the way it had openly tackled the problem of polarisation? There was scope, in their view, for economic gains by each one of the participants, and they frequently pointed to the five mechanisms which had been added to the original CARIFTA agreement in a deliberate attempt to provide the LDCs with positive opportunities to benefit from regional economic integration.

These were, firstly, the special provisions contained in the Reserve List,[33] a schedule of commodities which were not to be subjected immediately to free trade. Generally speaking, the LDCs were given a longer period in which to remove duties on goods on the Reserve List than the MDCs. The reasoning was obvious: their existing and potential manufacturing industries needed greater protection from outside competition and their exchequers were less able to afford a sharp and sudden reduction in revenue from import duties. Annex B of the agreement dealt with the need for protection. On three products – biscuits, coir products, and brushes made with plastic bristles – the MDCs had to remove duties immediately, whilst the LDCs were allowed a ten-year leeway. On another thirteen products, already made in the MDCs but which the LDCs were also actually, or hoped soon to start, producing, the LDCs were granted ten years and the MDCs five years in which to remove duties completely. Annex D, on the other hand, dealt with the revenue side of the Reserve List. On the first category of goods – beer, stout and ale; vodka and whisky; and petroleum products – all territories had to remove the 'effective protective element'[34] in revenue duties over a five-year period, whilst on the second category, which consisted solely of rum, the LDCs had ten years and the MDCs five. Lastly, the Revenue List provided that the LDCs could agree to eliminate immediately amongst themselves duties on reserved products or to reduce them more rapidly than with respect to the MDCs. As the Secretariat later put it, this allowed the LDCs 'to create "a small Free Trade Area" within "a larger Free Trade Area" '.[35]

Secondly, the new Article 39 of the agreement, much heralded by apologists of Caribbean economic integration as an example of 'the pragmatic, unorthodox and unique approach taken in

CARIFTA',[36] decreed than an LDC, on establishing an industry already in existence in one of the MDCs, could, in consort with other LDCs, seek the approval of the CARIFTA Council to set up in all the LDCs a protective tariff barrier against imports of similar products from the MDCs for as long as was felt necessary to put the LDC's infant industry on its feet.

Thirdly, there was the Agricultural Marketing Protocol (AMP), an integral part of the whole agreement, by which each member territory was required to declare every year its estimated production of some twenty-two agricultural commodities,[37] thus enabling the Secretariat (in theory at least) to allocate markets among all the territories according to the anticipated surpluses and deficits. The scheme derived from the realisation that free trade would in itself be insufficient to promote expanded intra-regional trade in agricultural products, chiefly because import duties on foodstuffs were either very low or completely non-existent in most territories, and that, in consequence, a more positive instrument was required. It was intended that the measure would particularly benefit the LDCs, where most of the region's agricultural production took place.

Fourthly, in accordance with the resolution adopted at the Fourth Heads of Government Conference in Barbados in October 1967, which was reproduced in full within the CARIFTA agreement as Annex A, the ECLA Secretariat was asked to undertake feasibility studies relating to industries which could be located in the LDCs.

Fifthly, and finally, there was a commitment to harmonise the fiscal incentives given to industry. Article 23 of the agreement gave the Council power to make recommendations in this direction, and the Heads of Government resolution requested another ECLA report on the subject. Incentives, we should note, were to be harmonised, not equalised, and the LDCs were promised that their special position would be recognised by allowing them to grant more generous incentives than the MDCs.

These various compensatory mechanisms do at least bear out the claim that the 1968 version of CARIFTA constituted something more than just a classical free trade area, but one wonders how much they really impressed the leaders of the

Leeward and Windward Islands. After all, freedom of movement of persons had been ruled out from the outset. Nor do concessions in a trading regime mean much unless there are goods to trade, and what the economies of LDCs lacked, above all, was actual production. Their real interest in Caribbean integration, as we have made clear, lay in the development funds they expected to receive from the CDB, their own bank, as it was universally seen in the capitals of the LDCs. Understandably, the delay in the establishment of the Bank caused by the row over its location and the final decision to site it in an MDC – with which, incidentally, they had agreed in order to block Jamaica's claim – provoked a reassessment of their position in the whole integration movement. The outcome was the signing on 27 April 1968 of an agreement to form an Eastern Caribbean Common Market (ECCM)[38] amongst the Associated States due to come into force in less than two months, on 15 June 1968: hence the desire to delay entry to CARIFTA till 1 July, when the ECCM would be operative. The ECCM had the same objectives as the CARIFTA agreement and was, of course, no more than the LDCs were permitted, and even encouraged, to institute within the terms of CARIFTA itself. It required the elimination of customs duties and quantitative restrictions between its member states, the removal of obstacles to the movement of factors of production, the harmonisation of tax structures, fiscal incentives and development policies, the establishment of a common policy on agricultural development and in the field of communications, and the imposition of common customs tariffs and commercial policies towards countries, including the MDCs, not parties to the agreement. If fully implemented, it meant that the construction of an integrated market would proceed at a more accelerated pace amongst the LDCs than amongst the Commonwealth Caribbean countries as a whole.

Nevertheless, the ECCM and the other 'concessions' contained within the structure of CARIFTA can only be said to have offered an *opportunity* and a *framework* in which to pursue economic development – in marked contrast to the tangible trading benefits which all the MDCs, except perhaps Guyana, the least industrialised of the four, could look forward to within weeks of the inception of free trade. Moreover, the day when the CDB began dispensing loans was manifestly still a long way off. It may be argued, then, that the Associated States' decision to enter CARIFTA on 1 July was not entirely justified in the scales of self-interest. There was, however, an additional commitment at the psychological level − some sense, in other words, of regional solidarity − and perhaps also the hope that ultimately economic integration would become political integration, which together tipped the balance and persuaded the LDCs to take their chance within the regional movement. As Edward Le Blanc, the Premier of Dominica, explained when he spoke on behalf of the Associated States at the ceremonial inauguration of CARIFTA on 30 April,

> this group of islands in the Eastern Caribbean stretching from Antigua in the north to Grenada in the south has demonstrated throughout the years that we are firmly committed to the dialogue of integration. We have participated in exercises of regional integration even when it was apparent that the dynamics for integration were bound up with the convenience of metropolitan countries. We have participated in federal efforts even when decisions seemed weighted in favour of other groups. During these desperate years of speaking for solidarity, the territories of the Eastern Caribbean have experienced many frustrations. But they have not lost faith ... To the cynical, we live in a fool's paradise of regionalism. To the unsympathetic, our goals seem comical. But to those who have a vision of a West Indian nation, speaking with one voice in countries of the world, and dedicated to the economic development of the peoples of the West Indies as a whole, our puny efforts assume heroic proportions.[39]

The Jamaican government, by contrast, completely rejected this sentimental approach to the issue of West Indian unity. Despite the boost that the Bank decision had given to the theory that the rest of the region was 'ganging up' on Jamaica to force her into a regional association, the implications of which had not been fully spelled out, the supporters of CARIFTA within Shearer's government were able all the time to point to the concrete benefits potentially attainable from free trade and to the consequences, moreover, of not joining, for then Jamaican goods would have had to compete with tariff-free products in the

Caribbean market whilst facing a duty barrier themselves. In the end they won the day: on 18 June 1968 the Jamaican House of Representatives approved a motion authorising the Jamaican government to seek membership of CARIFTA, and on 26 June the first CARIFTA Council, which at that stage consisted only of the representatives of Antigua, Barbados, Guyana, and Trinidad, approved applications from Jamaica and Montserrat (the latter still a colony and, therefore, not a party to the Associated States' declaration of intent to join) without seeking in any way to make alterations to the original terms of entry. Montserrat's concern about the loss of income from customs duties, on which it was especially reliant, was well understood by the rest of the region, but for Jamaica it was practically the last chance. The other MDC governments, attracted by the size of the Jamaican market, were, on balance, still willing to accept Jamaica's application. But in the weeks after Jamaica's withdrawal from the Bank and her decision not to enter CARIFTA on 1 May, the feeling had begun to develop, especially within the LDCs, that, so far from being a setback, Jamaica's non-participation would perhaps be a blessing in disguise. Unhampered by the inclusion of 'the Jamaican problem', could not the economic integration movement move ahead all the more swiftly? The potential market would still be $2\frac{1}{2}$ million people. Certainly, the prospect of Jamaica reaping the benefits of free trade within the markets of the LDCs, whilst rejecting any responsibility to help the less developed islands of the region by participating in the Bank, was viewed very unfavourably. It is more than possible that had the Jamaican application been received after 1 July by a CARIFTA Council enlarged by the presence of the LDC representatives there would have been an attempt to formalise the political connection between CARIFTA and the CDB. As it was, immediately after its first meeting the members of the Council felt it necessary to embark upon a hurried tour of the other states of the region to explain their decision to admit Jamaica and, in particular, to ask the Jamaican government to reconsider its position regarding participation in the Bank.

So by 1 August 1968 CARIFTA had been established, embracing ultimately the eleven leading states of the

Commonwealth Caribbean.[40] The claim was immediately made that, as a result of its creation, the West Indies was a more united region, at least at government level, and one cannot say that it was wholly untrue. The establishment of CARIFTA was a considerable achievement of its kind. One must be careful, however, not to overstate the case. The initial phase of the integration movement had not been without its moments of tension and drama. CARIFTA itself was still a very brittle structure. The CDB was not yet a reality and the commitments of Annex A remained paper ones only. Agreement had not yet been reached on the question of a regional airline and the attitude of the Jamaican government to the whole issue of integration was still an imponderable. What is more, the polarisation problem had clearly been only postponed, not solved. Caribbean integration was off the ground, but only just.

Notes

1. For a good summary of the arguments, see C. Eckenstein, 'Regional Integration among Unequally Developed Countries', in R. Preiswerk (ed.), *Regionalism and the Commonwealth Caribbean*, Port of Spain, 1969, pp. 41-55.
2. G. Myrdal, *Economic Theory and Underdeveloped Regions*, London, 1957.
3. W. G. Demas, 'Planning and the Price-Mechanism in the Context of Caribbean Economic Integration', in S. Lewis and T. G. Mathews (eds.), *Caribbean Integration. Papers on Social, Political and Economic Integration*, Rio Piedras, 1967, p. 83.
4. *Trinidad Guardian*, 29 October and 9 November 1967.
5. *Final Communiqué of the Fourth Heads of Government Conference*, Bridgetown, 1967.
6. B. Collins, 'The Caribbean Regional Secretariat', in Preiswerk (ed.), *op. cit.*, pp. 110-11.
7. *Ibid.*, p. 111.
8. *Ibid.*
9. R. Pico, *Financing for Economic Development*, San Juan, 1963, p. 153, quoted in F. Francis, 'The Caribbean Development Bank', in Preiswerk (ed.), *op. cit.*, p. 88.
10. Demas in Lewis and Mathews (eds.) *op. cit.*, pp. 99-100.
11. *Report of the Tripartite Economic Survey of the Eastern Caribbean, January–April 1966*, London, 1967, p. 250.
12. Francis in Preiswerk (ed.), *op. cit.*, p. 91. Francis was himself a member of the UNDP mission.
13. Statement by Shearer, Prime Minister of Jamaica, *Daily Gleaner*, 28

October 1967.
14. United Nations Development Programme, *Caribbean Development Bank*, United Nations SF/310/Reg.111, 1967, Section 2, paragraph 21. My emphasis.
15. *Ibid.*, Section 4, paragraph 46.
16. T. Wright, columnist, *Daily Gleaner*, 21 September 1961.
17. Editorial, *Daily Gleaner*, 4 November 1967.
18. The Political Reporter, *Daily Gleaner*, 5 November 1967.
19. Government of Jamaica, *Ministry Paper No. 57. Report on the Fourth Heads of Government Conference*, Kingston, 1967. Paper's emphasis.
20. *Trinidad Guardian*, 26 and 27 October 1967.
21. See statement by the Prime Minister, *Jamaica Hansard. Proceedings of House of Representatives 1968-9*, vol. 1, no. 1, 30 April 1968, p. 145.
22. Statement by A. Wright, Jamaican High Commissioner to Trinidad, *Trinidad Guardian*, 21 February 1968.
23. Brewster and Thomas provide empirical confirmation of the Jamaican manufacturers' argument that, in terms of labour productivity, they were at an absolute cost disadvantage in comparison with Trinidad. H. Brewster and C. Y. Thomas, *The Dynamics of West Indian Economic Integration*, Kingston, Jamaica, 1967, pp. 10-11.
24. See, for example, The Industrial Reporter, *Daily Gleaner*, 9 July 1968.
25. The cable noted Jamaica's acceptance of the principles and provisions of the CARIFTA agreement and promised appropriate steps to implement this acceptance in the Jamaican legislature. It was reprinted fully in the *Daily Gleaner*, 23 March 1968.
26. F. Burnham, 'Opening Speech to the Conference of Ministers of Finance on the Caribbean Development Bank, Georgetown, 25-26 March 1968', mimeo.
27. E. Seaga, 'Speech to the Conference of Ministers of Finance on the Caribbean Development Bank, Georgetown, 25-26 March 1968', mimeo.
28. *Ibid.*
29. E. Barrow, 'Speech to the Conference of Ministers of Finance on the Caribbean Development Bank, Georgetown, 25-26 March 1968', mimeo.
30. *Ibid.*
31. The Political Reporter, *Daily Gleaner*, 30 June 1968.
32. Voting was secret, but there is little doubt that these were the four countries who voted for Jamaica.
33. *Agreement establishing the Caribbean Free Trade Association*, Georgetown, February 1968, Annexes B and D.
34. *Agreement establishing CARIFTA*, Georgetown, 1968, Annex D, paragraph 1.
35. Commonwealth Caribbean Regional Secretariat, *CARIFTA and the New Caribbean*, Georgetown, 1971, p. 35.
36. *Ibid.*
37. The commodities are listed in *ibid.*, p. 31.
38. For details of the commitment made by the Associated States, see *Agreement for the Establishment of an Eastern Caribbean Common Market*, St George's, Grenada, 11 June 1968.

39. E. Le Blanc, 'Speech on behalf of the Associated States at the Ceremony to mark the signing of CARIFTA, Roseau, Dominica, 30 April 1968', mimeo.

40. The Bahamas and British Honduras were not members, but both countries had been visited in July 1968 by the members of the first CARIFTA Council and their governments had indicated a willingness to participate in the regional programme – the Premier of the Bahamas expressing an interest in supporting the Caribbean Development Bank and the Premier of British Honduras declaring his intention to apply for membership of CARIFTA. See *Guyana Journal*, vol. 1, no. 2, 1968, pp. 12-13.

CHAPTER FOUR

*The first
four years*

How did the integration movement develop during the first few years of CARIFTA's existence? It was not inevitable that it would survive for very long, and credit must be given, first of all, for the fact that it did so. CARIFTA nevertheless lived constantly in the same politically charged atmosphere in which it had been born. Fragility was always its most striking characteristic and disintegration an ever present possibility. Problems, in fact, arose from the very outset. Jamaica's belated accession to the agreement had done nothing to bridge the gap which separated her from the rest of the West Indies and, indeed, in the last few months of 1968 disaffection with Jamaica probably grew. To the annoyance of eastern Caribbean opinion the Jamaican government showed no sign of changing its mind on the question of its non-participation in the Development Bank. On the contrary, it worked assiduously, if secretly, to fashion a 'Western Caribbean Bank', with headquarters in Nassau, comprising Jamaica, the Bahamas and British Honduras.[1] The gulf was further widened by the 'Rodney incident' in October 1968 when Walter Rodney, a young Guyanese lecturer at UWI, was prevented from re-entering Jamaica after he had attended a Black Writers' Conference overseas. Shearer publicly blamed the ensuing demonstrations and violence at the Mona campus on the subversive activity of students and staff, who were predominantly, he said, West

Indians from the other islands.[2] Shortly afterwards Seaga spoke of the effect the non-Jamaicans at Mona were having in 'emasculating Jamaican nationalism' and revealed that the government had 'given thought' to the establishment of a Jamaican university.[3] The UWI was the longest-standing symbol of West Indian integration, and this threat to its existence immediately set off moves to call an emergency Summit of the region's leaders to discuss the future of the university and, at the same time, to try and reach some *modus vivendi* on the Bank issue. Shearer did not formally object, but he demonstrated his lack of concern for regional issues – and thus added to the ire of his colleagues – by three times finding proposed dates for the conference inconvenient.

When, finally, the Fifth Heads of Government Conference opened in Trinidad in February 1969, the issue at stake was not just UWI, or the Bank, but the future of Caribbean integration itself. The LDCs felt that Jamaica was being allowed to dictate the pace and direction of the integration movement in a way detrimental to their well-being, and only postponed a planned meeting to review their position in CARIFTA when, at last, dates for a full Summit conference were agreed. Their intention to take a hard-headed look at their role in Caribbean integration was not concealed for a moment. In the event, agreement was reached with surprising ease. It was decided to establish the Bank at the earliest possible date in 1969 and to proceed immediately with the recruitment of staff. Jamaica's 'special problems' were diplomatically recognised and, having refrained from reopening the debate about the Bank's siting, the Jamaican government was allowed to reserve its final decision on whether or not to take part till 31 May 1969.[4] At the same time the dispute over the future of UWI was allowed to dissipate of its own accord. In the end, the Jamaican government had been represented by neither Shearer nor Seaga, but by Lightbourne, whose conciliatory manner and personal commitment to the concept of regional free trade did much to clear the air. On his way to Trinidad he visited some of the Leeward and Windward Islands and managed throughout the conference to give the impression that, whatever the Jamaican government's position was on particular subjects, it was not rigidly and automatically opposed to the interests of the eastern Caribbean. For their part the LDCs were pleased with the decision to expedite the establishment of the Bank and, their irritation and impatience at least temporarily assuaged, they expressed a willingness to continue as members of CARIFTA. In so far, then, as it eased much of the tension in intra-regional relations and prevented the dialogue of Caribbean integration from completely breaking down, the conference must be adjudged a success.

In one important area, however, the discussion highlighted the existence of a clear difference of position between the various governments, a difference which developed during the course of the year into a bitter political wrangle. The issue in contention was the Trinidadian proposal that British West Indian Airways be established as the official air carrier of the region. BWIA has unquestionably had a troublesome history. It was first acquired by the Trinidad government in 1961 when its parent airline, British Overseas Airways Corporation (BOAC), indicated its intention to cease operations in the Caribbean. The original purchase was undertaken without consultation with either the other island governments or the then federal government and provoked a good deal of resentment. When, as a result, the rest of the region refused the offer of a share in the ownership of BWIA, the Trinidad government found itself in the increasingly desperate position of holding a large loss-making concern, which made bigger claims each year on the local exchequeur. It undoubtedly saw the establishment of CARIFTA as a chance to revive the possibility of the airline being taken into regional ownership as an instrument of integration. The proposal to set up a regional air carrier was therefore discussed at the Fourth Heads of Government Conference, and it was decided to set up a working party of officials to examine the matter further.

When complete, the working party report unequivocally favoured the idea of a regional airline and proposed that it should be based upon the operations of BWIA in the passenger sphere and the Guyana Airways Corporation in the cargo sphere.[5] These recommendations were no surprise, for in any objective assessment the case for the regional organisation of air transport in the Commonwealth Caribbean is practically irrefutable and has been made numerous times over the years.[6]

The first four years

International air transport is based upon the operation of a bilateral principle, by which the air traffic between any pair of nations is the monopoly of the airlines designated by the two governments in question and the internal 'cabotage' traffic the preserve of the national or nationally designated airline. During the colonial era, therefore, the Commonwealth Caribbean was counted as part of Britain for the purposes of air traffic agreements. With the advent of independence the four leading territories of the West Indies acquired the right to negotiate reciprocity arrangements with airlines wishing to use their airspace, and had either to establish their own national airlines, to designate foreign airlines to act as their national carrier, or to establish a regional air carrier. The latter policy had powerful advantages, chiefly in terms of the economy of running an airline and in the increased bargaining power over reciprocal route rights which it would generate; but, at the same time, it had disadvantages – political disadvantages in the loss of national control and prestige – which Caribbean governments have, on the whole, found more persuasive. Thus the offer of shares in BWIA was spurned because it was initially a Trinidadian airline. The Jamaican government preferred to set up a company, Air Jamaica Ltd, which leased aircraft from BWIA and BOAC to fly the lucrative routes from Kingston and Montego Bay to New York and Miami. Having made a small profit out of this 'paper' airline, it was sufficiently impressed with the viability of a 'national' carrier to want to extend its operation to include the actual purchase of aircraft. When, therefore, the issue of a regional air carrier came up for debate in 1969, Jamaica politely exempted herself from any discussion of the venture. Rather surprisingly, perhaps, this disclaimer did not provoke the hostile response one might have expected. On this occasion Barbados became the *bête noir* of integrationists.

At a ministerial conference held in July 1969 to discuss the report of the working party, the Barbados government firmly disassociated itself from a resolution supporting 'the earliest practicable establishment of BWIA as the Air Carrier of the region'.[7] Its objection to the proposal undoubtedly stemmed, in part, from a number of genuine doubts about BWIA's capacity to operate the services which it felt the Barbadian economy needed without frequent and considerable financial support from all the regional governments. Certainly the financial history of BWIA inspired no confidence in the Trinidad claim that the airline would show an operating profit by 1970. As Barrow knew only too well, it had lost money consistently throughout its existence and, by 1969, had accumulated massive debts. There was, however, a further and perhaps more telling reason why the Barbados government took up the position it did. Like the Jamaican government earlier, it too was thinking primarily of the well-being of its tourist industry. As such, it did not hide its wish to maximise air services to and through Barbados so as to continue and, if possible, accelerate the development of tourism, and admitted to a concern that a serious attempt to operate a regional air carrier efficiently might necessitate or provoke some restrictions on the number of established international airlines calling at Barbados. In short, it preferred to open its airport to all comers and, from the point of view of a Barbadian airline, to make the best deal it could with the giants of the airline business, acquiring, if possible, the promotional advantages of an apparently national airline without incurring the direct financial responsibility of owing a fleet of expensive jet aircraft.[8]

The Trinidad government was infuriated by this attitude and reportedly threatened in the heat of the moment to review its whole position in the integration movement.[9] From one point of view Barbados was only paying lip service to regional integration – 'Little England stabs CARIFTA in the Back', ran a headline in *The Nation*;[10] from the other, Trinidad was using blackmail in order to try and get her way in the matter of the airline. The issues soured relations between the two states throughout 1969. Although both governments subsequently remedied the omission, at the height of the row neither had a High Commissioner in the other's capital who could quietly explain his government's position behind the scenes. As a result, tension was allowed to spill over into other areas. In August 1969, for example, Barrow saw fit to describe a sensible enough Trinidad proposal that a CARIFTA mission be dispatched to Europe to hold talks with the EEC Commission as a complete waste of time. Caribbean leaders, he said contemptuously, should stop running after other people, begging them to 'let a few crumbs fall from their table'.[11] The remark was yet another illustration of the brittle nature of the personal relationships that bound together the West Indian leadership.

What the various leaders did have in common, however, was a determination to make regional economic integration serve the interests of the particular territories that they represented. In this light it is possible to detect an air of greater solidarity slowly permeating the integration movement as the MDCs, at least, began to garner some of the trading benefits promised by the advent of regional free trade. For, whilst the heads of government were indulging in crisis diplomacy over the establishment of a regional development bank and a regional air carrier, CARIFTA itself was working quite efficiently. There were, naturally, teething troubles – an early dispute over the entry into Guyana of paper bags produced in Jamaica and a clash over alleged Jamaican discrimination against Trinidadian textiles – and in keeping with the tension inherent in intra-regional relations the wrangling was conducted in an aggressive and declamatory fashion. Yet they were exceptional incidents, which belied the considerable efforts made by the CARIFTA Council and the Secretariat to ensure that the agreement functioned smoothly. CARIFTA was about trade and would be judged in the first instance by the extent to which it was able to generate a quick increase in intra-regional trade flows. On this score there was no doubt of its success, for from a very early date – even before detailed figures were publicly available – the delighted reactions of most of the leading businessmen of the region were evidence enough that intra-Caribbean trade was flourishing, especially between the MDCs.

Jamaica, for example, achieved a number of early successes in winning export orders in the eastern Caribbean market, especially for its manufactured goods – items like chemicals and paint, footwear and fabrics, matches, stoves and metal products generally. In fact, the extent of the rise in Jamaican exports to the rest of the region seemed to come as a pleasant surprise to most Jamaicans. In March 1969 the *Gleaner*'s 'Trade Reporter' wrote:

> there is no doubt that, in spite of what appeared at first to be

apathy or even distrust of closer economic association with the rest of the Commonwealth Caribbean the Jamaican businessman – manufacturer as well as exporter – has become fully alive to the fact that there is everything to be gained, and nothing whatsoever to lose, from trading with these neighbours of ours.[12]

CARIFTA, he concluded, 'has been a good thing for Jamaica'.[13] This change in Jamaican public opinion also fostered a more conciliatory attitude towards the Bank. Given the initial success of CARIFTA and growing awareness of the feeling widely held in the LDCs that Jamaica should not be allowed to reap the benefits of the latter without paying the costs involved in the former, the view began to develop that the government might, after all, be wise to have second thoughts about joining the CDB. It would be senseless, the argument ran, to provoke the LDCs and unnecessarily risk the disintegration of the free trade arrangements by giving the impression that Jamaica joined CARIFTA for purely selfish motives. Perhaps the contribution to the Bank's funds required of Jamaica should simply be regarded as an investment which would pay off in the form of increased trade benefits in the future? With this change of mood in Jamaica the JLP government's view of the regional experiment gradually changed too. If it never came to enthuse over economic co-operation, it grew at least to tolerate it.

On 28 May 1969 – just a day or so before the deadline set by the Fifth Heads of Government Conference – Shearer sent a telegram to his colleagues around the region, announcing Jamaica's willingness to participate in the Bank, 'subject to review of some aspects and provision of certain safeguards to be discussed'.[14] The reservations to which the telegram referred were thought to concern the siting issue (still), the terms under which the soft loan window operated, the contributions of extra-regional members and the placing of a limit on the amount of loans the Bank could make on multinational, as opposed to territorial, projects. By the time, however, a conference of plenipotentiaries met in Jamaica in October 1969 to consider and adopt an agreement establishing the Bank a series of ministerial and officials' meetings, held throughout the summer, had satisfactorily resolved all these points, mostly by making adjustments to the draft charter, but, in the case of the Bank's location, by devising a formula which provided for a final round in the long struggle for the acquisition of this particular prize. Thus it was that, appended to the text of the agreement establishing the Bank, was a protocol setting out a procedure for a vote to be taken at the inaugural meeting of the Board of Governors on the question of amending Article 36 of the agreement, the first part of which read: 'the principal office of the Bank shall be located in Barbados'.[15] There ensued once again a period of vigorous lobbying, and the Jamaican government may well have been hopeful that the decision would be reversed in the light of the disfavour in which Barbados was then held in the eastern Caribbean as a result of the BWIA imbroglio. It was not, however, to be. When the Governors met in Nassau on 31 January 1970, the vote, which excluded the representatives of Britain and Canada, the two extra-regional members, again turned against Jamaica – on this occasion by eight votes to five.[16] It seems that Jamaica crucially lost the support of the government of the Bahamas, which (according to one report) was seduced by the suggestion – allegedly deriving from a number of eastern Caribbean leaders, who had moved furtively in and out of the Bahamas in the months before – that, if the headquarters of the Bank were retained in Barbados, then the Bahamas itself would by the most suitable setting in which to establish a branch.[17] Jamaica accepted the decision, and some twenty-one months after the inauguration of CARIFTA the Caribbean Development Bank was at last able to begin work.

Its establishment came too late, however, to stifle the complaints of the LDCs that they were being harshly exploited by their more developed partners within CARIFTA. The actual operation of CARIFTA worked, as we have seen, to tie Jamaica more firmly to the regional movement by virtue of the boost it gave to her export trade; with the LDCs it worked in exactly the opposite way, since, as many indeed had expected, they were unable to increase their exports to the rest of CARIFTA to any appreciable extent. Their original doubts were enlarged, especially when this disappointing performance was set against the experience of the MDCs, excepting, perhaps, Guyana. Reviewing in May 1972 the achievements of the first four years of CARIFTA trade, the Secretariat affirmed that the exports of the four MDCs to the rest of the region had grown from EC$96 million in 1967 to EC$158 million in 1970 – a total increase of some 65 per cent for four years or approximately 18 per cent per annum. The level of Guyana's exports remained more or less static over the period, but Jamaican exports increased from EC$8·6 million in 1967 to EC$22·7 million in 1970 – the biggest annual percentage rate of growth, 38 per cent – and Trinidad's grew from EC$47 million in 1967 to EC$92 million in 1970 – the biggest growth in absolute terms. Barbados followed, with an annual average rate of increase of some 16 per cent – a growth from EC$10·3 million in 1967 to EC$16·2 million in 1970.[18] These developments should not, of course, have been particularly surprising. Such a pattern was the natural result of introducing free trade into a regional economy in which only Jamaica, Trinidad and Barbados possessed industrial sectors of any size. As we have seen, it had been fully anticipated by the architects of the Caribbean integration movement, who as a result created a number of special provisions which they thought would enable the LDCs to gain at least something from the experience of economic integration.

What, then, of the much-publicised compensatory mechanisms built into the movement? Did they not, in practice, have the effect intended of them? The answer must be a definite 'no'. The Bank, for example, we have looked at and seen enough to understand that it worked initially as an antagonising, rather than a conciliatory, agent. The publication of a document setting out its 'Financial Policies', in which a commitment was given that for the time being financing by 'special operations' (i.e. for loans deserving of low rates of interest or extended maturities) would be confined to the LDCs,[19] restored some of its standing in the Leeward and Windward Islands. It was the loans themselves, though, not just their promise, that the LDCs needed and needed quickly, and in this regard the Bank, under the presidency of Sir Arthur Lewis, soon made clear its intention to operate cautiously and deliberately in traditional banking style. Article 39 of the CARIFTA agreement, another of the supposedly 'benefit-equalising' provisions, was weak and rarely used, being applied in the first four years to just two products manufactured in the LDCs – beer in the case of Grenada and St Kitts-Nevis-Anguilla, and petroleum products in the case of Antigua.[20] Furthermore, the Agricultural Marketing Protocol, on which many hopes rested, proved to be equally disappointing in performance, despite the constant attention given to its efficient functioning by the region's agricultural technicians. An early report on its operation, in fact, concluded that even in potential it was 'less important than many people realised, in the sense that the quantity of intra-regional trade which it could generate, even if all went well, would be small compared with the quantities in the manufacturing sector and in rice and sugar'.[21] Moreover, all did not go well. The problems were manifold: inadequate and usually inaccurate crop forecasting, a lack of specialist knowledge of particular crops and, in some of the LDCs, the absence of marketing boards. The transport and communication facilities were also hopelessly insufficient. There was no telex system, for example, to expedite the exchange of market information on prices and production, and the informational data itself, given the paucity of proper statistical machinery and trained staff, again especially in the LDCs, was more often than not scanty and unreliable. In short, it was the MDCs who, because of their more sophisticated bureaucracies, were in the best position to take advantage of this so-called 'concession' to the LDCs, and both Barbados and Jamaica were able to expand their production of agricultural products, although in neither case by spectacular amounts. The fifth CARIFTA Council, meeting in January 1970, required governments which needed any of the twenty-two AMP products to approach first one or other of the LDCs and only to seek recourse to the MDCs as a secondary resort;[22] but the amendment seemed to have very little discernible impact upon the working of the protocol. In St Vincent a useful increase in the exports of carrots and peanuts was registered – thanks largely to the energy of a few officials in the government and marketing board – but that was definitely the exception rather than the rule.[23]

Whether, however, the LDCs were *worse* off or merely no *better* off as a result of regional economic integration was a question without an easy answer. What was the relevant criterion by which to pass judgement? McIntyre argued in the early 1960s in a much-quoted passage that:

> all integration should be required to do is to provide greater opportunities for each territory to increase its economic growth. It should not necessarily be expected that integration would allow all territories to enjoy the same rates of growth, or that it would equalize *per capita* incomes over the area as a whole. For the crucial test for each territory should be whether its rate of growth within an integrated market would be higher than outside of it, not whether it would enjoy the same rate of growth, or the same level of factor incomes as other participating countries.[24]

In essence, what he was saying was that as long as some territories in the integration movement did not actually lose development possibilities in net terms and become 'poles of stagnation' (or, more strictly, as long as they lost less within the integration movement than outside it), then the much-debated question of the 'equitable distribution of *benefits*' should not be a problem. 'In this respect', he went on to point out, 'historical examples which purport to show the tendency towards regional inequality in common markets, are largely irrelevant'.[25] In terms of cold logic, of course, McIntyre's argument is right. It was, however, picked up by the politicians and widely used in political debate in the Caribbean in defence of CARIFTA. Even if, it was said, the MDCs had the more substantive gains to show, and even if it could be shown that the operation of free trade had caused the LDCs to become victims of the polarisation effect, then they, the LDCs, had at least derived a host of almost intangible benefits from the various common services and co-operative programmes which formed part of the integration movement as a whole. They had not *lost* in an absolute sense by their participation in Caribbean integration. This was the propaganda and, like all good propaganda, it had the advantage and the disadvantage of being at the same time irrefutable and unprovable. On what criterion was a net judgement to be made? How could gains in one area (e.g. regional co-operation in meteorology) be balanced against losses in another (e.g. reduced attractiveness for industrial investment) ? It was both impossible and irrelevant. The practical world of politics does not deal easily with absolute judgements, but depends much more on *perceptions* of *relative* advantage or disadvantage. What counted, therefore, was the fact that the governments and peoples of the LDCs *felt* that the MDCs were using regional economic integration as a means of furthering their own economic development at the expense of their poorer less developed partners.

Their most direct experience of economic integration related, after all, to the prices at which CARIFTA goods were available for sale, and during the first two or three years of CARIFTA's existence prices in the region rose sharply. The view developed, moreover, that it was the operation of CARIFTA which was responsible for this acceleration of inflation – so much so that the third CARIFTA Council in March 1969 felt it advisable to distance itself from the businessmen of the region and place on record its condemnation of the way 'that manufacturers in the Commonwealth Caribbean have in certain cases sought to inflate prices of products entitled to area tariff treatment'.[26] In fairness, the rise in prices in the West Indies in the post-1968 period cannot be wholly attributed to the working of CARIFTA. As the Secretariat was keen to point out, there were a number of other factors to be considered – the effect, for example, of inflation in the metropolitan countries, from which important inputs were obtained; increased transport costs; the impact of the devaluation of the pound and all the Commonwealth Caribbean currencies in November 1967; and higher wage costs locally.[27] One must add, too, that many consumers in the Leeward and Windward Islands may somewhat naively have expected that the abolition of tariffs on intra-regional trade would lead to an actual *fall* in some prices, whereas, in practice, most governments recouped their revenue loss by imposing consumption taxes, which sometimes overcompensated and which, in any case, applied to all consumption of the product, whether imported from CARIFTA or elsewhere, or even produced at home. Having made all these provisos, though, it cannot be denied – and, indeed, was not, except by the manufacturers themselves – that the institution of CARIFTA was the occasion of a number of attempts by manufacturers to put up prices in order to increase their profit margins. The

Secretariat itself drew attention to the fact that circumstances existed in which producers had to increase their prices in order to be able to qualify for area tariff treatment in the CARIFTA market. It reminded us that:

> for a CARIFTA-made product to qualify for free entry to other CARIFTA markets, at least 50% of the export f.o.b. price must be made up of local payments, including profit. So by increasing his price in order to increase his profits, the producer may upgrade a product which did not have 50% local value added to one with local value added at 50% or more, and thereby qualify for area tariff treatment or (duty-free entry) to other CARIFTA markets.[28]

This, then, was the situation the LDC governments had to explain to the ordinary consumers who made up their electorates. It was little consolation to be informed that price inflation was unavoidably associated with the existence of a free trade area, and that, in any case, industries in developing countries almost always produce high-cost (and, for that matter, low-quality) goods. It was not LDC manufacturers who were pushing up the prices of their products in order to qualify for free trade treatment, because there were hardly any LDC manufacturers in existence. If, as was commonly agreed, it was the cost which had necessarily to be paid if the West Indies were to develop further its own manufacturing base, then the LDCs were entitled to ask: where was their share of that base? For all their scepticism, they had still hoped to gain some positive economic advantage from the introduction of free trade. In the event, not only were they themselves not developing industries, whereas the larger islands of the region were, but they were seeing the MDCs further reducing their chances of ever doing so by becoming ever more attractive poles of growth – and not only this: they were helping to pay the cost, and thus actively subsidising, MDC industrial development and their own concomitant stagnation. What price economic integration in these circumstances?

LDC discontent became, therefore, the major political problem facing the integration movement. Although the governments of the Leewards and Windwards were content for the most part just to complain, their disaffection would occasionally boil over into a demand for action on whatever issue was the most pressing at the time, and usually some sort of concession was made. For example, in January 1970, under LDC pressure, it was agreed that the Oils and Fats Agreement be reviewed and redrafted as a protocol to CARIFTA. This agreement had first been drawn up at the end of the Second World War as a means of upholding and encouraging the region's coconut industry and purported to require signatories to buy their copra from West Indian – which meant chiefly Windward Island – rather than extra-regional suppliers. It had never been strictly observed, but did not become a source of LDC grievance until 1969, during which year the regional supply of copra exceeded demand and the LDC producers were forced to sell on a depressed world market at well below the agreed area price.[29] Hence their demand that participants (especially beneficiaries) within CARIFTA should not neglect their responsibilities to the LDCs by remaining outside the former whilst enjoying the fruits of the latter.

In general, though, MDC opinion undoubtedly became more reluctant, as time went on, to appease every demand made by the LDCs. The establishment of the CDB in February 1970 was something of a watershed in this regard, for the MDCs clearly felt that, with the Bank at last in operation, they had fully delivered their part of the initial bargain with the LDCs. When the cries of exploitation continued, their exasperation and impatience with the LDCs mounted accordingly. MDC politicians began to suggest that the real explanation why the LDCs were not deriving much benefit from regional economic integration was to be found in the lack of enterprise and drive shown by their own governments and manufacturers. They were, it was said, waiting for the MDCs to develop them, rather than trying all they knew to help themselves.[30] There was, moreover, something in this. Businessmen in the LDCs, having been used for years to simply retailing imported goods, made little attempt to set up light manufacturing industries, despite the protection that could have been offered them under Article 39 of the CARIFTA agreement. For their part, the LDC governments cannot be said to have devoted much effort to acquiring the statistical data necessary to operate the AMP to their best advantage. Above all, in the eyes of the MDCs, the LDCs failed to make a reality of the Eastern Caribbean Common Market. The very idea of the ECCM demonstrated that, from the start, LDC governments realised the need to negotiate within CARIFTA from a position of combined strength, but, having resolutely insisted on drawing up the agreement before entering CARIFTA, they failed to put their weight behind its effective implementation. For instance, it took a number of years before a separate ECCM Secretariat was properly established, and even when this was done the governments often hampered its work by not providing the necessary data for projections and analyses. As a result, the only real achievement of the ECCM was the adoption of a common external tariff against third countries. The other ambitious commitments of the original agreement were never carried into practice, and thus the central purpose of the whole idea, namely the acquisition of the capacity to negotiate as a bloc with the MDCs, was negated.

In the final analysis the LDCs lacked the self-confidence to act independently of the MDCs. As one student of the Caribbean integration movement has put it, 'the Associated States continued to act as lone bargainers with the MDCs, each territory having its grouses, and putting forward its views as an individual unit in spite of the fact that the areas of discontent tended to be very similar'.[31] Their debilitating sense of impotence was induced principally by their tiny size and limited resources, relative even to their regional neighbours. In global terms, Jamaica and Trinidad are micro-territories, but in the Commonwealth Caribbean environment they are giants, without whom the LDCs feel they cannot survive and to whom they look instinctively as benefactors. This was the attitude which increasingly irritated the MDCs. In a speech in June 1970 Kamaluddin Mohammed attacked the constant grumbling of the LDCs and exhorted them to make full use of the opportunities afforded them by mechanisms like the AMP. He loftily put their disaffection down to their 'colonial mentality' and said that if they wished to withdraw from the regional economy and trade elsewhere, they could. If they stayed in CARIFTA, though, they would benefit in the long run.[32]

This latter point became the new refrain of the integration

movement. 'Hold strain', 'bear up', and, in time, the benefits of economic integration would reach the LDCs. It was realistic in that it admitted that the LDCs had little to gain in the short term from economic integration as conceived in the Caribbean; but, as a rallying cry, it only drew attention to the slow pace at which the governments of the region had approached the task of advancing the integration process – the so-called 'deepening' phase, as envisaged in the various forward commitments of Annex A to the CARIFTA agreement. The studies themselves were set in motion without too much delay. The Secretariat, assisted by a technical advisory panel drawn from member governments, embarked upon an investigation into the feasibility of establishing a common external tariff for the region, either in whole or in part, and the Caribbean office of ECLA was asked to undertake two studies, concerning, firstly, the harmonisation of fiscal incentives to industry, bearing in mind the special needs of the LDCs, and, secondly, the industrial development of the region as a whole, but with a view both to the establishment of 'integration industries' and to the location of industries in the LDCs. Not itself possessing the personnel resources for this latter task, the Commission contracted it out to the United Nations Industrial Development Organisation (UNIDO). All this was, of course, merely the first stage of the 'deepening' process. When it was first known that the regional integration resolution passed by the Fourth Heads of Government Conference was to be incorporated within the CARIFTA agreement as a testament to the long-term intentions of the architects of Caribbean integration, critics had immediately pointed out that the commitment merely to *study* a number of steps towards closer regional integration was not evidence *per se* of a burning and irrevocable commitment actually to institute them.[33] Events, in fact, proved how accurate their forebodings had been.

By the time the Sixth Heads of Government Conference met in Jamaica in April 1970, decisions had still not been taken in any of the three areas mentioned above. The report on the feasibility of a common external tariff had been held up by problems in assembling the team of experts originally chosen and was not yet complete.[34] On the other hand, both ECLA and

UNIDO had submitted their reports as scheduled in mid-1969,[35] only to see them consumed, almost without trace, within the laborious system of intergovernmental discussion and consultation. In his opening address to the Heads of Government Conference, Burnham, for one, betrayed his impatience at the region's failure to move on more positively to the next phase of the integration movement. Speaking of the challenges facing the region, he said:

> we should like to see the study on a Common External Tariff carried out. ... we should like to see decisions taken on the Harmonisation of Fiscal Incentives, another of the resolutions passed in 1967 ... we should like to see the region as a whole come closer towards adumbrating a policy with respect to the location of industries. We are prepared to make our contribution towards the region deciding on the integration industries. These are subjects which we discussed way back in 1967; and though one can understand quite clearly how much time a study in depth normally takes, one becomes anxious to see that positive steps are taken for the implementation of the resolutions which we passed ... This Conference will have to make serious decisions. We will have virtually to decide whether CARIFTA is the be-all and the end-all or whether it is merely part of a larger picture.[36]

Despite this exhortation to action and the warning that Burnham went on to deliver about 'the seething ferment and incipient revolution in our midst',[37] the heads of government were unable to speed up the process of decision-making on key issues and had to resort to demanding more studies and reports in other areas of economic integration. They set up a Joint Consultative Committee, consisting of officials drawn from the Secretariat and the member governments, to consider the question of ownership and control of regional resources, including land, and the whole issue of foreign investment; established another intergovernmental committee to consider ways and means of preserving the interests of the West Indies in the negotiation of taxation agreements with metropolitan countries; and, lastly, mandated the Secretariat to recommend whatever additional measures were necessary to enable the LDCs to benefit from regional integration.

There is no doubt that the technicians and officials of the Caribbean were worked hard in the cause of furthering the regional movement, nor that they responded valiantly to the demands placed upon them. At the beginning of 1970 the Trinidad government released Demas to assume the job of Secretary General of CARIFTA, for which many had always thought him incomparably suited,[38] and for the first time the Secretariat was given a sense of leadership and purpose. By mid-1971 the governments had in their possession positive recommendations in all the areas just previously outlined, but on none of them – not even the most long-standing, like the common external tariff and the harmonisation of fiscal incentives – had an agreement to act been reached. Shridath Ramphal, the Guyanese Attorney General and Minister of State for External Affairs, summed up the situation in a speech delivered at the time:

> there is not good reason to believe that agreement will be reached on any of these matters within the foreseeable future. This is a serious indictment of us all, and it is not one that I make lightly. I should be surprised, however, if any Minister, indeed, if any official, who has sat, as I have sat, at each of the eight meetings of the Council of the Free Trade Association or at the annual conferences of Caribbean Heads of Government that followed the 1967 meeting in Barbados, would dispute that prognosis.[39]

What, then, were the obstacles? It is difficult to answer the question categorically because very little information about the discussions was made public. One can say, however, that Guyana, Trinidad and Barbados were broadly in favour of 'deepening' CARIFTA, albeit perceiving the need to do so with differing degrees of urgency, and were prepared to consider proposals to improve the position of the LDCs. The countries in doubt were the LDCs themselves and Jamaica. The LDCs correctly saw both the common external tariff and the harmonisation of fiscal incentives as MDC issues, i.e. advances which would favour the MDCs, rather than themselves. The former was certainly not in their interest. Generally speaking, the Leeward and Windward Islands had very low import duties (for the obvious reason that most of their internal consumption was imported) and so an increase in duty to the level needed to meet the requirements of a common external tariff for the region as a whole would have been bound to increase the cost of living in the LDCs without any real gains for them in the way of genuine incentives to expand production; moreover, their markets would have been that much more open to the infiltration of MDC manufactures if external imports were thus made more expensive. With regard to the harmonisation of incentives, they were just as dubious, being particularly disturbed by the recommendation contained within the ECLA report that special concessions should be given to depressed areas within the MDCs themselves.[40] As the Dominican Minister of Finance, Trade and Industry explained just before the ninth Council meeting, 'this would make nonsense of increased incentives to less developed countries. In this way all industries will tend to gravitate towards the less developed areas in the more developed countries.'[41] To offset, therefore, what they saw as the worsening in their economic position, which would have been brought about by these two measures, the leaders of the LDCs pressed the MDCs to make a much greater commitment to their problems than before. More and more throughout 1971 they began to talk of political integration as the solution. Although this mood contributed in part to the signing of the Grenada Declaration in November 1971 – to be discussed more fully later[42] – it was utterly unrealistic to expect that the political integration of the West Indies would be accepted by the MDCs as the *quid pro quo* for a further commitment to regional economic integration. The latter had been undertaken, as we made clear at the start, precisely because it offered some of the advantages of regional co-operation without necessitating the embrace of an overtly political arrangement. Unable to get satisfaction in this sphere, the LDCs remained highly sceptical of the vague and inexplicit MDC promises of further compensatory measures and did their best to stall the talks on 'deepening'.

Jamaica, though for different reasons, was no more keen than the LDCs to press ahead with 'deepening' the movement and was, in reality, a more serious obstacle. The eastern Caribbean MDCs felt – not without reason – that at the last moment the

LDCs would always fall in with the demands of regional integration because, to put it bluntly, 'they had nowhere else to go'. By comparison, the readiness of the Jamaican government to disrupt regional integration in the cause of national advantage was only too well proven: Shearer was linked, after all, by a direct line of succession to Bustamante. The JLP government insisted quite correctly that it was only formally committed to regional free trade – economic *co-operation* – and that it had never hidden its disinclination to advance to a set of arrangements which would be construed throughout Jamaica as fully embracing economic *integration*. Four years of regional economic collaboration – to adopt a neutral intermediate term – had done little to alter its cautious and calculating approach. There was inevitably a certain loss of decision making freedom in the harmonisation of fiscal incentives, which was a negative point in the eyes of the Jamaican government, and, since Jamaica's tariffs were high already, there was arguably no economic advantage to be gained from the adoption of a common tariff code throughout the region. It was felt that free trade alone would bring, and indeed had already brought, what trading benefits there were to be obtained from the regional connection. In short, there appeared to the Jamaican government to be no good reason for altering its well tried policy of keeping the eastern Caribbean at arms length. Very much the opposite, in fact: the rest of the region's brief flirtation with political integration at the end of 1971 (the Grenada Declaration episode) merely tended to confirm Jamaican suspicions about the deeper motives of a number of eastern Caribbean states, whilst the increasingly radical economic policies of the Burnham government in Guyana – illustrated, in particular, by the nationalisation of the Alcan bauxite holdings[43] and the creation of a state buying agency called the External Trading Bureau – were anathema to the conservative philosophy which characterised Jamaican Cabinet and establishment opinion. Indeed, at one stage, Lightbourne felt it necessary to make a speech to American businessmen in New York, reassuring them of Jamaica's continuing desire to attract foreign investment and specifically rejecting the idea that Jamaica might 'do anything foolish',[44] as he put it, in its relations with foreign concerns in the island. With regard, finally, to the position of the LDCs within the integration movement, the Jamaican government was totally unsympathetic: it was by tradition and practice always more concerned, one might say, with Miami than with Montserrat.

For all these reasons, therefore, the 'deepening' approach met with stubborn and effective resistance from the Jamaican government, which favoured instead the idea of simply 'widening' the scope of regional economic integration – in other words, extending the size of the available tariff-free market – to include new members.[45] Belize (as British Honduras was now known) had joined at the beginning of May 1971, but her accession had always been intended. By the concept of 'widening' was meant the inclusion within CARIFTA and the CDB of countries in the wider Caribbean with a Spanish, French or Dutch heritage. On the whole, it received little support, and Guyana in particular was fiercely opposed. Ramphal eloquently expressed his government's view of the 'widening' proposal and of the regional integration scene in general in mid-1971 when he said:

> it would be bad enough if all we faced was delay, however avoidable, in moving upward to a more intimate economic association; but we face the real possibility that while we delay we may be encouraged to take steps that would render vertical development impossible, or at least utterly improbable. Already it has been suggested that what we should be doing is to expand the Free Trade Area horizontally – that is, to broaden its membership by going beyond Commonwealth Caribbean countries ... Suffice it to say at this point that in moving in a direction which dilutes the intimacy of the Association, by introducing at this formative stage states that bring to it totally different social, political and constitutional norms, a new language, a new culture and new methods of operation, we must in the nature of things enormously increase the difficulties of securing consensus for our joint progress upward toward an economic community.[46]

Caught between all these conflicting views, Caribbean economic integration was effectively immobilised.

It is probably true to say that this institutional stagnation would not alone have led to the demise of the movement, as some integrationists feared, although it is, of course, possible to construct scenarios by which this could have occurred. What made disintegration a very real danger indeed was the simultaneous failure of the Commonwealth Caribbean governments to reach agreement on a common policy towards the European Economic Community. To understand the background to this situation, we must move back in time to the summer of 1969. Observers in the Caribbean, as elsewhere, realised immediately that President Pompidou's assumption of office in France in place of General de Gaulle considerably enhanced the prospects of British entry into the EEC, again making the need to preserve the region's special trading arrangements with Britain the foremost priority of West Indian governments. The fourth CARIFTA Council, meeting in July 1969, decided that a delegation of regional ministers and officials, led by Lightbourne, should proceed post-haste to Europe in order to draw attention to the special position of the Commonwealth Caribbean countries. So began more than two years of discussion on the subject — with the EEC, with Britain, and within the Commonwealth Caribbean itself. Lightbourne's mission made its tour and won a promise from the Labour government in Britain that it would stand by the assurances it had first given in 1967. A year later, in September 1970, he was back in London with another ministerial mission, receiving similar undertakings from the new Conservative government. For all this diplomatic activity, and the apocalyptic rhetoric used by Caribbean leaders to describe the consequences of a failure to safeguard the region's traditional markets, the opening of negotiations between Britain and the EEC took place with the territories of the Caribbean still unclear about the type of association agreement they favoured. The seventh Council had agreed in November 1970 that the CARIFTA countries should seek, as a group, to negotiate a single form of relationship with the expanded European Community, but ended without specifying the actual policy to be followed in negotiation.

In fact, the decision facing the region was an extremely awkward one, because of the two different stages of constitutional development represented within CARIFTA — independence and Associated Statehood. The LDCs, as Associated States of Britain, were automatically eligible for association with the EEC under Part IV of the Treaty of Rome,[47] an option not available to the four independent MDCs, and it was thought that their acceptance of this arrangement would inevitably bring about the destruction of the Caribbean integration movement. For, under Part IV, the Associated States would be required to extend duty-free entry to EEC manufactured products with which, obviously, the output of the nascent industrial sectors of the MDCs could not hope to compete. CARIFTA could hardly be sustained in circumstances such as these. To the LDCs, of course, its demise may not, by this time, have loomed very large, and the possibility of the LDCs opting for Part IV was openly voiced by several of their leaders.[48] It seems, moreover, that the British government, feeling no doubt that a weakened and divided Caribbean would reduce some of the pressure on its own bargaining position with the EEC, especially over the contentious question of sugar imports, sought to persuade the Associated States that it was indeed in their best interests to accept Part IV.[49] As we have seen, the LDCs did eventually agree to pursue a policy of group negotiations, but they always knew that they had the option of Part IV in reserve – as a sort of insurance policy. It is also worthy of note in this context that amongst the LDCs only Antigua and St Kitts had any exportable sugar surplus and thus a direct stake in the future of the Commonwealth Sugar Agreement. This – perhaps the most difficult aspect of the negotiations – was therefore very much an MDC concern, one which the LDCs for their part could (just about) afford to view with equanimity.

In consequence it was the MDCs who found themselves at a comparative disadvantage and who, for the sake of their own bargaining position with the EEC – not to mention the future of CARIFTA – had to preserve the negotiating alliance which had been agreed in general terms with the LDCs in November 1970. They were seriously handicapped, however, by their own inability to agree upon the most suitable *form* of association to aim for. Under the 1963 EEC 'declaration of intent', developing Commonwealth countries had been given the choice of three models of association, an offer which was eventually repeated in the post-1970 negotiations. The available options, in descending

order of intensity, were:
1. Association along with eighteen French and Belgian ex-colonies in Africa under a third five-year Yaoundé Convention.
2. Association *sui generis* under Article 238 of the Treaty of Rome, involving 'mutual rights and obligations, particularly in matters of trade', as negotiated by the East African territories of Uganda, Kenya and Tanzania in 1968 in what was called the Arusha Agreement.
3. A simple trade agreement, involving either discriminatory or non-discriminatory reductions of tariffs on imports of selected items of interest to both parties to the Agreement.[50]

Although the discussions on the subject were clouded in secrecy, it is possible to detect some of the differences of position between the West Indian governments. Trinidad and Guyana were interested most, it is probably fair to say, by the more limited idea of a straightforward commercial agreement involving just those commodities critical to the stability of the Caribbean economy, although they were also attracted, perhaps to a lesser extent, by the notion of a special *sui generis* arrangement for the Caribbean. Although the obligations of associations under Article 238 extended to the concession of rights of establishment to individuals and enterprises belonging to the EEC, they did not involve the need to have prior consulation with the Commission before the imposition by the associate of quantitative restrictions for protective purposes, nor did they demand the granting of reverse preferences to the Community on more than a small number of items. Trinidad and Guyana were certainly disinclined to adopt the Yaoundé approach, which provided for the formation of a free trade area between each associated territory and the EEC. EEC goods would thus have to be allowed free access to Caribbean markets, and since defensive duties or quantitative restrictions could, unlike the Arusha Agreement, only be imposed after consultation with the Yaoundé Association Council (permission being far from automatic), the region's industrial development could have been seriously inhibited. Nor, for that matter, would the region's exports of sugar and bananas have been effectively protected under Yaoundé. Sugar was regulated by the Common Agricultural Policy of the EEC, whilst West Indian bananas would still have been vulnerable to competition from other associated countries, many of which had substantially lower costs of production. In the view of Owen Jefferson, a lecturer in economics at the University of the West Indies, Yaoundé was without doubt 'the least desirable type'[51] of agreement on offer to the region.

It was, however, the arrangement which the British government preferred that the Caribbean MDCs accept, since, as Jefferson pointed out, a Yaoundé-type agreement would afford British exports to the West Indies a useful tariff advantage over American goods.[52] More seriously, from the West Indian point of view, the Jamaican government also favoured Yaoundé – attracted presumably by the financial and technical assistance provided under the Convention – and so stood alone on yet another major regional issue. When, therefore, in March 1971 it was learnt that Lightbourne, having just absented himself from a CARIFTA Council meeting, was in Brussels talking to EEC officials, suspicions were naturally aroused that Jamaica was trying to make a bilateral association deal with the Community. Whether or not they were justified on this particular point, there is no doubt that the region *was* sharply divided over EEC policy – an editorial in the *Trinidad Guardian* talked of a 'carefully covered up dogfight'[53] between the members of CARIFTA – and that this situation held serious implications for the stability of CARIFTA and Caribbean integration in general.

If the need to prepare for the impending negotiations (scheduled for the summer of 1973) represented one obvious source of stress upon the integration movement, then so too did the continuing discontent of the LDCs, and so too the impasse into which the 'deepening' approach had run. All three problems were, of course, intertwined, and *in combination* they undoubtedly contained the possibility that the first four years of CARIFTA would constitute practically the total life span of this latest attempt at Caribbean integration. We should pay heed to the warning given to the region by Ramphal in November 1971. Referring to the plethora of problematic issues queuing up within the decision making system of the integration movement, he said:

> if we fail to agree upon all these, or even to commit ourselves to them, there is danger, indeed, and it is a real and pressing danger, that we may not merely fail to achieve our objectives but that through protracted and increasingly angry argumentation we may impair that measure of identity which was our starting-point.[54]

There was, as he well knew, no inevitability that the degree of regional consensus necessary to preserve and advance Caribbean economic integration would be forthcoming.

Notes

1. No formal reference is available: in the nature of the policy, it could not be admitted to in public.
2. *Daily Gleaner*, 19 October 1968.
3. *Ibid.*, 3 November 1968.
4. See *Final Communiqué of the Fifth Heads of Government Conference*, Port of Spain, 1969.
5. See *Guyana Journal*, vol. 1, no. 4, 1970, p. 44.
6. The most pertinent example is S. De Castro, *Problems of the Caribbean Air Transport Industry*, Kingston, Jamaica, 1967. This was one of the UWI Studies.
7. *Press Release of Conference of Commonwealth Caribbean Ministers on the Regional Air Carrier*, Port of Spain, 1969.
8. This policy led shortly to the creation of 'International Caribbean Airways' as the so-called Barbadian national airline. It was owned by a leading British aviation entrepreneur and flew between Barbados and Luxembourg.
9. *Trinidad Guardian*, 23 July 1969.
10. *The Nation*, vol. 12, no. 44, 25 July 1969.
11. *Barbados Advocate-News*, 29 August 1969.
12. *Daily Gleaner*, 9 March 1969.
13. *Ibid.*
14. Quoted in *ibid.*, 30 May 1969.
15. *Agreement establishing the Caribbean Development Bank*, Kingston, Jamaica, 18 October 1968, Protocol to Provide for Procedure for Amendment of Article 36 at the Inaugural Meeting of the Board of Governors.
16. Although the voting was again secret, the result was not.
17. The Political Reporter, *Daily Gleaner*, 22 February 1970.
18. Commonwealth Caribbean Regional Secretariat, *From CARIFTA to*

Caribbean Community, Georgetown, 1972, p. 36.
19. Caribbean Development Bank, *Financial Policies*, Bridgetown, 1970, paragraph 6.
20. See Secretariat, *From CARIFTA to Caribbean Community*, p. 40.
21. P. L. Yates and G. E. Buckmire, 'Agricultural Trade and Development in the Commonwealth Caribbean', Commonwealth Caribbean Regional Secretariat, Georgetown, mimeo, 1972, p. 47.
22. See Secretariat, *From CARIFTA to Caribbean Community*, p. 38.
23. Yates and Buckmire, *op. cit.*, p. 48.
24. A. McIntyre, 'Some Issues of Trade Policy in the West Indies', in N. Girvan and O. Jefferson (eds.), *Readings in the Political Economy of the Caribbean*, Kingston, Jamaica, 1971, p. 178.
25. *Ibid.*
26. *Final Communiqué of the Third CARIFTA Council*, Georgetown, 1969.
27. Commonwealth Caribbean Regional Secretariat, *CARIFTA and the New Caribbean*, Georgetown, 1971, pp. 42-3.
28. *Ibid.*, p. 43.
29. See J. G. M. Compton, 'Budget Address by the Premier and Minister of Finance of St Lucia, 30 December 1969', mimeo.
30. For diplomatic reasons such comments were not made openly, but they were widely aired behind the scenes at intergovernmental meetings.
31. R. E. Wiltshire, 'Regional Integration and Conflict in the Commonwealth Caribbean', unpublished PhD thesis, University of Michigan, 1974.
32. *Trinidad Guardian*, 30 June 1970.
33. See, for example, M. Segal, lecturer in economics at UWI, 'CARIFTA must move ahead quickly', *Trinidad Express*, 20 July 1968.
34. It was eventually completed in January 1971.
35. ECLA, Office for the Caribbean, *Report of the United Nations Expert Team on Harmonisation of Fiscal Incentives to Industries in the Caribbean Free Trade Area*, E/CN. 12/845, 1969; UNIDO, *The Establishment of Integrated Industries in the Caribbean and the Location of Industries in the Less Developed Countries*, 1969.
36. *Guyana Journal*, vol. 1, no. 4, pp. 4-5.
37. *Ibid.*, p. 6.
38. He was considered for the post when it was created in March 1968, but he was then Permanent Secretary in the Ministry of Planning in Trinidad and not at that stage available for secondment to the Secretariat.
39. S. S. Ramphal, *West Indian Nationhood. Myth, Mirage or Mandate?*, Georgetown, 1971, p. 19.
40. ECLA, *op. cit.*, p. 51.
41. R. O. P. Armour, *Trinidad Guardian*, 4 October 1971.
42. See pp. 259-63.
43. For a discussion of Guyana's bauxite policy, see N. Girvan, 'The Guyana–Alcan Conflict and the Nationalization of Demba', *New World Quarterly*, vol. 5, no. 4, 1972, pp. 38-49.
44. *Daily Gleaner*, 14 July 1970.

45. The CARIFTA agreement did imply that at some stage the geographical scope of the movement should be widened. The Preamble looked forward to 'the ultimate creation of a viable economic community of Caribbean Territories'. *Agreement establishing the Caribbean Free Trade Association*, Georgetown, 1960, Preamble.

46. Ramphal, *West Indian Nationhood*, p. 20.

47. Part IV of the Treaty of Rome was the regime under which the dependent territories of the original six members of the EEC had initially been associated with the Community.

48. Wiltshire, *op. cit.*, p. 71.

49. *Ibid.*, p. 72.

50. For a wider discussion of these three alternatives in the context of the Caribbean, see I. Hawkins, 'The Choice of Agreement', *West Indies Chronicle*, January 1972.

51. O. Jefferson, 'Caribbean and the EEC', *Daily Gleaner*, 13 February 1972.

52. *Ibid.*

53. *Trinidad Guardian*, 3 April 1971.

54. S. S. Ramphal, *Dialogue of Unity. A Search for West Indian Identity*, Georgetown, 1971, p. 15.

CHAPTER FIVE

From crisis to CARICOM

In the event, the ultimate crisis of disintegration was avoided. The necessary reinvigoration of the integration movement came just in time, and from the most unlikely source. In February 1972 Shearer's JLP government in Jamaica was heavily defeated at the polls and was replaced by a People's National Party (PNP) government, led by Michael Manley. Although the reasons for the JLP's loss of office had little to do with regional integration and the issue itself played no part in the election campaign, the change of government in Jamaica did significantly alter the environment in which the movement had to survive.

Historically the PNP had a very different record from the JLP on the question of Caribbean integration. It was the party which had supported the Federation and which campaigned to stay in during the notorious Jamaican referendum of September 1961. Michael Manley himself was the son of Norman Manley, a lifelong supporter of the federal concept in the West Indies. Although the PNP formally opposed entry into CARIFTA when the issue came to a vote in the Jamaican House of Representatives in 1968, it did so on the grounds that free trade was a weak form of economic integration – 'neither fish nor fowl or red herring', as its spokesman put it at the time.[1] It has been suggested too that the phenomenon of 'opposition politics' was instrumental in dictating PNP tactics on this occasion,[2] and on the whole the party did remain true to the regional ideals of its founder. The problem was that the PNP tended to be afraid of espousing regional integration too enthusiastically because its own loss of power in 1962 in the elections immediately following the referendum had been almost universally attributed to its support for the Federation.

Michael Manley understood the dichotomous position into which the PNP seemed to have been driven and was determined to lead his party away from it. In an article entitled 'Overcoming Insularity in Jamaica', which appeared in the American journal *Foreign Affairs* at the end of 1970, he expressed his own commitment to CARIFTA in particular and regional economic integration in general. He wrote:

> although many counsel caution − and indeed, this may be the price of ultimate success − one wishes that a greater sense of urgency attached to the whole exercise ... Clearly, regional economic development provides a more ample prospect in a situation where peaceful progress cannot be more than a marginal possibility. Yet, although the aisle is clearly marked, we seem to come to the altar of history like a reluctant bride with faltering step and lowered gaze.[3]

What was needed, he suggested, and what indeed he appeared to possess, was 'a tough-minded recognition that national survival, like business survival, is a matter of margins and that regionalism can provide the framework in which internal markets are increased, external bargaining power enhanced and international recognition maximised'.[4] For the benefit of those who were still dubious, he outlined four specific advantages which, in his view, Jamaica stood to gain from regional integration: firstly, the potential fulfilment of what he saw as an urgent need for all the countries of the region to 'develop techniques for handling trade and other relations with the outside world on the basis of a common policy';[5] secondly, the increased negotiating strength which could be achieved by handling major foreign capital interests, like the bauxite companies, on a common basis; thirdly, the provision of a base from which to enter the mainstream of Third World politics; and fourthly, the intangible benefits offered by the psychological boost which regional integration would give to the security and dignity of the West Indies. In Manley's estimation the choice lay between 'a low road of self-imposed, insular impotence and a high road of adventure into Caribbean regionalism leading on to the wider possibilities of third-world strength'.[6] The rhetoric may have been over-dramatic, but it was not wholly misplaced. If the appearance of a PNP government in Jamaica in February 1972 had less adventurous consequence for integration than Manley's peroration might have led one to expect, it certainly denoted a marked change of strategy as far as Jamaica's policy towards the development of CARIFTA was concerned.

The integration movement took on new life immediately. In a number of post-election interviews, widely reported throughout the region, Manley spoke eloquently of Jamaica's new interest in economic integration and of his government's continuing and unqualified support for the regional character of the University of the West Indies.[7] At the time the University was embroiled in a dispute over a Jamaican proposal to reduce the level of entry qualifications and institute a preliminary year of study in a number of departments. The suggestion had been fiercely opposed by Williams, partly out of a characteristically Oxonian desire to maintain 'academic standards' of entry and partly out of a reluctance to subsidise (in effect) the education system in islands which, unlike Trinidad, had inadequate secondary schools. Under questioning, Manley at least showed signs of flexibility on this point. A more concrete indication of the new government's attitude came in connection with a row which had broken out between Trinidad and Jamaica over the imposition in Jamaica of new controls on the import of textiles from Trinidad. Soon after taking office, the new Jamaican Minister of Trade and Industry acted to defuse the tension by announcing that Jamaica would revert, without further ado, to the import licensing arrangements previously obtaining. It was a move which was clearly meant to be seen as a gesture of intent.

For their part, the technocrats of the Secretariat responded eagerly to the opening that was being offered them. They had long been trying to secure the former Jamaican government's agreement to the 'deepening' programme and had grown increasingly frustrated at their inability to do so. Soon after the new government's election, Demas himself visited Jamaica and in a very short space of time organised the preparation of a booklet designed to give publicity to the various issues confronting the regional movement. *From CARIFTA to Caribbean Community* was published in July 1972 and set out the further steps which the Secretariat thought were needed to achieve what it referred to as 'meaningful economic integration'.[8] The programme embraced most of the issues over which the regional governments had been deliberating, but getting bogged down, since 1967 – a common external tariff and protective policy, the harmonisation of fiscal incentives, a common policy on foreign investment, the rationalisation of regional agriculture, the development of a regional industrial policy, co-operation in tourism and in fiscal and monetary affairs, agreement on external commercial policy especially towards the EEC, the adoption of further measures to enable the LDCs to benefit from regional economic integration and the extension of functional co-operation into new areas – but also contained some items which had yet to be discussed, like the co-ordination of foreign policy.[9] The significant factor, however, was that for the first time all these diverse ideas and proposals had been brought together and conceived as a package. For, as the Secretariat admitted, what was really being proposed was more than just an injection of new life into CARIFTA: it was that the time had come

> to take the decisions necessary to convert CARIFTA into a Caribbean Common Market. At the same time, as common services and areas of functional co-operation generally are extended, a certain amount of tidying up is required. These two processes ... point to the need to give a formal juridical basis to the entire complex of regional co-operative arrangements, including the Heads of Government Conference, which is the apex of the entire regional movement.[10]

Thus was born the idea of a Caribbean Community.

When, therefore, the tenth CARIFTA Council opened on 10 July 1972, the political atmosphere in which the ministers met to consider the 'deepening' approach was strikingly different from that prevalent when the ninth Council had come to an indecisive conclusion just nine months earlier. As if to symbolise the need to carry the LDCs along with the movement, Demas invoked his special powers as Secretary General to convene the Council, not in the usual venue, the Secretariat in Georgetown, but in the capital of one of the LDCs, namely Roseau, Dominica. Partly because of this, and partly because they wanted to take advantage of the relative vulnerability of the MDCs on the EEC question, the LDCs prepared their position more thoroughly than usual and took the initiative at the Council, making demands rather than merely accepting whatever concessions the MDCs were prepared to offer. As a result, the tenth Council provided the first signs of a breakthrough. With regard to the position of the LDCs, proposals for increased technical assistance from the MDCs in the training of manpower at professional, administrative and managerial levels were formulated and conditions for the transfer of civil servants from the MDCs to the LDCs made easier. The MDCs also gave an undertaking to purchase, aside from the AMP, a number of agricultural commodities capable of increased production in the LDCs, and, most important of all, acquiesced in the suggestion that a 'location of industries task force', comprised of representatives of the Secretariat and the private sector, be established to prepare positive plans for the industrial development of the LDCs. In return the LDCs agreed that the 'deepening' process should be allowed to advance hand in hand with the adoption and implementation of the new measures specially designed to benefit them. Significantly, too, the Council reaffirmed the view that the CARIFTA countries should seek a group relationship with the enlarged EEC, not only in order 'to obtain the best possible terms at minimum cost through joint bargaining', but to 'preserve the integrity of the present CARIFTA arrangements'.[11] The LDCs, in other words, were setting out their terms for not breaking up the team.

The real advance towards closer integration, however, came at the Seventh Heads of Government Conference, held at Chaguaramas in Trinidad in October 1972, the first in the series for over two years and perhaps the most productive in the entire history of Caribbean integration. By the time the conference ended, the heads of government had reached agreement to convert CARIFTA into a common market with effect from 1 May 1973, the fifth anniversary of its foundation, and to form a

From crisis to CARICOM

Caribbean Community, embracing the new common market, foreign policy co-ordination and several areas of functional co-operation, and had appointed a committee of Attorneys General of all the member territories of CARIFTA, plus the Bahamas, to examine the legal implications of their decisions and to prepare a draft treaty for the new Community.

What did the proposed common market and Community involve? That question can perhaps best be answered by outlining the most important of the many decisions taken at the conference. They divide into three groups. The first concerned the 'deepening' of the economic integration side of the movement. The centrepiece here was the agreement to implement a common external tariff and common protective policy from 1 May 1973, subject to the negotiation of special provisions for the LDCs. A scheme for the harmonisation of fiscal incentives to industry was also to be introduced from the same date. In the area of fiscal, financial and monetary co-operation the heads of government adopted a draft treaty on intra-regional double taxation and accepted the report of the Joint Consultative Committee on double taxation arrangements with developed metropolitan countries. They also agreed that the countries of the Caribbean should pursue closer co-operation with respect to exchange rate policy and the exchange of information and representation in international economic forums. In the field of agriculture, the conference agreed to the pursuit of a programme for the rationalisation of agricultural production in the region as a matter of urgency and, with regard to the exploitation of natural resources, it called for the greatest possible exchange of information and the formulation of joint policies for the exploitation of such resources. To give operational effect to these aspirations, they also agreed to the drawing up of a long-term regional perspective plan, based on the identification of regional natural resources and a projection of direct and indirect demand for agricultural, industrial and mineral products, and giving special attention to development opportunities open to the LDCs.

The second group, in their turn, were measures designed specifically to bring benefits to the LDCs. In the first place, the CARIFTA agreement was to be substantially amended in their favour – in respect of Article 5, by lowering from 50 per cent to 40 per cent the percentage of the export f.o.b. price of an LDC product which had to be contributed locally if the product was to be allowed area tariff treatment; in respect of Article 17, by allowing the LDCs to give certain aids to their exports which were denied to the MDCs; in respect of Article 18, by allowing LDC governments to discriminate in their procural policies in favour of an LDC product on a basis other than purely commercial; in respect of Article 39, by allowing the LDCs as a group to protect their markets against MDC exports whilst denying to the MDCs, except Barbados, any right of retaliation; and in respect of the Reserve List, by delaying from 1978 to 1983 the date by which the LDCs had to remove the remaining duties applicable to goods coming from CARIFTA territories. In addition, in the scheme for the harmonisation of fiscal incentives the LDCs were to be allowed to give greater benefits than the MDCs, including longer tax holidays, and in respect of the common external tariff they were to be given a longer time to adjust to the new regional tariff level. The conference also adopted certain proposals made in the report of the 'task force' on the location of industries in the LDCs, which had been set up at the tenth Council. These included the establishment of a multinational Caribbean Investment Corporation, the creation of an export credit insurance scheme to be operated by the CDB, the provision of more technical assistance to the LDCs by the public and private sectors of the MDCs, and the use by the LDCs of the industrial and technical research facilities available in the MDCs.

The third group of decisions concerned the initiation of new areas of integration. The majority of these were simply extensions of the range of functional co-operation. Rather more significant, though, was the decision to establish a standing committee of ministers to deal with matters of common interest in foreign policy. Foreign policy co-ordination was a new departure in the context of Caribbean integration, but one which was immediately given some substance by the publication of two conference declarations on foreign policy questions, one announcing that the four independent states of the Commonwealth Caribbean would, on a joint basis, seek the early re-establishment of diplomatic relations with Cuba, the other condemning the exclusion of certain West Indian states from the so-called Inter-American System built around the Organisation of American States (OAS).

These, then, were the main resolutions passed. It has been necessary to set them out fully in order to be able to explain the politics of the conference. For, without doubt, the key to the conference's success was the vast amount of ground it managed to cover. Within the wide range of proposals to which broad assent was given, there was something for everybody – LDCs and MDCs alike. Whereas the notion of a 'package' had only been implicit in the deal which led up to the establishment of CARIFTA, it was quite undisguised on this occasion. The bargaining was preoccupied almost wholly with the task of reconciling the positions of the two sides, rather than accommodating a dozen or so different viewpoints. LDC and MDC delegations tended to meet privately in between formal sessions to prepare common positions, and there was clearly an element of tension in the discussions. On one day of the conference the *Trinidad Guardian* reported the recollection of 'Conference sources' that at one stage there had been an extraordinary period of 'almost fifteen minutes of silence as delegates from all sides stared at each other, each hoping that someone would start the discussion'.[12] It does seem, though, that the MDCs regained the initiative in the negotiating sessions and resumed their customary position of ascendancy in the integration movement, enforcing agreement on all the issues of most concern to them and merely making the minimum necessary concessions to the LDCs, rather than being forced to agree to definite redistributive demands. The LDCs, as always, were torn between an unwillingness to continue as makeweights in the integration process and a lack of confidence in their ability to 'go it alone', the latter in the end proving the stronger. Even so, their continued participation within the regional integration programme was probably only brought about by the novel idea of establishing an investment company charged with the responsibility of providing equity capital for industrialisation projects in the smaller islands. Its attraction was that, if successfully implemented, it would eliminate one of the most troublesome bottlenecks in the economic development effort of the LDCs – namely their inability, more often than not, to raise the capital needed to match CDB loans, the Bank itself being restricted by its charter from taking an equity share in the projects it supported.[13]

For what it was worth, Demas's view was that the controversial issues of the Summit, by which he meant those dividing the MDCs and LDCs, had been resolved broadly down the middle, 'with perhaps the edge going in favour of the LDCs'.[14] Again, whether this was really so or was merely presentation on Demas's part mattered less than what the LDC leaders themselves believed. Trapped in the glare of publicity that surrounded the Heads of Government Conference, nonplussed by the intense and continuous pressure of their MDC colleagues and the Secretariat personnel, and only too aware that rejection of the 'deepening' programme and the common negotiating posture towards the EEC might well again bring about the ignominy of another collapsed attempt at West Indian integration, for which this time they would get the blame – in the face of all these pressures the LDC leaders may have felt that they had achieved the best deal available in the circumstances. However, once they were back in their island capitals, and thus temporarily insulated from the seductive pull of emotional appeals to West Indian unity, some began to find that, subjected to close and dispassionate scrutiny, their negotiating achievements in Trinidad were somewhat less substantive than they first realised. In January 1973 Austin Bramble, the Chief Minister of Montserrat, announced that his territory would not be joining the proposed common market, because it simply could not afford the increased cost of living which would ensue, via higher levels of duty, if Montserrat was actually to adopt the common external tariff.[15] In February Ronald Armour, Dominica's deputy Premier, declared that the Associated States were unlikely to take part in the next Heads of Government Conference, scheduled for Guyana in April,[16] and just a week later Paul Southwell, a leading figure in the St Kitts government, repeated the threat, warning that 'if the undertakings, extracted almost with blood in Trinidad, are being frustrated by the antics of some Caribbean countries in the area, then, let them understand we will not be there'.[17]

These outbursts reflected the continuing distrust felt in the Leeward and Windward Islands about the *bona fides* of the MDCs. Armour even went so far as to allege that 'subtle attempts are being made to erode the clear decisions taken at the last Heads of Government meeting and the "package" is being broken into with the larger countries attempting to extract only those items which please them'.[18] Without being privy to the minutes of the many meetings of officials and ministers which occupied the months after October 1972, we can do no more than draw attention to the allegation. At no stage did Armour endeavour to substantiate the charge, other than to observe that by the end of 1972 – some two and a half months after the decision to set up a Caribbean Community had been taken – the LDCs still had no extra benefits to show for their renewed commitment to Caribbean integration. The serious point behind this and other LDC complaints was their understandable concern to ensure that their support for the proposed 'great leap forward' was rewarded by *concrete* measures to promote their essential economic interests. With no room to manoeuvre, economically or politically, within their own islands, they felt they could not afford to be outwitted again in the regional stakes, still smarting as they were from their experience of the 'special provisions' associated with CARIFTA. The attitude of the LDCs to the proposed common market can, therefore, be simply summarised as 'once bitten, twice shy'.

Far from applying the finishing touches to the new Community and common market arrangements, as they had anticipated, the various West Indian leaders attending the Eighth Heads of Government Conference in Guyana in April 1973 found themselves faced with the task of rebuilding the political consensus that had been tenuously and, as it turned out, temporarily forged between the LDCs and MDCs at Chaguaramas just six months previously. In the end, all the LDCs were represented, although they attended only with a view to redrawing the terms on which they were prepared to endorse the institutional development of the movement. Their demands were contained in a position paper submitted by Montserrat,[19] first to the thirteenth CARIFTA Council which immediately preceded the conference, and then, when that was deadlocked, to the heads of government themselves. The Montserrat paper, as it quickly came to be called, was not just another recitation of familiar LDC grievances and inadequacies but was an altogether more substantial document. As one academic observer noted, it was 'reasonably argued in terms of the literature about economic development and economic integration' and 'had to be taken seriously'.[20]

The main theme of the paper was that the economic integration programme proposed for the region did not 'give anything like adequate recognition to the dangers of polarisation in the Commonwealth Caribbean context' and, by itself, would not 'arrest, let alone reverse, current trends' in that direction.[21] The adoption of joint protective policies would, on the contrary, reinforce 'the concentration of economic activity in those territories that already have an industrial headstart'.[22] They were the ones which would benefit from the additional production, employment and income created by the further increase in their intra-regional exports, whilst the less developed net importing territories would be faced with the dubious alternative of continuing to import goods from outside the region, but at a greater cost to the consumer because of the higher protective tariff, or buying more costly products from fellow common market members. Given that this was likely to be so – and nobody disputed the economic analysis underpinning the LDC case – the paper argued that 'an important ingredient of the Commonwealth Caribbean Regional Integration Movement must be a feasible regional economic development strategy which places emphasis as strongly on the economic development of the less developed territories as on free trade and market protection', and thus 'ENSURES – repeat ENSURES – that the people in all territories enjoy a fair share of the new employment, the greater economic activity, and the profits and beneficial effects brought about by economic integration'.[23] The government of Montserrat accordingly put forward an eight-point plan of action, which became the focal point of the summit discussions:

    1. Precise development objectives, plans and programmes for

the integration movement should be comprehensively documented and integration instruments drafted to provide for the implementation of the said plans and programme and the achievement of the objectives.

2. In the light of the weak competitive position of the LDCs for industry, the production of some specific commodities should be allocated to and reserved for the LDCs. Specifically the manufacturing enterprises identified by the E.I.U. as being suitable for establishment in the LDCs should be reserved and MDCs should not give any encouragement or incentives for development or expansion of those industries in their territories.

3. In order to attract appropriate staff to the Industrial Evaluation and Promotion Unit in the ECCM Secretariat and to facilitate the establishment of Industrial Development Corporations in the LDCs, a fund should be established out of which local salaries for the specialist posts of these organisations could be topped up to competitive levels.

4. A technical committee should be set up immediately to prepare a regional perspective plan which should show among other things the level of investment required to generate production in the LDCs commensurate with their consumption capacities.

5. In order that the Caribbean Investment Corporation might make a satisfactory contribution to the Industrial Development of the LDCs provision should be made in the integration instruments for periodic replenishments of its resources.

6. The Caribbean Investment Corporation should be required to work to agreed performance and time targets.

7. A broad-based and powerful commission should be established to guard the rights of Caribbean consumers. This commission should be required among other things to –

(i) oversee the setting and enforcing of proper standards of quality for regional products;
(ii) make regulations and take all actions necessary to protect consumers from monopolies;
(iii) make regulations and take action to prevent unfair 'price fixing'.

8. There should be established a provision to give effect to Article 2 – Objectives of the CARIFTA Agreement – '(e) to ensure that the benefits of free trade are equitably distributed among the Member Territories;' and also to Article 3 – Objectives of the Common Market which states that ... the sustained expansion and continuing integration of economic

activities, the benefits of which shall be equitably shared taking into account the need to provide special opportunities for less developed Member States.
Such a provision would be analogous to the Distributable Revenue Pool of the East African Community.
In the case of the Commonwealth Caribbean Common Market this provision should be for MDC countries enjoying trade surpluses with LDCs to pay each LDC annually a sum equal to 10% of the f.o.b. value of the surplus on trade in industrial products for the preceding year. (Petroleum products should be exempted). Such a provision would be a powerful incentive for LDC countries to take all possible steps to divert the maximum import trade from extra-regional sources to MDC sources. Any money thus paid to the LDCs should be used only for economic development and any LDC country which contravened this regulation should forefeit its right for the following year.[24]

As it stood, the Montserrat paper was unacceptable to the MDCs. They considered demands like the direct transfer proposal to be both unreasonable in terms of equity and – more to the point – impossible to implement politically. As they were wont to point out, *all* the countries of the region, no matter whether in the terminology of the integration movement they were MDCs or LDCs, were underdeveloped in a global context and were, therefore, prohibited in a very real sense from supporting the economic development of the LDCs to the full extent requested. The MDCs were only being realistic too in recognising that there was a limit beyond which they could not go for fear of possible domestic repercussions. Even such a mild 'equalising measure' as the differential in favour of the LDCs in the proposed scheme for the harmonisation of fiscal incentives to industry provoked the editorial column of the *Daily Gleaner* to ask witheringly whether it would 'be possible for the Jamaican Government to explain to the thousands of Jamaicans who do not have jobs that they will have to wait until countries thousands of miles away catch up'.[25] In Trinidad as well there were those who observed that, if the LDCs had very few manufacturing industries, then the same could be said of Tobago and even more so of Chaguanas or Siparia or Toco or many other outlying areas of Trinidad itself.[26] To be fair, the LDC negotiators accepted that there were constraints upon the ability – to make no mention of the willingness – of the MDCs to embark upon a severely redistributive strategy of integration. They realised that the regional movement was not *that* firmly established in any of the MDCs, despite the trading gains delivered by CARIFTA, but still held strictly to the view that the limits imposed on the MDCs were a good deal less stringent than the MDC leaders themselves appeared to believe.

Consequently, some tough bargaining took place across the negotiating table in Guyana, and it was not until the very last moments of the conference (around dawn on the day after the meeting was scheduled to end) that a deal was finally concluded – in LDC–MDC terms, somewhere between the consensus reached at the Seventh Heads of Government Conference and the demands made in the Montserrat paper. The Georgetown Accord,[27] as the agreement was dubbed, affirmed that the Caribbean Community and Common Market were still to be established but not until 1 August 1973, three months later than originally planned, and comprising initially just the four MDCs, Barbados, Guyana, Jamaica and Trinidad and Tobago. For their part, the governments of Belize, Dominica, Grenada, St Kitts-Nevis-Anguilla, St Lucia and St Vincent agreed to sign the Community treaty on the prescribed date, 4 July 1973, with a view to becoming contracting parties to it on 1 May 1974, whereupon CARIFTA was to cease to exist. The missing signatories, therefore, were the representatives of the governments of Antigua and Montserrat, who promised only 'to give urgent consideration'[28] to joining in the Accord, a commitment which was formally noted by the other governments. The lack of total unity, both in respect of the timetable and the hesitancy of two members of CARIFTA, was a genuine disappointment, and the general response to the Accord was somewhat less than euphoric for that reason. Nevertheless, the MDCs were certainly relieved that the 'deepening' programme was to go forward in essentially unaltered form. Set against the success which this represented in their eyes, the additional concessions which the LDCs had eventually won were comparatively superficial, involving few actual *costs* as far as the MDCs were concerned.

What, then, were the new gains made by the LDCs at this Eighth Summit? Firstly, in a clear application of the principle of the deposit, they won agreement that the Caribbean Investment Corporation was to be established by the earliest possible date, 1 June 1973, two months even before the common market was to become operative and very nearly a year before the LDCs had committed themselves to join. The harmonisation scheme was to be implemented on the same day, but with a new feature negotiated at the conference: namely, that no enterprise within a list of thirty-five industries, set out in an annex and drawn from the industrial activities considered by the EIU report as suitable for establishment in the LDCs, should be eligible for the receipt of new or extended fiscal incentives in the MDCs for a period, in the first instance, of five years.[29] In addition, the Accord reaffirmed the right of the LDCs to choose their own form of association with the EEC, promised them special provisions in the Regional Perspective Plan and the scheme for the rationalisation of agriculture, which were being talked of, and declared the intention of the signatories to establish a Regional Commission by 1 May 1974 'for the purpose of safeguarding the rights of Caribbean consumers with regard to standards and prices',[30] an area which, as we have seen, had been a constant source of LDC complaints. In respect of the common external tariff, an earlier commitment was made good: for the items on which the rates of the Caribbean Common Market and the ECCM tariffs were not identical (about 40-45 per cent of all tariff items), provision was made in the Accord for consultation, review and phasing in on an average of an eight-year period by the LDCs ending on 1 August 1981, with no compulsion, however, to begin before 1 August 1977. In the meantime their existing tariffs under the ECCM agreement were deemed to fulfil their initial obligations to the common market. Finally – in what some saw as the most important of all the concessions – it was agreed that there should be 'an annual review by the Heads of Government Conference of the need for strengthening existing mechanisms or introducing new ones to provide greater benefits to the Less Developed Countries'.[31]

The Secretariat later claimed that, in combination with the special provisions agreed at the Trinidad conference in October

From crisis to CARICOM   155

1972, these various concessions represented nothing less than a 'New Deal for the LDCs',[32] indicative of 'a high degree of commitment'[33] to the cause of a fair and just process of regional integration on the part of the four MDCs. 'In no other integration arrangement', it argued, was there 'such a wide range of measures in favour of the economically weaker members of the grouping.'[34] The Secretariat itself had much to do with the fact that this was so. Both at the time and in retrospect, LDC leaders have been more than ready to pay tribute to the extent to which the technicians of the Secretariat, and in particular Demas, the Secretary General, sought to defend the interests of the LDCs during the negotiations and to win for them the best deal available. Had it not been for this influence it is at least possible that a common market would have been set up comprising just the MDCs without any commitment by the LDCs to join at a later date. The Guyana government was certainly prepared for this, if necessary.[35] Demas, however, wanted the entire region to move ahead together and worked assiduously to persuade the governments of the LDCs that, whilst the special concessionary measures did not, and could not, by themselves guarantee the LDCs either economic development or even a higher level of participation in intra-regional trade, they did 'provide the kind of opportunities that would hardly be available to the Less Developed Countries outside of the context of Caribbean integration'.[36] Pitching his case in this low-key manner – regional integration *faute de mieux* – in the end he was remarkably successful in keeping the region united, carrying with him all but two of the governments, for whose reluctance there were, in fact, special reasons, as may be quickly explained.

Montserrat occupied a unique position in the Commonwealth Caribbean: on that virtually everybody could agree. It was the smallest of the CARIFTA member countries, both in population – some 12,000 people – and size – being just thirty-two square miles in area – and its economy, although superficially prosperous, in fact rested on extremely artificial foundations. Most of its income came (and still comes) from external sources: emigrants' remittances, capital and recurrent grants-in-aid from the United Kingdom treasury and the expenditure of foreign residents who spend part of the year in Montserrat in 'second homes'. There was little agricultural production and, not surprisingly with such a tiny home market, hardly any industry. Its balance of trade was always in deficit, exports in 1971 amounting to EC$279,000 and imports a relatively huge EC$8,558,000.[37] 1972 was no better: exports increasing to EC$369,000, but imports by even more to EC$12,100,000.[38] Accordingly, the special nature of Montserrat's problems, to which its government had persistently drawn attention during the existence of CARIFTA, were given a sympathetic hearing by the rest of the region. The island had for a long time received more technical assistance from the MDCs than any of the other LDCs and had recently been assigned a higher *per capita* allocation of loan funds from the Caribbean Development Bank than, again, any of its neighbours.[39] In addition, the Georgetown Accord laid down that Montserrat had until 1981 before it need begin to phase in the common external tariff and until 1985 to complete the job, and promised further 'special arrangements or mechanisms . . . to meet the particular position of Montserrat'.[40] In pursuit of this pledge, a team of ministers and officials from the MDCs, accompanied by Demas, visited Montserrat shortly after the end of the Eighth Heads of Government Conference and drew up jointly with the island's government a set of special development proposals. The measures agreed were an offer by the MDCs to help in the formulation of a national development plan for Montserrat and to make available to the island experienced personnel in the fields of industrial planning, agriculture, public administration and port development, both as part of, but also beyond, the terms of the Commonwealth Caribbean Technical Assistance Programme; a further undertaking to absorb the exportable production of industrial enterprises located in Montserrat and to urge the Caribbean Investment Corporation to give priority to the financing of projects in the island; and, finally, the acceptance by the Secretariat of the need to initiate studies immediately on the improvement of air and sea transport arrangements for cargo in relation to Montserrat.[41] They obviously did not meet the demands contained in the Montserrat paper, but even in that document, critical as it was of the actual stance of the economic integration programme, the Montserrat government had declared its 'unequivocal' commitment to the *'principle'* of Caribbean integration.[42] In that light, the 'special regime' for the island proved to be enough to make the difference, and the Montserrat government duly signed the Accord before the end of 1973.

Antigua, however, was a different case. The central feature of the explanation offered by the Antiguan government for its decision not to join the new Community and common market was the argument advanced repeatedly by all the governments of the LDCs during the course of the lengthy discussion of the whole 'deepening' programme within the region: viz. that the introduction of a common external tariff and a common protective policy would curtail their ability to import goods as cheaply as possible from developed countries and force them to subsidise without benefit to themselves the industrialisation of their more developed partners.[43] Persuasive as this objection was on its own merits, it could not be argued that Antigua would be *worse* affected by the establishment of a Caribbean Common Market, with all its ramifications, than other LDCs like St Kitts or St Lucia. It did not face the special economic difficulties of Montserrat, and for all the Antiguan government's contention that the preservation and development of the island's tourist industry − by 1973 the prime mover in its economy − necessitated the maintenance of an 'open' economy, this again was insufficient to establish the exceptional character of Antigua's difficulties. Indeed, a note prepared by George Rampersad, the deputy director of the ECLA office in Port of Spain, for the Executive Secretary of the ECCM concluded that 'on technical grounds' there was no sound reason for Antigua, in particular, to elect to opt out, and suggested − although without elaboration − that the decision appeared 'to be politically motivated'.[44] The observation was well taken. One must remember that Antigua, in the person of Vere Bird, had been one of the originators of the first CARIFTA agreement, signed at Dickenson Bay in 1965. However, Bird's Antigua Labour Party (ALP) government was defeated in the general elections of 1971 and was replaced by a Progressive Labour Movement government, led by George Walter, which gave the impression of being antagonistic to any and every policy – regardless of merit – associated with its predecessor in office, including within this blanket disapproval the promotion of regional integration. The question of whether or not to sign the Georgetown Accord and join the proposed Community and common market thus became the focus of domestic political strife. Trying to take full advantage of the Walter government's virtual isolation in the region, the ALP opposition actually handed to the Regional Secretariat a party resolution, expressing readiness 'as the alternative government of Antigua and Barbuda' to 'indelibly affix' its signature to the Georgetown Accord.[45] Antigua, in fact, was probably the only territory in the region where the 'deepening' issue was politicised at the level of the general public – albeit crudely and superficially. The writer saw, for example, a number of pro- and anti-common market slogans daubed on the walls of public buildings in St Johns, the island's capital.

Whatever the explanation for Antigua's reluctance to align herself with the rest of the region – and one cannot pronounce categorically on the subject – what was demonstrated quite explicitly was the lack of sympathy her action aroused amongst the other states of the West Indies, especially the MDCs. 'Who don't sign, don't sign,' declared Williams, before adding, 'but I want to know where they are going to go.'[46] Barrow too spoke in a similar blunt vein in an extraordinary television interview given shortly after the signing of the Community treaty on 4 July 1973 by Barbados, Guyana, Jamaica and Trinidad. Without specifically mentioning Antigua and, in fact, widening his attack to embrace all the LDCs, he said:

> I do not believe in molly-coddling what I describe as a geographical expression, the lesser Antilles. What is happening in this exercise is that nothing is being done by the leaders of the lesser developed countries, better known as the Associated States, to develop the economies of their countries, but they want us to do what God and the British Government did not do for 300 years ... I have gone along with the proposals which have been made, not because we need their votes or anything like that, but for humanitarian reasons. But I do not think it is going to work out, and what we have done is to allow them to enjoy all the advantages of being in a Common Market with none of the responsibilities.[47]

From crisis to CARICOM

Although the other MDC leaders neither denied nor endorsed Barrow's remarks and the furore engendered by them died down relatively quickly, his outburst did dramatically illustrate the superior and condescending attitude with which the MDCs viewed their poorer, less fortunate brethren in the other islands. LDCs were to be pitied, helped where possible, but not allowed to divert MDCs from the pursuit of their basic interests.

Indeed, in many ways the most striking feature of the entire negotiating period – from the tenth CARIFTA Council in July 1972 onwards – was the unanimity and determination displayed, at least in public, by the four MDCs. It surprised the LDC leaders at the Seventh Heads of Government Conference in Trinidad and was subsequently so visible and, indeed, compelling that it was, in fact, the LDC grouping which split, Montserrat and Antigua breaking ranks in Georgetown. As Dr Vaughan Lewis, a West Indian political scientist from St Lucia, has observed,

> it is clear to all of us now, and clear to the LDCs in particular when they go to these Heads of Governments meetings that the movement towards integration is not a movement based on sentiment as was characteristic of the period of, say, 15 years ago. The More Developed Countries wish to engage in cooperation with each other or in cooperation with the LDCs because it is necessary in terms of the protection and advancement of their own individual interests that such a system of cooperation should be devised ... One can easily see that in this kind of situation the MDCs are going to advance their interests and so advance the cooperation or integration movement in so far as it protects themselves, and whether or not the Less Developed Countries are interested in coming along.[48]

Whereas in the days of the Federation it was the smaller islands of the region which were most enthusiastic about some form of regional integration and, by and large, the larger territories who were more cautious, the position was reversed with the advent of CARIFTA and the launching of the economic integration movement. In recent years it has been the governments of the larger states who have been keen to proceed and to organise closer forms of integration, and the LDCs who have tended to hesitation and reluctance.

Why the change? There are, of course, many reasons, to which we have drawn attention during the preceding narrative, most of them a function of the way in which economics has come to the fore of the regional movement. One point, however, deserves further emphasis here. It is the difference of outlook brought about by the way in which the MDCs – much more than the LDCs – have had to engage since 1962 in a variety of negotiations and activities in the *international* arena. The attitude of the MDCs to regional integration is very much an expression of their perception of certain needs forced upon them by their participation since independence in the world of inter-state bargaining. They soon came to realise, for example, that nation states tended increasingly to deal with each other on the basis of interrelationships between different economic and political groupings, and that to survive in this world, and certainly to make their voice heard, the Caribbean states also had to organise themselves diplomatically on a collective basis. The EEC negotiations were obviously a particularly pressing illustration of this need, for, as the MDCs undoubtedly understood, to make any impression in these negotiations with respect to the kind of economic arrangements they felt to be necessary for themselves and the region as a whole, they had to be talking on behalf of a coherent entity – the Commonwealth Caribbean grouping. CARIFTA was better than nothing as a negotiating base, but better, the MDCs rightly believed, to deal with one common market (the EEC) as another (the Caribbean Common Market). Quick agreement, therefore, on a common external tariff and a common protective policy was called for as much by the necessity to deal with the EEC negotiators as by the desire, in itself, to 'deepen' the integration movement. Hence the determination and the speed with which the MDCs and the Secretariat pushed the process of negotiating the new Community and common market structure.

By contrast, the LDCs were not subordinated to the pressures of the international environment to the same extent. To quote Dr Lewis again – and much of our understanding of this important difference of perspective between the MDCs and LDCs derives from his insight – there seemed to be still a degree of protection – material and psychological – that stems from the fact of responsibility of the British Government for various areas of the external relations of these countries. Thus the problems have not been placed before them in the way they have been placed before the Government of, for example, Trinidad and Tobago trying to bargain with the other oil-exporting countries about its oil.[49]

For this reason, if for no other, one has to say, with Lewis, that Associated Statehood performed a disfunction and disservice to the LDCs in shielding them from the demands that international power politics increasingly makes on developing countries. Under the terms of their constitution, for example, they had no power to fix the par value of their currency, which moved automatically in alignment with sterling; they did not have to defend their interests at international conferences, at the United Nations or within the councils of the OAS; and, above all, as the integration movement had been forced to recognise, their virtual right to association under Part IV meant that they did not necessarily have to negotiate with the EEC. In short, they were insulated from first-hand experience of the necessity for collective endeavour at the level of international representation. As a result the LDCs have tended to see the Caribbean Common Market and Community in the single dimension of economic integration – in terms of trading benefits, investment patterns and tariff levels, and in these terms alone – and thus to underestimate the strength of the integration argument, as it was perceived by the MDCs. This also partly explains their demand, in the common market negotiations, for almost more than the MDCs were willing to concede.

Notwithstanding the fact that the CARIFTA era had reverberated with the sound of LDC leaders calling for the advent of a deeper and more meaningful form of economic integration calculated to bring real benefits within their grasp, the advance to a common market and a Caribbean Community took place only when the governments of the four MDCs came to agree upon its necessity. This is really the central point. The interests of the LDCs were considered, and special measures devised in their name, *but* only such provisions as were compatible, or at least not incompatible, with the position of the MDCs. In the end, all the LDCs came in. The Antiguan government appointed a committee to re-examine the question of joining and eventually signed the Community treaty, urging the ECCM states to act as a fifth bloc within the integration movement 'on terms' with the four MDCs.[50] The committee apparently advised the government that, being a part of the Caribbean, Antigua could not realistically stay out of the Caribbean Community. All the other LDCs assembled to sign the treaty in time for 1 May 1974, as prescribed in the Georgetown Accord, and all did so, except, however, for St Kitts, whose Premier, Robert Bradshaw, walked out of the signing ceremony as a protest against British government advice that he could not sign the treaty on behalf of Anguilla, which, in the aftermath of its 'secession' from the St Kitts-Nevis-Anguilla unit, was being directly governed by Britain. Administrative measures were adopted to allow St Kitts to continue enjoying the free trade arrangements of CARIFTA, and representations made to Britain by the various governments of the region. Its gesture made, the St Kitts government subsequently signed the treaty on 26 July 1974.[51] In doing so, it completed the final stage in the process of building CARICOM – the acronym by which both the Community as a whole and the common market as a separate institution have subsequently been known.[52]

The full establishment of the Community also marks the end of the first part of this study. The emphasis changes now from description of the historical origins and emergence of the Community to analysis and evaluation of the way it has worked in the crucial first years of its life.

Notes

1. *Jamaica Hansard. Proceedings of House of Representatives 1968-9*, vol. 1, no. 1, 18 June 1968, p. 251.

2. By the phenomenon of 'opposition politics' is meant 'the dictum that Opposition parties oppose'. R. E. Wiltshire, 'Regional Integration and Conflict in the Commonwealth Caribbean', unpublished PhD thesis, University of Michigan, 1974, p. 131. For a wider discussion of the relationship between political opposition and regional integration in the Commonwealth Caribbean, see *ibid.*, pp. 106-33, and for a particular

From crisis to CARICOM

discussion of the problem in its Jamaican context, see *ibid.*, pp. 124-8.
3. M. Manley, 'Overcoming Insularity in Jamaica', *Foreign Affairs*, vol. 49, no. 1, 1970, p. 106.
4. *Ibid.*
5. *Ibid.*, p. 107.
6. *Ibid.*, p. 110.
7. See *Trinidad Guardian*, 16 and 19 March 1972.
8. Commonwealth Caribbean Regional Secretariat, *From CARIFTA to Caribbean Community*, Georgetown, 1972, p. 5.
9. *Ibid.*, pp. 57-112.
10. *Ibid.*, p. 125.
11. *Final Communiqué of the Tenth CARIFTA Council*, Georgetown, 1972.
12. *Trinidad Guardian*, 13 October 1972.
13. *Agreement establishing the Caribbean Development Bank*, Kingston, Jamaica, 18 October 1969, Article 13(c). The restriction was not lifted until 1976.
14. *Daily Gleaner*, 23 October 1972.
15. *Trinidad Guardian*, 14 January 1973.
16. *Ibid.*, 7 February 1973.
17. *Ibid.*, 16 February 1973.
18. *Ibid.*, 7 February 1973.
19. Government of Montserrat, 'Montserrat's Proposals on the Caribbean Common Market', Georgetown, mimeo, 30 March 1973.
20. V. A. Lewis, *The Idea of a Caribbean Community*, New World Pamphlet No. 9, Kingston, Jamaica, 1974, p. 3.
21. Government of Montserrat, *op. cit.*, p. 2.
22. *Ibid.*, p. 3.
23. *Ibid.*, p. 4. Government's emphasis.
24. *Ibid.*, pp. 4-5. The reference to the E.I.U. in paragraph 2 is to the Economist Intelligence Unit, *Eastern Caribbean and British Honduras Industrial Survey. Final Report*, London, 1972. The survey was commissioned by the Caribbean Development Bank.
25. *Daily Gleaner*, 6 November 1972.
26. See, for example, *Trinidad Guardian*, 5 March 1973.
27. *The Georgetown Accord*, Georgetown, 12 April 1973. The Accord is reprinted in full in Caribbean Community Secretariat, *The Caribbean Community: A Guide*, Georgetown, 1973, pp. 83-6.
28. *Ibid.*, Section 1(5).
29. *Ibid.*, Section 4(2).
30. *Ibid.*, Section 7.
31. *Ibid.*, Section 9(d).
32. Caribbean Community Secretariat, *Guide*, p. 45.
33. *Ibid.*, p. 91.
34. *Ibid.*
35. During the tenth CARIFTA Council, Ramphal, the Foreign Minister, was reported as saying 'a start must be made' on the 'deepening' of the integration movement, even if it meant that not all the members took part immediately. *Trinidad Guardian*, 10 April 1973.

36. Caribbean Community Secretariat, *Guide*, p. 91.
37. *Ibid.*, p. 50.
38. Government of Montserrat, *op. cit.*, p. 1.
39. Caribbean Community Secretariat, *Guide*, p. 50.
40. *Georgetown Accord*, Sections 9(c) and B.
41. Memorandum, Chief Minister's Office, Government of Montserrat, no date, pp. 4-5.
42. Government of Montserrat, *op. cit.*, p. 2. My emphasis.
43. G. Walter, Premier, report of address to a public meeting in St John's, Antigua, *Trinidad Guardian*, 15 August 1973.
44. G. Rampersad, 'Antigua, ECCM and CARICOM', note prepared for the Executive Secretary of the Eastern Caribbean Common Market, Port of Spain, mimeo, 1973.
45. *Resolution of the Antigua Labour Party on the Caribbean Community and Common Market*, St John's, 29 October 1973.
46. *Trinidad Guardian*, 9 July 1973.
47. *Ibid.*, 5 August 1973.
48. Lewis, *op. cit.*, pp. 4-5.
49. *Ibid.*, p. 4.
50. See *Trinidad Guardian*, 13 June 1974.
51. For further information on these events, see Caribbean Community Secretariat, 'One Year of CARICOM', Georgetown, mimeo, 1974, pp. 11-12.
52. See W. G. Demas, *West Indian Nationhood and Caribbean Integration*, Bridgetown, 1974, p. 33.

PART II

Analysis and evaluation

CHAPTER SIX

Economic integration

We must make clear immediately that for all its preoccupation with matters of economics the Caribbean Community is not a Caribbean *Economic* Community. The economic integration of the member states is the first and the overriding objective of the Community, but it is provided for by a Common Market regime, the details of which are set out in an annex to the Community Treaty.[1] The use of the phrase 'Common Market' can, however, itself be misleading. The conventional understanding of economic integration among developed countries usually distinguishes between a number of different forms that represent varying degrees of integration. Balassa, for example, lists five escalating stages:

(*a*) a free trade area, in which tariffs and other trade barriers between participating countries are abolished, but each country retains its own tariffs against non-members;

(*b*) a customs union, which involves in addition the equalisation of tariffs in trade with non-member countries;

(*c*) a common market, where not only trade restrictions but also restrictions on factor movements are abolished;

(*d*) an economic union, which combines the suppression of restrictions on commodity and factor movements with some degree of harmonisation of national economic, financial and monetary policies in order to remove discrimination that was due to disparities in these policies;

(e) total economic integration, which presupposes the unification of the policies listed above and requires the setting up of a supranational authority whose decisions are binding for the member states.[2]

This kind of textbook classification is not so relevant to new states, among which an integration grouping that goes beyond a free trade area is either called a common market or an economic community without necessarily implying any specific economic structure. This is the case with CARICOM. In view of the Secretariat's claim that the Common Market represents the successful 'deepening' of the Caribbean integration movement, the question we must ask is simply: how deep a form of economic integration does the Caribbean Common Market represent? We need, therefore, to examine thoroughly the various constituent parts of the Common Market arrangements. They embrace altogether five spheres of activity.

Trade liberalisation

Trade liberalisation is still very much the cornerstone of Caribbean economic integration, even though CARIFTA formally disappeared with the inauguration of CARICOM. Chapter III of the Common Market Annex[3] re-established the free trade regime much as it stood between 1968 and 1973 – preserving the arrangement by which pre-CARIFTA undertakings to impose import duties or quantitative restrictions on certain listed products were respected and, in general, setting out the rules of free and fair competition. The only significant changes concerned the extra concessions made to the LDCs: the extension of the period afforded them for removing duties on the items on the Reserve List; the right to use government aids to subsidise their exports to the MDCs, with the exception of Barbados, and to purchase supplies from their own producers on other than strictly commercial grounds; the reduction of the percentage of local 'value added' required to qualify a product for free trade; and the considerable protective opportunity represented by Article 56, which was the strengthened version of Article 39 of the CARIFTA agreement.

Nevertheless, the great bulk of intra-regional trade is liberalised, and was indeed so from the inauguration of CARIFTA.[4] In this respect the establishment of CARICOM made little difference. Although lack of data still makes a comprehensive appraisal of the economic impact of trade liberalisation in the region a difficult task, there is no doubt that the level of intra-area trade has increased considerably. The figures by themselves are certainly impressive: compared with 1967, the year before CARIFTA began, intra-regional trade had by 1974 more than quadrupled in value, imports rising from US$ 47.5 million to US$ 247.3 million and exports from US$ 49.8 million to US$ 232.8 million.[5]

There are, all the same, a number of cautionary notes to be entered. In the first place, the increase in trade cannot with certainty be attributed entirely to the effect of tariff liberalisation, for there is no knowing what increase might otherwise have taken place.

Secondly, the ratio of intra-area trade to gross domestic product is still small, which suggests that trade liberalisation has yet to make a substantial structural impact on the production pattern of the regional economy. The figures are shown in Table 1.

TABLE 1
Intra-area trade and gross domestic product, 1967–72

	Imports from CARIFTA as % of GDP			Exports to CARIFTA as % of GDP		
	1967	1970	1972	1967	1970	1972
Barbados	7.0	9.9	12.5	2.9	4.1	6.4
Guyana	6.9	8.1	9.9	5.9	5.7	8.4
Jamaica	0.5	0.8	2.3	0.7	1.1	1.5
Trinidad and Tobago	1.2	1.6	2.0	3.3	5.0	5.7
ECCM [a]	13.3	19.2	19.4	2.3	2.3	3.1
CARIFTA [a]	2.5	3.4	4.4	2.3	3.1	3.9

(*a*) Excludes Belize.

Source: *ECLA Bulletin for Latin America*, vol. xviii, nos. 1 and 2, 1973, table 8, p. 146.

Economic integration

Thirdly, the expansion of intra-Caribbean trade has been uneven in terms of its commodity composition. Prior to CARIFTA, intra-area trade was made up primarily of petroleum products from Trinidad, fertilisers, some chemicals and cement from Trinidad and Jamaica, rice from Guyana and root crops from the Leeward and Windward Islands.[6] Since the beginning of regional free trade the trade flows reveal a relative decline in the trade in petroleum and petroleum products, an increase in food and beverages and, above all, a substantial expansion in the trade in manufactured goods, i.e. goods coming under SITC sections 5-8. The details are presented in Table 2.

TABLE 2

Percentage increases and composition of intra-CARIFTA domestic exports

SITC sections	% increase, 1967–71	Composition % 1967	Composition % 1971[a]
0 Food	78.1	28.9	30.0
1 Beverages and tobacco	94.2	2.6	3.0
2 Crude materials (except fuels)	62.2	4.8	4.6
3 Fuels and lubricants	– 6.8	26.1	14.2
4 Vegetable oils and fats	67.1	1.5	1.4
5 Chemicals	56.7	15.5	14.2
6 Manufactured goods by materials	65.8	14.2	13.8
7 Machinery and transport equipment	759.6	0.3	1.4
8 Miscellaneous manufactured articles	398.3	5.9	17.2
9 Miscellaneous transactions	66.0	0.2	0.2

(a) Excludes Antigua, Grenada and St Vincent; 1970 figures used for Barbados and 1969 figures for Belize and Dominica.

Source: *ECLA Bulletin for Latin America*, vol. xviii, nos. 1 and 2, 1973, table 6, p. 144.

Food is still the largest category of merchandise traded between the countries of the region, but manufactures are clearly the items to have benefited most from free trade. Indeed, by 1972 Trinidad was consigning 34 per cent of its export of manufactured goods to other CARIFTA countries, Jamaica 49 per cent, Barbados 40 per cent and Guyana 66 per cent[7] – all very sizeable proportions. The drawback is that, because of the particular pattern of economic development pursued by the region, there is a relatively small regional 'value added' in the production of manufactured goods – small, that is, in relation to the previous trade. For example, in the older trade, concentrated, as it was, on agriculture and petroleum, 'value added' was virtually 100 per cent; in the new manufacturing trade it is only about 50 per cent in the upper reaches and, in many cases, considerably below that percentage. This sort of trade is, of course, underwritten by the Basic Materials List, which, for the purpose of defining rules for area tariff treatment, confers local origin on materials which are not, and never have been, produced within the region, but which are needed to sustain previously established light manufacturing industries. Moreover, with the establishment of the Common Market, the list was extended beyond the seventy-three items it contained under the CARIFTA regime to no fewer than 199.[8] For this reason it must be said that 'a great deal of CARICOM trade from a strictly economic point of view may not be all that beneficial to the member countries who are exporting'.[9]

As Demas himself has admitted, the 'rules of origin' constitute one of the real deficiences of the CARICOM Treaty. The Basic Materials List is 'far too long', he has written, and 'includes products which could either be produced within the Region or for which regional substitutes are or can become available'.[10] Even without this loophole, the percentage requirements did not demand a very substantial element of regional 'value added'; even overhead costs could be used to form part of the qualifying criteria. Moreover, the rules, which were awkward to operate, even with the best of intentions, were constantly open to abuse and sharp practice by regional businessmen and were the cause of the few alarums that upset the largely harmonious pattern of trading relations under CARIFTA. After the establishment of CARICOM the origin system came under increasing criticism. It was pointed out that attempts – as by the Guyanese government – to change consumer tastes away from imported goods, and to protect local agriculture by imposing restrictions on the import of certain food items from third countries, were being frustrated because those items were on the Basic Materials

Economic integration

List and were being imported by other CARICOM countries, minimally added to in value and then exported under the free-trade regime to the very country seeking to prohibit their entry in the first place. By this means, for example, apple juice could be readily available in the shops of Georgetown even though the region grew no apples and direct importation of the fruit had long been banned in Guyana!

The Secretariat had for some time recognised the difficulty, and throughout 1974 devoted a lot of time to re-examining the rules of origin. Its objective was to draw up, at long last, a Process List, by which goods would qualify for free-trade treatment by reference to the nature of the industrial process they underwent in the region. This commitment had originally been part of the CARIFTA Treaty,[11] but had never been pursued. The sixth CARICOM Council, held in Jamaica in July 1975, formally recognised that 'the existing intra-regional trade arrangements are in need of adjustment' and urged the acceleration of work on the Process List, including appropriate deletions from the Basic Materials List.[12] Agreement was reached and new origin requirements, based on the 'transformation principle' that 'where a product is produced from imported materials or components then the manufacturing or processing operation performed within the Common Market must result in a change of classification under the Brussels Tariff Nomenclature (BTN) between these imported starting materials and components and the finished product',[13] were scheduled at one time to come into operation for all CARICOM member states on 1 January 1977. Although the existing percentage 'value added' criterion was temporarily retained within the scheme for certain of their products, the LDCs nevertheless took fright and withdrew their consent to the new proposals before the projected date of implementation. Since then several other deadlines have slipped by and in mid-1979 the new origin rules were still not in operation. In reality the LDCs are unlikely to agree at any time to an origin system in which the amount of regional processing required for goods to qualify for area tariff treatment is sufficient to exclude most of their 'final touch' industrial production from free trade. Given that this is so, there must be some doubt whether even the long-delayed introduction of the Process List will be sufficient to overcome the more fundamental economic argument that trade liberalisation has worked primarily to encourage the intra-regional trade of manufactures in which little 'value added' accrues to the region and in which, therefore, there is little developmental gain.

Fourthly, the steady increases in intra-regional trade, so marked in the years of CARIFTA, have not been maintained. The value of intra-regional imports, for example, betwen 1970 and 1977 is shown in Table 3.

TABLE 3

CARICOM intra-regional imports c.i.f., 1970–77
(US $ million)

	1970	1974	1975	1976	1977
Barbados	13.5	35.2	35.6	41.0	31.9[a]
Guyana	18.9	67.3	73.6	81.7	80.9
Jamaica	9.1	71.5	94.4	63.7	42.3
Trinidad and Tobago	13.4	30.1	42.1	53.7	39.9[a]
Sub-total MDCs	54.9	204.1	245.7	240.1	(195.0)
ECCM	24.3	39.5	55.7[b]	n.a.	n.a.
Belize	2.4	3.7	3.1	n.a.	n.a.
Sub-total LDCs	26.7	43.2	58.8[b]	62.0[b]	64.0[b]
Total CARICOM	81.6	247.3	304.5[b]	302.0[b]	295.0[b]

(a) Data for January–September. (b) ECLA estimate. n.a. Not available.

Source: ECLA, Office for the Caribbean, *Economic Activity – 1977 – in Caribbean Countries* (CEPAL/CARIB 78/4), Port of Spain, 1978, p. 38.

The data are still incomplete and some of the figures are estimates, but it seems likely that the level of trade in 1976 and 1977 actually fell below the peak figure registered in 1975. Certainly a sharp halt was brought to the rate of increase. The background to this situation was the general recession in the world economy that resulted from the fourfold increase in the price of oil in 1973. Trinidad and Tobago, as a petroleum-exporting country, was to some extent insulated from the consequence of the recession, but all the remaining territories of the region, including the other MDCs, suffered recurrent budgetary and balance of payments deficits. Guyana and Jamaica were particularly hard hit[14] and in 1977 were forced to restrict imports from CARICOM partner states as a means of alleviating their financial situation.

As one would imagine, this produced a very real crisis in CARICOM, to the point where fears were expressed about the whole future of the economic integration movement. Not only did the import restrictions illustrate forcefully that much of the trade within CARICOM was not in products deemed essential in periods of foreign exchange shortage,[15] but, more important, it also aroused widespread fears that there would be retaliation, notwithstanding the fact that Article 28 of the CARICOM Treaty clearly permitted the imposition of quantitative restrictions on regional goods in the face of serious payments difficulty. Despite this, scant sympathy was aroused by the position of Jamaica and Guyana, and Trinidad, in fact, announced its intention of instituting its own system of quantitative controls on the import of regional goods. An official committee was appointed which identified companies seriously affected by the restrictions in CARICOM trade and recommended twenty-three products for protection.[16] In the event, no administrative action was taken on the recommendations, and the immediate crisis passed. Both Jamaica and Guyana have recently given commitments to restore the value of their imports from the rest of the region to at least 1975 levels and there are signs now that the level of trade within CARICOM is recovering from the decline which was so evident during 1977 and the early part of 1978.[17] Nevertheless, the spill-over effect of the crisis into other areas of the integration movement was considerable and, as will be seen shortly, has not yet been eradicated. There is no avoiding the fact that, by so dramatically exposing the fragility of the free trade regime, which is the mainstay of CARICOM, the affair revealed a serious weakness in the whole structure of Caribbean economic integration.

The Common External Tariff and Common Protective Policy

The second important feature of the Common Market — constituting, in the Secretariat's estimation, 'the main pathway from CARIFTA to CARICOM'[18] — is the Common External Tariff (CET) and the Common Protective Policy.[19] The establishment of a CET had been a source of debate and dissension in the integration movement ever since the initial commitment was made in 1968 in Annex A to the CARIFTA agreement. Five years later, in July 1973, the Agreement Establishing the Common External Tariff for the Caribbean Common Market was signed, and the CET came into effect for the MDCs in that August. However, it has still not yet been fully implemented. Where differences existed between national tariff rates and the CET, lengthy phasing-in periods were granted. Montserrat, as we know, was given until 1 August 1985; the rest of the LDCs an eight-year period ending on 1 August 1981, with no compulsion to begin before 1977; Barbados up to five years for most products and eight on a few others; and Jamaica, Trinidad and Guyana a maximum period of three years, expiring on 1 August 1976. A further problem was constituted by the widespread, but differing, national practices of exempting certain industrial inputs from import duties. To overcome this difficulty, the CET agreement established an Exemptions List of those industries where member countries would continue to allow duty exemptions for imported inputs on a discretionary basis. In practice this list covers almost every existing industrial activity in the Commonwealth Caribbean. Thus there is not only to be a long period of disharmony in tariff levels, but an extremely large number of goods can still be imported duty-free into the Community. The CARICOM Common External Tariff is far from being common to all the states of the region.[20]

Moreover, the realisation of the so-called Common Protective Policy is no nearer. The thinking was that a CET alone would not be enough to protect and develop the industrial base of the Common Market or to reshape the consumption pattern of the region away from the well known West Indian predilection for high-status metropolitan goods. Tariffs work slowly, sometimes

Economic integration

too slowly to prevent dislocation in local industries, whilst in comparison with the rates operative in other developing countries the level of the CARICOM CET is still relatively low. Because of these various factors, the planners saw the need for a companion measure to the CET – a Common Protective Policy, by which they simply meant a common regime of quantitative restrictions (QRs). QRs are not only easier to impose than tariffs, but they are also more effective in the short term and especially useful in the Caribbean context (it was argued) because of the need, not merely to 'replace' imports from abroad by local production, but to 'displace' them altogether from the consumption pattern of the region – encouraging, for example, the use of sorrel instead of Coca-cola and cassava flour instead of wheat flour. However, the provision actually made for a common QR policy was strikingly weak and undemanding. The relevant article of the Common Market Annex merely required that:

> during the transitional period, that is, until 1st August 1981, Member States individually or otherwise undertake to pursue such policies regarding quantitative restrictions on imports from third countries as would facilitate the implementation of a common protective policy for the Common Market as soon as practicable after the transitional period.[21]

In other words, nothing before 1981, and then only as soon as practicable – a distant prospect, given the very large differences in existing national QR regulations. In the meantime there was nothing to prevent unfair competition in a number of lines of industrial production, with, for example, different CARICOM countries pursuing very different policies with regard to the import of raw materials needed for the region's manufacturing industries. Under pressure from the regional private sector, the CARICOM council meeting in Jamaica in 1975 admitted the problem and called for the design of a comprehensive QR regime. However, preparatory work on the scheme was delayed for a long while by difficulties in securing the necessary technical assistance and, as a result, was still unfinished in mid-1979.

Factor mobility

Provision is also made in the Treaty – in Chapter V of the Annex[22] – for rights of establishment, the tender of services and the movement of capital within the Common Market. The particular commitments are not, however, very strong. Article 35 on 'Establishment' 'recognises that restrictions on the establishment and operation of economic enterprises therein by nationals of other Member States should not be applied, through accord to such persons of treatment which is less favourable than that accorded in such matters to nationals of that Member State' – and here is the catch – 'in such a way as to frustrate *the benefits expected from such removal or absence of duties and quantitative restrictions* as is required by this Annex'.[23] The legalistic terminology may obscure the point, so let us quote the hypothetical example used to illustrate it by Edwin Carrington, until very recently a senior member of the CARICOM Secretariat:

> We are going to Jamaica to set up a factory to make shoes. The Jamaican Government can say, Well, look I am going to give a certain concession to my Jamaican business – not fiscal incentive. I may give him factory shells or something else and this he doesn't give to you. He can do that within the context of the Treaty. He can give him other incentives that are not debarred by the Treaty; incentives you cannot claim as of right. You can only cry foul when he does something which derogates from your rights due to you on account of the freedom of goods from tariff or quantitative restrictions.[24]

As Demas put it, the article is 'so weak as to be meaningless'.[25] Despite its existence, the government of a CARICOM member state can still effectively prevent nationals of other member states from setting up economic enterprises or buying land or making investments in its territory. Nor is the succeeding article, dealing with the 'Right to Provide Services', much better. It merely states that nationals of other member states must be given preference over nationals of third countries. However, some flesh has since been added to these Treaty provisions. A majority of CARICOM states have now signed an agreement setting up the so-called CARICOM Enterprise Regime, which is designed to allow the establishment of companies substantially owned by nationals of at least two member states.[26] When the agreement finally comes into force, it should certainly facilitate the spread of regional business projects.

This prospect raises the question of the free movement of capital within the region. This is something which most common markets aim to promote, but which the planners of CARICOM were forced to avoid in its fullest form. It was felt that in the particular economic circumstances of the Caribbean complete freedom of movement would mean that what investment capital was available in the LDCs would immediately be attracted to business ventures in the MDCs, thereby accentuating even further the polarisation problem which all the other special LDC measures had been designed to counter. The Treaty, therefore, only commits the Council to 'examine ways and means for the introduction of a scheme for the regulated movement of capital',[27] paying special attention to the needs of the LDCs. What this means in any detail is left, and still remains, unexplored. The only associated development concerns the establishment of the Caribbean Investment Corporation as a means of channelling business capital towards the LDCs, and in practice even this relatively limited project has proved to be a disappointment. At the outset, the region's private sector gave a commitment to provide EC$ 2 million (or 40 per cent) of the CIC's initial share issue, but by the end of 1978, some five years or more since the CIC was established, their contribution was still some EC$ 551,200 short.[28]

By comparison, the rejection of the free movement of labour has been quite categoric – even to the point of including an article in the Common Market Annex, declaring in a very forthright manner that 'nothing in this Treaty shall be construed as requiring, or imposing any obligation on, a Member State to grant freedom of movement to persons into its territory whether or not such persons are nationals of other Member States'.[29] In view of the brouhaha the issue aroused during the life of the Federation, such a disclaimer was only realistic. The governments of the MDCs undoubtedly viewed with dismay the prospect of a massive influx of unskilled labour from the LDCs, which would almost certainly follow the implementation of a free movement of labour scheme, even though it was the MDCs (especially Jamaica) which tended to have the highest levels of unemployment within the Common Market. This alone was enough to render the scheme a political impossibility, despite the fact that the LDCs themselves were strongly in favour. Making a virtue out of necessity, the Secretariat put to them the point that, in all probability, freedom of movement would also deprive them of the few skilled and trained persons in their work-force, whom they badly needed to support their own development efforts.[30] It offered instead – in the so-called 'special regime' – the fond hope that development opportunities, and thus employment, could actually be brought to the LDCs.

The idea, in sum, was to provide a 'functional substitute' for the free movement of labour. It dates back in the Caribbean to the short discussion of regional economic integration written by Alister McIntyre in the mid-1960s, in which he had argued as follows:

> Had the main object of economic integration been sufficiently recognised, it might have been possible to avoid the crisis which occurred over 'freedom of movement' within the Federation. For the central theoretical justification for the free movement of factors within an integrated area is that free trade in goods and services alone would not bring about the full equalisation of factor incomes within the area. Had it been demonstrated to the smaller islands that their interests really lay in securing a faster rate of growth rather than equality of income with the larger territories, and if the arrangements for Customs Union had indicated clearly enough what opportunities these islands had for growth within an integrated market, the debate might not have embittered inter-West Indian relations in the way it did.[31]

The planners of CARICOM followed his advice and have succeeded so far in preventing the issue becoming divisive. Groups of countries are permitted to establish unrestricted freedom of movement between their territories (as in the case of the parties to what was called the Petit St Vincent Agreement – Grenada, St Lucia and St Vincent)[32] or to set up planned resettlement schemes where the requisite land space is available; but, apart from these more limited possibilities, the whole issue has been removed from the agenda. Efforts have, instead, been devoted to removing some of the obstacles to travel within the Community by nationals of member states.[33]

Co-ordination of economic policies

CARICOM further diverges from the standard classification of a common market by virtue of its attempt to co-ordinate a number of the economic policies of member states.[34] The Treaty affirms that the countries of the region 'recognise that the economic and financial policies of each of them affect the economies of other Member States', and accordingly they express their readiness 'to pursue those policies in a manner which serves to promote'[35] the general cause of regional economic integration. The broad areas in which it is intended that this process of co-ordination and harmonisation should take place are then enumerated.

The first is the harmonisation of fiscal incentives to industry, an old familiar from Annex A of the CARIFTA agreement, but since July 1973 a functioning part of the Common Market arrangements. Under the Harmonisation Agreement one common incentives scheme has been established, whereby benefits are granted by all CARICOM countries in accordance with an agreed scale and in relation to the contribution made by the benefiting industry to the home economy. The maximum number of years of income tax relief that can be given is less for the MDCs than for the LDCs,[36] but is still by no means ungenerous.

The second is the negotiation of agreements on the avoidance of double taxation, both intra-regionally and extra-regionally. Although the territories of the Commonwealth Caribbean have long had double taxation agreements with the United Kingdom and other metropolitan countries, they have not until recently had similar relationships amongst themselves, relying instead on the application of certain outdated 'empire relief' arrangements.[37] As a result, there was very little incentive for an entrepreneur in one West Indian territory to invest in another, since he could have been taxed in both places. The Common Market Annex, therefore, provided for a complete set of intra-CARICOM Double Taxation Agreements, of which to date, however, only the inter-MDC–LDC agreement has been brought into effect.

The third is the area of monetary, payments and exchange rate policy, which is dealt with by the CARICOM Treaty in particularly broad and sweeping style, seeking little more than the co-ordination of relevant aspects of policy.[38] To supervise this process, the Treaty established as a Community institution a Standing Committee of Ministers of Finance. Its main concern since inception has inevitably been the severe balance of payments crises which have lately confronted nearly all the region's territories, and in this connection in 1976 it set up an Interim Balance of Payments Facility, known as 'the safety net'.[39] The arrangement was put into use immediately in June 1976 when Barbados, Guyana and Trinidad extended short-term support of approximately US$25 million to Jamaica as part of what came to be called the 'Port of Spain Agreement'. At the same time Jamaica was also provided with some US$55 million of longer-term budgetary support, Trinidad being the main lender under both parts of the agreement.[40] Trinidad, of course, was a substantial beneficary of the new high price of fuel, and to the extent that it was concerned about the fate of the still embryonic CARICOM it showed itself willing on this and a number of other occasions to come to the aid of its partner territories.[41] Whether or not Trinidad's various proposals constituted the most effective form of aid that could have been offered has been questioned,[42] but there is no doubt that in the circumstances they were very welcome, even as they stood, and were evidence of the existence of some sort of regional solidarity in the face of a general world economic crisis. This solidarity did not, however, survive Jamaica's and Guyana's emergency imposition of regional import restrictions in 1977. Further loan applications to Trinidad from these two countries in October 1977 were refused and there is every indication, culminating in the Trinidad government White Paper on CARICOM issued in April 1979, that Trinidad has finally tired of shoring up the economies of countries which, in its eyes, have broken the spirit of the CARICOM Treaty.[43]

The provision of emergency balance of payments support has been the most dramatic activity undertaken by the Committee of

Finance Ministers, but it has not been its only contribution to regional economic integration. The opportunity of establishing a single currency in the Caribbean passed with the demise of the Federation and the gradual acquisition of the trappings of monetary independence – a national currency and a new central bank or monetary authority – by most of the states of the region during the post-colonial era, but member states have nevertheless recognised in the CARICOM Treaty the desirability of harmonising their exchange rate policies.[44] The recent record of the Caribbean has been notoriously bad in this area, but a step in the right direction was taken in 1976 when, after much persuasion, Belize, Trinidad and the member countries of the Eastern Caribbean Currency Authority agreed to follow the Bahamas, Barbados, Guyana and Jamaica in pegging their currencies to the US dollar, thus establishing a common intervention currency for all the Commonwealth Caribbean countries.[45] This means that the currencies of all the CARICOM states now have a fixed daily relationship to each other via the US dollar, which will benefit the flow of trade and money within the region.

Finally, in talking of monetary co-operation, mention should be made of the CARICOM Multilateral Clearing Facility which came into effect in June 1977.[46] This replaced the previous bilateral clearing arrangements between central banks and monetary authorities and provides for the multilateral settlement of payments between participating countries up to an agreed credit ceiling. Under the facility, a given country's net surplus with one partner can be used to offset its net deficit with another. Thus only the overall regional deficits have to be settled in sterling or US dollars, thereby economising on scarce foreign exchange.

The fourth area in which CARICOM aims to induce a process of policy co-ordination concerns the ownership and control of regional resources. This is dealt with by Article 44 of the Annex, which reads:

1. Member states recognise the need for continuing inflows of extra-regional capital and the urgent necessity to promote development in the Less Developed Countries.
2. Member States shall keep under review the question of

ownership and control of their resources with a view to increasing the extent of national participation in their economies and working towards the adoption as far as possible of a common policy on foreign investment.[47]

It is worth quoting in full, because the two clauses of the article reflect a very real contradiction in Caribbean economic policy between a continuing desire to attract foreign investment and a growing awareness of the need to contain its adverse effects. As a result, it has proved impossible so far to reach agreement on a common policy on foreign investment.[48] A Draft Agreement on Foreign Investment and the Development of Technology, which had been prepared in great secrecy, was submitted to the Ninth Heads of Government Conference in July 1974, but was referred back to the working party of officials from which it had derived. It had put forth a policy of 'localisation' of the regional economy with the eventual goal of excluding foreign participation from some key sectors altogether. The policy had been formulated in such a way as to be flexible enough to accommodate the different approaches to foreign investment in existence in the region in national policy and to permit continued inflows of capital under conditions conducive to the development of the region, and it included generous provision for the LDCs, but it still proved to be an unacceptable basis for agreement. According to Axline's information, all the MDCs were prepared to support the proposal, with Guyana being ready to go further than the Draft Agreement and Barbados being the least enthusiastic, but the LDCs were adamantly opposed and effectively blocked agreement on a common policy.[49] In the meantime, the absence of an agreed stance on foreign investment constitutes a major gap in the fabric of regional economic integration.

The fifth area of policy co-ordination to be mentioned in the Treaty was that of agricultural development. Whilst the arrangements for the marketing of oils and fats and other agricultural products that were worked out during the time of CARIFTA were naturally continued and incorporated within the Common Market[50] – indeed, the AMP is currently being revised – CARICOM placed its main emphasis in the agricultural field on the rationalisation of production within the region, by which is meant the promotion of a complementary web of national agricultural programmes.[51] A Standing Committee of Ministers of Agriculture exists to give political direction to these efforts, and a good deal of technical work has been done in preparing the rationalisation scheme.

Sixthly, and lastly, there is the question of collaboration in the promotion of tourism,[52] where it has to be said that, despite the considerable scope for co-operation, hardly any progress has been made. The Secretariat has so far made little effort to alter that situation.

Production integration

The remaining clauses dealing with the co-ordination of economic policies are best treated separately, because they bear, or are said by the Secretariat to bear, upon the much-discussed question of 'production integration', the alternative strategy of integration proposed in the mid-1960s by the UWI economists. The approach to this question adopted by CARICOM was set out in three articles of the Common Market Annex.

Article 45 provided for the preparation of a long-term Perspective Plan for the Common Market as a means of identifying opportunities for the complementary development of the various economies of the region. Member states also agreed to consult each other in drawing up national medium-term operational development plans, and a committee of officials in charge of national planning agencies has been assembled to promote this collaboration. Article 46 looked to a process of regional industrial programming aimed at achieving the following objectives:

(a) the greater utilisation of the raw materials of the Common Market;
(b) the creation of production linkages both within and between the national economies of the Common Market;
(c) to minimise product differentiation and achieve economies of large scale production, consistent with the limitations of market size;
(d) the encouragement of greater efficiency in industrial production;
(e) the promotion of exports to markets both within and outside the Common Market;

(*f*) an equitable distribution of the benefits of industrialisation paying particular attention to the need to locate more industries in the Less Developed States.[53]

To oversee the implementation of these aims, the Ninth Heads of Government Conference decided to establish a Standing Committee of Ministers responsible for Industry, advised by a working party of industrial planners. Finally, Article 47 recorded the intention of the members of CARICOM to work towards the development of joint projects for the increased utilisation of the natural resources of the region and to collaborate in promoting research and exchanging information in these areas, and estabished a further Standing Committee of Ministers — those responsible for Mines and Natural Resources — to recommend how these particular goals might be achieved.

It is on the basis of these commitments that Demas has argued that CARICOM now embraces within its compass the UWI concept of 'production integration'. He has, in fact, asserted that:

> it is difficult to see how the allegation that the Treaty does not provide for the integration of production can be sustained. Perhaps the political and economic pundits in the Region who make these statements have not even bothered to study the Treaty carefully, the first duty of a pundit or a scholar. Or perhaps they fail to understand that the provisions of a Treaty must necessarily be couched in somewhat general and 'permissive' terms.[54]

Various points are made here. Demas is undoubtedly right to point out that the scope of the CARICOM Treaty stretches well beyond the CARIFTA agreement, and he is probably right to suggest that the flesh of the UWI strategy could be fitted on to the bones of the CARICOM Treaty if all the member governments were so committed. The aims and provisions of the relevant articles are sufficiently 'general and "permissive" ' not to be prohibitive of that sort of approach. The argument really concerns the advisability of adopting a highly flexible stance to an extremely contentious aspect of economic integration. Although the Secretariat apparently held the view that, 'generally speaking, the procedures for establishing regionally integrated industries should not be hamstrung by any formal

Protocol or Agreement on a Regime for regionally integrated industries',[55] that argument can be turned on its head. Flexibility is one side of the coin that has woolliness on the other. In fact, the harsh political truth is that the CARICOM Treaty was couched in general terms, precisely because this was the only level at which agreement could be reached between the governments on the range of issues which Demas and the Secretariat wanted the Treaty to embrace. Their aim, bluntly stated, was to postpone the struggle and go for a superficial unanimity over a wider number of subjects.

In some areas the strategy has clearly worked, and more substantive agreements have been negotiated in the period since the Treaty was signed, but this has not occurred in the field of 'production integration'. There was a time at the end of 1974 when the formulation of plans for a number of regional production projects seduced Demas into claiming that those provisions of the Treaty covering the integration of production and the joint development of natural resources were already being implemented,[56] but events since then have tended to belie his optimism. The most spectacular of these projects was announced in June 1974 when the governments of Guyana, Jamaica and Trinidad made public their intention to build two aluminium smelters, one in Trinidad and one in Guyana. The Trinidad smelter, which it was hoped would be established by 1977, was to derive its power from the island's natural gas and was to be jointly owned by the three governments, with the Trinidad government holding 34 per cent of the equity and the Jamaican and Guyanese governments 33 per cent each, whilst the Guyana smelter, which was not due to be completed until 1980, was to use hydro-electric power and was to be owned 52 per cent by the Guyanese government and 24 per cent each by the other two. It promised to be a major step towards the integration of regional production, but, because of the way it has subsequently become embroiled in a bitter intergovernmental dispute between Trinidad and Jamaica about the role to be played within the regional economy by powers outside the Commonwealth Caribbean – of which more later[57] – the whole project has been abandoned and Trinidad is to 'go it alone' with a national smelter project.[58] Less spectacular but at least still alive are the scheme for a cement plant, located in Barbados but based on a joint enterprise between Barbados and Guyana, and the corn and soya bean project to be established in Guyana under the joint ownership of the governments of Guyana, Trinidad and St Kitts-Nevis-Anguilla. However, even these schemes have suffered setbacks. Very little progress has been made on the cement plant,[59] whilst the corn and soya bean project has experienced severe implementation problems in connection with staff, supplies and finance.[60]

This leaves just the Region..' Food Plan to sustain the argument that CARICOM has moved towards the 'production integration' approach of Brewster and Thomas. The Food Plan is designed specifically to reduce the large and rapidly growing regional food import bill and has very ambitious production targets.[61] Implementation of the plan is the responsibility of the Caribbean Food Corporation (CFC), a regionally owned holding company established in 1976 which is mandated to operate on a profit-making basis whilst at the same time taking into account social and political considerations.[62] It is still early to pass judgement on the scheme. To date, it has only a few thousand acres under cultivation and the CFC is still experiencing difficulty in acquiring qualified senior staff. Even at the conceptual level, though, there must be doubts as to whether the Plan matches up to the notion of 'production integration'. The CFC has been given wide enough powers to enable it to plan and undertake productive activities on its own initiative,[63] but it is still 'seen essentially as a management and service company, that would work with Member Governments and their respective private sectors'.[64]

Conclusion

Some overall assessment of Caribbean economic integration is now needed. Let us begin by admitting that, at heart, CARICOM is still a free trade area, albeit glorified by the addition of a (more or less) common external tariff, a modest degree of monetary co-operation and a harmonised set of fiscal incentives, and looking forward to a uniform QR regime and increased freedom of capital movement. As such, it represents

Economic integration

an elaborate form of economic integration, but one which is still rather limited in conception. It is limited in the sense that it derives its rationale from an analysis of Caribbean economic underdevelopment – Demas's early 'small size' thesis – which focused overwhelmingly on just *one* of the economic problems facing the region. CARIFTA and CARICOM have been designed, in the first instance, to overcome the constraints upon the economic growth of the region imposed by small size. The 'deepening' movement was thus intended primarily to extend the thrust of the original approach from a tentative venture in market expansion to something approaching more closely to full market integration. On the whole it has been successfully implemented. Economic integration has unquestionably revitalised the light industrial sector of the regional economy and has significantly advanced the process of regional import substitution in manufactures. To a large extent, therefore, economic integration in the Caribbean has achieved what it was initially established to achieve.

However, even the architects of CARICOM, as well as the critics, are coming to agree that what it has not done is perhaps of even greater importance. In January 1977 a special meeting of regional technicians took place in Georgetown and was presented with a report, jointly prepared by Demas and Alister McIntyre, which contained an intensive analysis of the accomplishments and future development of CARICOM. Their report, which came to be known as the Demas–McIntyre Report,[65] began with a very significant statement, recognising the shortcomings of the 'market integration' approach which had been adopted in Georgetown ten years earlier and advancing the case for the 'production integration' approach which had then been rejected. It said:

> One cannot repeat too often the well-known proposition that the main benefits from integration are derived not so much from the freeing of trade as from the development of complementary structures of production and demand.[66]

The report went on to identify a number of the main flaws in the existing integration arrangements and ended by making several recommendations for future action. Amongst these were the adoption of a common external trade policy, a common policy on foreign investment and the transfer of technology, a co-ordinated regional programme for technological development and adaptation and a common regime for regional industrial programming.[67] In short, the thinking underlying the analysis closely followed the conception of regional integration put forward by Brewster and Thomas in 1967.

It would, however, be a mistake to assume from this that 'production integration' as a strategy is now acceptable to the region's governments. Indeed, the very reverse is still the situation. The broad thrust of the approach is scarcely more viable politically in 1979 than it was when it was first unveiled twelve years ago. The intervening years have undoubtedly witnessed changes in the *laissez-faire* economic policies which were then dominant in the region, but the changes have been neither fundamental nor universal. Guyana certainly has moved, via the nationalisation of its bauxite holdings and the vast Bookers conglomeration, to a position where the bulk of the gross national product of the country is in the control of the government, and both Jamaica and Trinidad have acquired partial ownership of a number of the international enterprises operating in their territories. But neither of these latter two states has wanted to escape completely from dependence on foreign ownership and investment with all the attendant costs that that might imply, and Barbados, for its part, still vigorously pursues a policy of 'industrialisation by invitation'. The same can also be said of the LDCs, which continue to offer generous fiscal incentives to potential investors. In such a context, the speed of the convoy is that of the slowest ship. If the analogy does not quite apply to the pace and pattern of Caribbean economic integration because of the weak negotiating position in which the LDCs have usually found themselves – they have sometimes had to be towed – it does highlight the fact that the overall economic stance of the integration movement cannot be determined by the outlook of the most progressive member government. 'Production integration' will only become a politically practicable proposition when the governments of *all* the leading territories of the West Indies accept the thinking

Economic integration

behind it. Anything less – as at present – is not enough.

By virtue of its inability to adopt this strategy of integration, CARICOM is exposed to the criticisms originally made of Demas's thesis by Lloyd Best, one of the UWI economists. In a seminal review[68] of Demas's *The Economics of Development in Small Countries*, Best argued that the basic fallacy of the theory was its almost exclusive emphasis on 'natural' variables, such as size, as opposed to 'societal', and therefore 'manipulable', policy variables.[69] In his view, Demas failed to demonstrate 'that smallness necessarily places economies at a disadvantage in the exploitation of their own "endowment" of resources' and often seemed to imply that 'the significant feature of the development of what he classifies as transformed and wealthy nations was the fact that they *began* as economies with large populations and favourable resource endowments'.[70] Might it not have been, Best asked, 'that the crucial factor was their ability to discover and exploit whatever resources they had?'[71] If, as Best believed, the answer was in the affirmative, then it followed that 'there may be a path of innovation which may lead to the fullest transformation of a small economy'[72] and that, from an analytic point of view, 'the bulk of the potential for explaining economic growth – even in small countries – has still to come from more systematic examination of the instruments that control rather than of the "natural" variables themselves'.[73] In short, should not political economists place emphasis as much upon the organisation of Caribbean economies as on their size?

This perspective finds no place within CARICOM. Economic integration has not been used as a tool to *reorganise* the regional economy, as the UWI team advocated. There has not been a concerted attempt to take control of the terms on which the West Indian economy is integrated into the world economy and to replace these subordinate extra-regional linkages with a real regional economic interdependence. Even the attempt to establish a common stance on foreign investment was a failure. Instead the prime 'instruments of control' – the international corporations – have been allowed free rein within the regional market, and indeed in the manufacturing sphere they have had their position underwritten by the existence of the Basic Materials List, with the result that much of the benefit from the trading gains promoted by free trade will have seeped out of the region. Nor have those international corporations involved in the exploitation of some of the region's resources, like sugar and bauxite, had to face a united challenge to their position by the CARICOM governments. Whether or not all this matters in any important sense is a point of ideological dispute and a question which only serves to illustrate the difficulties inflicted upon the integration movement by the lack of consensus within the region on the meaning of 'economic development'. There can be no suggestion, though, that CARICOM has been motivated by this kind of analysis.

Notes

1. By adopting this arrangement, the Annex could, if necessary, be 'detached from the rest of the Treaty and, with minor changes, operated as a separate Agreement'. Caribbean Community Secretariat, *The Caribbean Community: A Guide*, Georgetown, 1973, p. 79. It also had the advantage of enabling a state to join the Community but not the Common Market, whilst making it difficult for a country to enjoy the benefits of membership in the Common Market without identifying with the Community. See D. E. Pollard, 'Institutional and Legal Aspects of the Caribbean Community', *Caribbean Studies*, vol. 14, no. 1, 1974, p. 47.
2. B. Balassa, *The Theory of Economic Integration*, Homewood, 1961, p. 2.
3. *Treaty establishing the Caribbean Community*, Chaguaramas, 4 July 1973, Annex – the Caribbean Common Market, Articles 13-30.
4. According to the Secretariat, over 90 per cent of intra-regional imports by the MDCs were free of all barriers to trade by the end of 1973 and the corresponding figure for the LDCs was well over 80 per cent. A. McIntyre, 'Evolution of the Process of Integration in the Caribbean and the Current Situation and Perspectives of CARICOM', address to the Management and Staff of the Inter-American Development Bank, June 1976, mimeo, p. 5.
5. ECLA, Office for the Caribbean, *Economic Activity – 1976 – in Caribbean Countries*, (ECLA/CARIB 77/5), Port of Spain, 1977, pp. 68-9.
6. See A. McIntyre, 'Aspects of Development and Trade in the Commonwealth Caribbean', *Economic Bulletin for Latin America*, vol. 10, no. 2, 1965, pp. 145-6.
7. ECLA, 'The Impact of the Caribbean Free Trade Association (CARIFTA)', *Economic Bulletin for Latin America*, vol. 18, nos. 1 and 2, 1973, p. 144.
8. *Treaty establishing Caribbean Community*, Annex, Schedule II, Appendix – Basic Materials List.

9. W. G. Demas, 'The Caribbean Community and the Caribbean Development Bank', speech delivered at a Seminar on Management in the Caribbean, Port of Spain, 2 December 1975, mimeo, p. 5.
10. W. G. Demas, *West Indian Nationhood and Caribbean Integration*, Bridgetown, 1974, p. 62.
11. *Agreement establishing the Caribbean Free Trade Association*, Georgetown, February 1968, Article 5(1) (b).
12. *Final Communiqué of the Sixth Common Market Council*, Montego Bay, 1975.
13. *Press Release. New Origin Rules to Govern Intra-regional Trade*, Caribbean Community Secretariat, Georgetown, May 1976.
14. See R. Ramsaran, 'CARICOM: the Integration Process in Crisis', *Journal of World Trade Law*, vol. 12, no. 3, May–June 1978, p. 211.
15. For a discussion of this point, see A. McIntyre, 'Statement by the Secretary-General of the Caribbean Community Secretariat to the 7th Annual Meeting of the Board of Governors of the Caribbean Development Bank, Port of Spain, 27-8 April 1977', mimeo, p. 3.
16. *Financial Times* (London), 2 February 1978.
17. See *Press Release. Common Market Council Sees very Significant Improvements in Intra-regional Trade*, Caribbean Community Secretariat, June 1979.
18. Caribbean Community Secretariat, *op. cit.*, p. 32.
19. *Treaty establishing Caribbean Community*, Annex, Articles 31-4.
20. See W. G. Demas, *Creating National and Regional Linkages in Production* (address to the eighth Annual Meeting of the Board of Governors of the Caribbean Development Bank), Bridgetown, 1978, p. 25.
21. *Treaty establishing Caribbean Community*, Annex, Article 33.
22. *Ibid.*, Annex, Articles 35-8.
23. *Ibid.*, Annex, Article 35. My emphasis.
24. E. Carrington, 'CARICOM – After One Year: its Achievements and Prospects', amended version of Address given to Trinidad and Tobago Economic and Statistical Society, Port of Spain, 6 August 1974, mimeo, p. 24.
25. Demas, *West Indian Nationhood*, p. 63.
26. See Caribbean Development Bank, *Annual Report 1977*, Bridgetown, 1978, p. 26.
27. *Treaty establishing Caribbean Community*, Annex, Article 37.
28. Caribbean Investment Corporation, *Annual Report and Statement of Accounts for the Year ended 31 December 1978*, Castries, 1979, p. 7.
29. *Treaty establishing Caribbean Community*, Annex, Article 38.
30. See Caribbean Community Secretariat, *op. cit.*, p. 29.
31. A. McIntyre, 'Some Issues of Trade Policy in the West Indies', in N. Girvan and O. Jefferson (eds.), *Readings in the Political Economy of the Caribbean*, Kingston, Jamaica, 1971, p. 178.
32. This agreement was the product of a weekend meeting between the Premiers of Grenada, St Lucia and St Vincent in June 1972, in which they agreed that there should henceforth be complete freedom of movement between the islands for the nationals and permanent residents of the three

states. See *Trinidad Guardian*, 21 June 1972. However, the agreement had little effect and lapsed after a change of government in St Vincent.

33. See *Final Communiqué of the Ninth Heads of Government Conference*, Castries, 1974.
34. *Treaty establishing Caribbean Community*, Annex, Articles 39-50.
35. *Ibid.*, Annex, Article 39 (1).
36. See Caribbean Community Secretariat, *op. cit.*, p. 33.
37. See *ibid.*, p. 34.
38. *Treaty establishing Caribbean Community*, Annex, Article 43.
39. Caribbean Development Bank, *Annual Report 1976*, Bridgetown, 1977, p. 18.
40. *Ibid.*, pp. 18-19.
41. A number of aid schemes have been established by Trinidad, some funded via the CDB, others direct from the Trinidad exchequer. For details, see Caribbean Development Bank, *Annual Reports, 1974-78*, Bridgetown.
42. See T. Farrell (UWI lecturer in economics), 'How Should Trinidad and Tobago help the CARICOM Countries?', *Tapia*, vol. 4., no. 25, 23 June 1974.
43. For an analysis of the White Paper, see 'Trinidad's criticism of CARICOM Partners', *Caribbean Contact*, vol. 7, no. 1, May 1979.
44. *Treaty establishing Caribbean Community*, Annex, Article 43 (2) (b).
45. Caribbean Development Bank, *Annual Report 1976*, Bridgetown, 1977, p. 17.
46. Caribbean Development Bank, *Annual Report 1977*, Bridgetown, 1978, pp. 25-6.
47. *Treaty establishing Caribbean Community*, Annex, Article 44.
48. For a good account of this area of policy, see W. A. Axline, *Caribbean Integration: The Politics of Regionalism*, London, 1979, pp. 136-57.
49. *Ibid.*, p. 145.
50. *Treaty establishing Caribbean Community*, Annex, Schedules VIII and IX.
51. *Ibid.*, Annex, Article 49.
52. *Ibid.*, Annex, Article 50.
53. *Ibid.*, Annex, Article 46 (1)
54. Demas, *West Indian Nationhood*, p. 60.
55. Commonwealth Caribbean Regional Secretariat, *From CARIFTA to Caribbean Community*, Georgetown, 1972, p. 87.
56. Demas, *West Indian Nationhood*, p. 65.
57. See pp. 212-17.
58. *Financial Times* (London), 6 October 1977.
59. Caribbean Development Bank, *Annual Report 1977*, Bridgetown, 1978, p. 42.
60. Caribbean Development Bank, *Annual Report 1978*, Bridgetown, 1979, p. 48.
61. For a general discussion of the Food Plan, see Caribbean Community Secretariat, *CARICOM Feeds Itself*, Georgetown, 1977.
62. *Agreement Establishing the Caribbean Food Corporation*,

Georgetown, 1976.
63. *Ibid.*, Article 5, 'Power and Functions'.
64. McIntyre, 'Evolution of the Process of Integration in the Caribbean', p. 11.
65. 'Towards the More Effective Functioning of the Caribbean Common Market', Report of Special Meeting of Technicians, Georgetown, 17-18 January 1977, cited in Axline, *op. cit.*, p. 179.
66. *Ibid.*, p. 1.
67. *Ibid.*, p. 22.
68. L. Best, 'Size and Survival', in Girvan and Jefferson (eds.), *op. cit.*, pp. 29-34.
69. *Ibid.*, p. 29.
70. *Ibid.* Best's emphasis.
71. *Ibid.*
72. *Ibid.*
73. *Ibid.*, p. 31.

CHAPTER SEVEN

Functional co-operation

We turn next to the second major objective of the Caribbean Community, the development of functional, non-economic cooperation between member states – in the words of the Treaty, 'the efficient operation of certain common services and activities', 'the promotion of greater understanding' among the peoples of the Community and 'the advancement of their social, cultural and technological development'.[1] Functional co-operation in the West Indies considerably pre-dates the establishment of the Caribbean Community. A prominent theme of the federal era, it not only succeeded in surviving the collapse of the Federation but was considerably expanded in scope during the lifetime of CARIFTA. Since the inauguration of the Community, however, schemes of functional co-operation have grown still further, both in number and sophistication. In fact, the CARICOM Treaty lists no fewer than fifteen areas in which member states have agreed to make every effort to co-operate. Let us, therefore, look briefly at the activities which have been undertaken, or are being planned, in each of these fields. It is in such matters of detail that theory begins to be translated into practice. The machinery will not work without the nuts and bolts.

Shipping

Since it is made up of a number of units all separated by sea – and is, incidentally, the only integration movement among developing countries to be so comprised – the efficient functioning of CARICOM depends crucially upon the existence of an adequate and reasonably cheap shipping service between the islands. The organisation upon which this responsibility falls is the West Indies Shipping Corporation (WISCO), set up in 1961 by the federal government for the purpose of operating the two Canadian gift ships, the *Federal Palm* and the *Federal Maple*, and preserved after the federal collapse. The two ships operated from Trinidad and Jamaica, one sailing north and the other south, and provided a leisurely, fortnightly service to all the islands in between. With the establishment of CARIFTA and the resulting expansion of intra-regional trade, the service came under pressure and began, with reason, to attract the ire and the derision of the region's business community. Essentially, the ships were not suited to the task at which they were deployed. Being multi-purpose vessels (cargo, deck-passenger and cabin-passenger), they had insufficient freight-carrying capacity to cope with the growth of trade and were, in addition, notoriously unreliable mechanically. The service was also susceptible to political interference by heads of government who insisted that the ships call at their islands on every trip, even when there was not enough cargo to make it economically worthwhile.[2] As a result, WISCO lost money steadily and required regular subsidies from the region's governments to keep it afloat.

Various remedies were tried – the transfer of responsibility for the two ships from a private contractor to the direct management of WISCO, the chartering of more suitable freighter vessels, rate increases, even the sale of one of the ships – but the corporation remained beset by problems of finance and efficiency. Not until 1974, however, was any move made to reorganise WISCO in a far-reaching way. The key was the decision to mandate the Secretariat to prepare a five-year investment programme of fleet expansion, involving the acquisition of specialist cargo boats to replace the one remaining federal ship. A loan was successfully negotiated from the Caribbean Development Bank to purchase a container ship, and that vessel, *CARICOM Enterprise*, came into service in November 1976. The CDB has approved a loan for the purchase of a second vessel, and finance is being sought for two more. With Guyana deciding to join service, it was also decided to have WISCO serve two routes in future – the 'trunk' route comprising Jamaica, Barbados, Trinidad and Guyana, on which the bulk of the cargo moves and which was conceived as a profit-making route, and the 'through' route passing through the Windward and Leeward Islands from Trinidad to Jamaica, which was expected still to require subsidy. Finally, a decision was taken to establish a standing committee of Transport Ministers in order to provide a new policy-making framework in which the service could operate. This new body, the Regional Transportation Council, held its inaugural meeting in April 1976 to mark the entry into force of a new agreement amongst Community members, reformulating WISCO with more commercially directed principles and procedures, giving it greater autonomy and placing ultimate responsibility for its functioning in the hands of the Transportation Council. This agreement terminated the existence of the old Regional Shipping Council, the ministerial body which had had overall responsibility for WISCO since the time of the Federation.

In respect of extra-regional services, the Caribbean is almost wholly dependent upon foreign-owned shipping facilities and is thus thrust into the hands of the shipping cartels, in particular the Association of the West India Trans-Atlantic Steam Ship Lines (WITASS), which is responsible, *inter alia*, for the fixing of the freight rates charged by all its members on the transatlantic route. In recent years, the Caribbean countries have had to face several sudden increases in WITASS rates,[3] which obviously have an injurious effect upon the general standard of living of the region. In 1970, in a vain attempt to prevent or restrain such increases, the governments got together in the so-called Eastern Caribbean Consultative Committee and met the representatives of WITASS, only to find them unwilling to negotiate seriously. In reality, the only escape from this particular form of dependence lies in the governments themselves establishing a West Indian-owned extra-regional shipping service, and, although this has been discussed, nothing has yet come of it.[4]

Air transport

Except for joint representation at the International Civil Aviation Organisation and the establishment of an Air Fares Advisory Committee, which examines and advises the governments on each fare or rate charge requested by the airlines flying into and out of the Caribbean, there has been no progress at all in developing a regional approach to air transport. The various governments, like many newly independent governments in the developing world, seem not yet to have realised that this is an area where it is wasteful to duplicate the provision of large international airports, where there may be fruitful opportunities to share technical facilities, and, above all, where it is necessary to pool their bargaining power in order to regulate the operation of foreign airlines in their own best interests.

As for the establishment of a single regional air carrier, that is not only as far from achievement as it has ever been, but is still one of the most divisive issues in the integration effort. The lengthy and acrimonious history of this question acquired a new chapter when, in August 1974, Court Lines, the British firm which owned the tiny Leeward Islands Air Transport Company (LIAT), went into liquidation. So far from moving swiftly to take the airline (which, as the only air link between many of the small islands in the eastern Caribbean, was a vital cog in the mechanism of regional integration) into joint ownership, the governments of the region were unable to come to any satisfactory agreement, despite holding a series of emergency meetings. In the end it took a huge bridging loan from Venezuela to keep the airline flying. As far as the LDCs were concerned, the question of whether or not the MDCs were prepared to take an equity share in a reconstructed LIAT became an issue of confidence, a test of their commitment to regional integration as a whole. Jamaica, Barbados and Guyana agreed to the plan, but the Trinidad government (flush, as the LDCs saw it, with oil money) refused and agreed only to the provision of a soft loan equivalent in sum to the equity stake it had been asked to put up. Its position was that the Trinidad taxpayer had already suffered enough in carrying the whole of the burden of supporting BWIA, which continued to serve all the main Caribbean islands.[5] Trinidad eventually relented, but from a regional point of view the whole bitter episode was a sorry business.

In short, the only consolation available to integrationists in the field of air transport is the fact that Air Jamaica, BWIA and International Caribbean Airways, the pseudo-national airline of Barbados, tend to fly different routes and thus do not often compete directly with each other. It is possible at least to hope that they can co-operate between themselves and secure valuable economies by way of the standardisation of equipment, the pooling of parts and the joint administration of ticket agencies and booking facilities. Responsibility for this sort of collaboration now lies with the Regional Transportation Council.

Meteorological services and hurricane insurance

Whilst member governments of CARICOM maintain their own national meteorological services, they co-operate to provide certain common services in this field to the region as a whole. The Caribbean Meteorological Council, which was first set up in July 1962 in the aftermath of the collapse of the Federation, is the ministerial body responsible for policy-making at this level. Under the terms of a new agreement which entered into force in May 1974, the ambit of the council embraces the work of the Caribbean Meteorological Institute, originally a WMO/UNDP Special Fund Project, which was taken over by the region in May 1972 and thus continues to provide training facilities for meteorological personnel as well as conducting research and collecting and publishing meteorological data, and a Caribbean Meteorological Foundation, a new body established to raise funds for the promotion of study and research on meteorological and allied sciences at the Institute. The Council is served by a Headquarters Unit, located in Trinidad, which is being organisationally integrated with the Community Secretariat.

One long-standing project of the Meteorological Council has been the preparation of a regional hurricane insurance scheme. Following the favourable report of a UN expert, a meeting of officials in September 1973 agreed on the need for such a scheme and circulated a number of practical recommendations amongst member governments, at which point the matter has come to rest.

Health

Although it was only recently considered to be an appropriate field for functional co-operation, health has, of late, been one of the busiest of all areas. It was not until February 1969 that a standing body of Caribbean Health Ministers was inaugurated and not until October 1971 that a Health Desk was created in the Secretariat. Nevertheless, the health programmes which have been set in motion are many and varied − ranging from the adoption of a plan of vigilance against certain diseases, to attempts to strengthen the health services for mothers and children, and a co-ordinated effort to improve the quality of drinking water supplies in the region. The Health Ministers now meet annually. They try to define common problems and promote co-operative solutions in all areas of health care.

Intra-regional technical assistance

First proposed by the Premier of St Lucia in October 1967, the Commonwealth Caribbean Technical Assistance Programme came into force in November 1970. It was primarily an attempt to formalise and place on a multilateral basis arrangements for technical assistance which was already being made available bilaterally in such forms as geological surveys, the sharing of laboratory facilities and the provision of teaching assistance and doctors' services. There was also a redistributive element in that the programme was seen as a means of MDCs displaying their commitment to regional integration by offering technical assistance to the LDCs. In the early days relatively few of the requests for assistance met with the desired response − the MDCs themselves were often short of qualified personnel − but more recently the confidence of member governments in the scheme seems to have grown. Jamaica, Guyana and especially Trinidad have all provided a number of technical services required by the smaller islands. Even so, the seventh CARICOM Council, which met in January 1976, gave instructions that the operation of the programme be examined with a view to improving its efficiency and widening its scope.

Intra-regional public service arrangements

The Public Service Agreement came into effect in October 1972 and makes provision for the transfer of officers from the public service of one country in the region to the public service of another or to regional organisations like the Secretariat without their losing their pension rights in respect of their previous service. However, such transfers require the prior approval of the governments by whom the officers are employed.

Education and training

There are a number of bodies concerned with co-operation in education. Foremost amongst them is the University of the West Indies, which is divided into three campuses – at Mona in Jamaica, at St Augustine in Trinidad and at Cave Hill in Barbados. Established as long ago as 1948, in anticipation of the Federation, the University has just about succeeded in maintaining its regional character in the face of all manner of obstacles. However, this has only been achieved at the expense of a general trend to give more autonomy to each campus, which has led to the duplication of certain facilities on all three sites. In this context, the step from autonomy to independence is small and could feasibly be taken by either of the two larger campuses in Jamaica and Trinidad. Indeed, in October 1977 the Trinidad government published a White Paper in which it demanded fundamental changes in the structure of the University and proposed the establishment in Trinidad of a National Institute of Higher Education, specialising in science and technology.[6] Part of its criticism of the University was that it had become out of touch with the region's overall development aims, and certainly there has been little sign of the participant governments hastening to implement the demanding Demas plan for the future of UWI, which emerged from an intergovernmental committee set up under his chairmanship in December 1975 and which looked precisely to bring the work of the University more in line with the current needs of the region.[7]

Of more recent origin than UWI is the Council of Legal Education, which has been entrusted with the responsibility for providing education and especially professional training for Caribbean students wishing to qualify for the law.[8] Although it was in 1963 that a committee was first established to enquire into the desirability of introducing a system of legal education into the Commonwealth Caribbean, the Council did not hold its inaugural meeting until September 1971. It must be said too that the delay was largely due to the difficulties experienced by the governments in agreeing at which campus the UWI Law Faculty was to be located — yet another jealous struggle for one of the perks of the integration movement. As a result, the teaching of law in the University did not begin until October 1970, the first students did not graduate until July 1973, and the first wholly Caribbean-trained West Indian lawyers did not emerge until July 1975.[9]

The Caribbean Examinations Council, another long-delayed regional educational project, is also now in existence, having held its first meeting in January 1973. The idea of preparing a new system of examinations more suited to the needs of the Caribbean than those provided by metropolitan examining boards dates back, in fact, to the days of the Federation. It was revived in 1964, approved by the Fourth Heads of Government Conference in 1967, brought to the verge of establishment by the Montserrat Accord of November 1971, which was essentially a declaration of intent to establish an Examinations Council subscribed to by all the territories of the region, and finally came into being in mid-1972. The inaugural regional examinations took place in the summer of 1979.[10]

Finally, as one might now expect, there has been established under the CARICOM Treaty a Standing Conference of Ministers responsible for Education, which works to co-ordinate the various areas of intergovernmental collaboration in the educational field.

Broadcasting and information

The development of the media as a force for informing and unifying the peoples of the Caribbean is another issue that has been engaging the attention of the region's governments since the late 1960s. The Caribbean Broadcasting Union was established in 1970, but it cannot be said to have greatly assisted the exchange of radio and television programmes between the different countries of the region. It is hoped that the long-awaited Caribbean News Agency, which is now also in existence, will be more successful in building up a community consciousness by its transmission of local news around the region. In addition to those two organisations, UNESCO has, since 1972, provided three experts to help radio and television broadcasting, especially in the Leewards and Windwards, and to train local personnel in all aspects of mass communications.

Culture

The Seventh Heads of Government Conference, meeting in October 1972, decided that a Cultural Officer should be based at the Secretariat to work in close liaison with the Education Desk in the promotion of cultural activities in the Caribbean. After an unsuccessful attempt had been made to secure external funding, money was found from within the Secretariat's budget and the post eventually filled in November 1975. An extremely popular Caribbean Festival of Arts (CARIFESTA) was held in Guyana in 1972 and is intended to become a regular feature of regional life, rotating in venue between the various territories. A second CARIFESTA was held in Jamaica in 1976 and a third in 1979. However, outside these organised celebrations, the number of cultural exchanges between the territories in the form of inter-island visits by drama groups, dance theatres, steel bands and the like, is still surprisingly few.

Harmonisation of the law and legal systems of member States

Uniformity of legislation in certain key areas has been

recognised as a necessary means of assisting the smooth functioning of the integration and co-operation movement. Agreements on the harmonisation of fiscal incentives to industry and the avoidance of double taxation are already in operation, and a scheme has been prepared for harmonising company law between the various territories. There are also a number of other areas where it is planned to examine the feasibility of unifying national legislation.

The harmonisation of the legal systems of the region has, however, proved more difficult to engineer. In particular, there has been no progress on the proposal, first advanced at the Sixth Heads of Government Conference in 1970, that consideration be given to the establishment of a Commonwealth Caribbean Court of Appeal to replace the Judicial Committee of the Privy Council as a final court of appeal. It is not that there is any shortage of legal talent or ability in the region, but rather that some are concerned about the cost of the court in relation to the number of cases it might be expected to hear, whilst others are reluctant to sever the link with the Privy Council in London. And so, as yet, no decision has been taken.

The position of women in Caribbean society

At the Seventh Heads of Government Conference it was agreed that the Secretariat should conduct a study with the aim of identifying specific ways in which women could play a more meaningful role in Caribbean affairs. Many areas in which existing laws and conventions discriminated against women were discovered, and the Secretariat is attempting to catalogue these impediments with a view to initiating appropriate remedies. A women's affairs officer has recently been appointed in the Secretariat.

Travel within the region

Consideration has also been given to ways of making it easier for West Indians to travel from one country to another within the region by relaxing some of the forbidding immigration formalities which had become a tiresome adjunct to intra-regional travel. A significant step in this direction was taken at the Ninth Heads of Government Conference in July 1974 when it was decided that nationals of member states of the Community should be allowed to travel within the region on a common travel document − devised previously by a meeting of ministers responsible for immigration − thus avoiding the necessity to possess and present a full passport. At least two states, Barbados and Guyana, immediately indicated that they would also be prepared to accept as a valid travel document an identification card issued by the government of any member state to its nationals.

Labour administration and industrial relations

Recognising the part which regional policies in the field of labour and industrial relations had necessarily to play in the expansion of employment within the Commonwealth Caribbean, the Seventh Heads of Government Conference agreed to the establishment of a Standing Committee of Ministers of Labour and the creation of a Labour Administration Desk within the Community Secretariat. To date, the committee's work programme has been concerned with the development of a regional approach to such policy areas as vocational training, workers' education, the training of labour officers and family welfare education.

Technological and scientific research

One of the areas in which the West Indies as a region is most deficient is in the provision of facilities for technological and scientific research into industrial and agricultural needs. This is not a problem in respect of the traditional export crops of sugar, and citrus, but it is in the sphere of domestic agriculture and livestock production and as far as industrial use of locally available raw materials is concerned. Because of the expensive nature of the sort of research that is required, the redress of these omissions is an obvious case for regional co-operation. Accordingly, the Trinidad government's offer to the LDCs to make use of the facilities of the Caribbean Research Institute, established since 1970 in Trinidad at the St Augustine campus of UWI, has been accepted, and representatives of the LDC governments sit on the Institute's board of management. The Regional Research Centre (a part of UWI) has also been reorganised and converted into a Caribbean Agricultural Research and Development Institute, required − much more than in the past − to gear its research activities to the actual implementation of national and regional agricultural development programmes. Finally, there is to be established in Jamaica a regional drug testing laboratory.

Social security

In an effort to ensure that workers would not lose their social security rights by moving between the various countries of the region, the Seventh Heads of Government Conference agreed that steps should be taken to examine the case for establishing reciprocal arrangements for social security. A working party was set up and has been discussing a draft agreement for the application of a convention on social security in the Caribbean, under which benefits can be transferred without loss of rights from one country to another within the Community.

Conclusion

There is, in fact, not much to be said by way of conclusion. We have given brisk accounts of the main fields of functional co-operation in the belief that in this area the facts speak largely for themselves. There are clearly many co-operative programmes and common services in existence. The only conclusion it seems fair to draw is that in an underdeveloped part of the world which is not overburdened with spare resources, these are all wholly valuable enterprises. They not only save money and share skills, but tend intangibly to promote a sense of regional destiny which facilitates the execution of other areas of co-operation and integration. Of course, it can be objected that the programme of functional co-operation does not go far enough − it never will; or that there is too often a gap between intention and deed − we have tried to point out where this has occurred; or that too much emphasis has been placed upon the establishment of committees, councils and associations at the expense of ensuring that they do something once they come into being – which may be so, but the one precedes the other; or even that emphasis has been placed upon functional co-operation because sufficient advances cannot be achieved in the major arenas of integration – a view which can only be sustained by an implicit assumption that the projects we have described in this chapter are not worthwhile in themselves. In addition, some of the more extreme critics of the Community have argued that the proliferation of co-operative schemes in technical areas has been a manoeuvre 'to mask the true content of regional integration',[11] which they condemn. Even if their criticisms of the fundamental stance of CARICOM are valid (and these we have considered elsewhere), it is not evident that ancillary forms of co-operation deserve to be decried merely by association. Unheroic though it may have been, the overall programme of functional co-operation must be adjudged to have made a useful contribution to the general well-being and quality of life of the people of the West Indies.

Notes

1. *Treaty establishing the Caribbean Community*, Chaguaramas, 4 July 1973, Article 4(c) (i) and (ii).

2. E. Carrington, 'CARICOM – After One Year: its Achievements and Prospects', amended version of Address given to Trinidad and Tobago Economic and Statistical Society, Port of Spain, 6 August 1974, mimeo, p. 16.

3. See Caribbean Community Secretariat, *The Caribbean Community: A Guide*, Georgetown, 1973, p. 52.

4. Jamaica and Guyana have, in fact, begun to make their own arrangements. Jamaica, in partnership with a Mexican company, has formed Jamaica Merchant Marines Ltd and Guyana a company called Guyana Shipping Ltd. Both companies concentrate on carrying bauxite and alumina.

5. *Trinidad Guardian*, 28 September 1974 and 7 February 1975.

6. Government of Trinidad and Tobago, *National Institute of Higher Education (Research, Science and Technology)*, Port of Spain, 1977.

7. 'First Report of the Inter-governmental Committee on Caribbean University Education', mimeo, March 1976.

8. See *Agreement Establishing the Council of Legal Education and the Supplemental Agreement in Relation to the Council of Legal Education*, Georgetown, May 1974.

Functional co-operation

9. Students now read for the LL.B. degree at the Faculty of Law — eventually established at the Cave Hill campus in Barbados — and then receive their formal professional training at one of the two Law Schools which have been set up in the region — in Jamaica and Trinidad. The division of the facilities between the three campuses was typical.
10. See *CARICOM Bulletin*, No. 1, August 1978, pp. 10-14.
11. C. Y. Thomas, 'Neo-colonialism and Caribbean Integration', *Ratoon*, April 1975, p. 25.

CHAPTER EIGHT

The co-ordination of foreign policy

We come, thirdly, to the co-ordination of foreign policy, the one area of integrative activity embraced by CARICOM which had no place within the structure of CARIFTA. Foreign policy is inevitably an integral part of the general development strategy of small, structurally open economies like those of the Commonwealth Caribbean. It has a considerable impact upon the volume, quality and sources of aid, private investment, trade and technical assistance. In an area which had devoted so much effort to the promotion of economic integration, some attempt to co-ordinate the foreign policy of the region's governments was, if anything, overdue when, in 1973, it was formally promulgated as the third major objective of the new Caribbean Community. To this end, Article 17 of the Community Treaty provided for the establishment of a Standing Committee of Ministers responsible for Foreign Affairs and required it to make recommendations to the governments of member states with a view to bringing about 'the fullest possible co-ordination of their foreign policies within their respective competences' (thereby confining representation on the committee to the independent states of the region) and adopting 'as far as possible common positions in major international issues'.[1] These aims are not over-ambitious, but can be said to demand that member states should have at least worked out amongst themselves a common position on the question of association with the EEC, on the appropriate relationship to have with the 'wider' Caribbean, on the stance to adopt towards major international issues and, finally, on the merits of shared diplomatic representation abroad. These four 'issue-areas' stand, therefore, as tests of the Commonwealth Caribbean's willingness to enter seriously the field of integration in foreign policy.

The EEC

For nearly two decades the EEC question has been the fulcrum upon which the future of the Commonwealth Caribbean has seemed to turn. With just cause, the region's leaders have been fearful of the social, political and economic disruption liable to result from failure to protect adequately the markets of the ten or so West Indian products traditionally exported to the United Kingdom under tariff preferences or other special arrangements – if and when Britain joined the EEC. As we have seen, this concern, which was shared in one way or another by all the territories, has worked consistently to unite the region and to give impetus to the integration movement. The transmutation of CARIFTA into CARICOM, for example, owed a lot to the successful conclusion to which British negotiations were brought in 1972. It might be expected, then, that if there was one area in which the member states of the new Community would be able to co-ordinate their foreign policies it would be over the question of association with the EEC.

And so, indeed, it proved. Throughout the negotiations, the several territories of the Caribbean Community adhered resolutely to the original decision of the CARIFTA Council that the region should negotiate with the enlarged EEC as a group. At the opening conference in Brussels in July 1973, Ramphal, Guyana's Foreign Minister, informed the EEC that all the territories of the region had chosen 'to sit together at this table under the single label of the "Caribbean Countries" ',[2] and even though the Caribbean grouping was subsequently incorporated within an African, Caribbean and Pacific (ACP) negotiating front, it continued to behave as a united bloc amongst the ACP countries. A senior member of the Secretariat staff reported that at the joint ACP–EEC ministerial meeting held in Jamaica in

July 1974, which in many ways constituted a breakthrough in the negotiations, the region again

> had one spokesman ... For the first time you could have relaxed and said we were not likely to split the thing this time. We were really united. We spoke as one group and I think it did our cause well. In fact, it wouldn't be immodest to say that much of the intellectual fuselage used in the battle with the EEC by the African, Caribbean and Pacific side, emanated from the Caribbean group.[3]

Because, however, they were not independent, the Caribbean LDCs could not formally be a party to the negotiations. They were listed, after all, for association under Part IV. Nevertheless, their representatives often took part in, and were always kept closely informed of, the Caribbean group's discussions,[4] and the independent territories of the region did receive from the EEC negotiators a promise that the new Part IV arrangements would be no less favourable than those for the ACP states and would take full account of the aims and aspirations of the Caribbean Community. At the time this was taken to be sufficient, but difficulties later arose. When a communication from the British government to the non-independent Part IV states of the Caribbean about their allocation of aid from the European Development Fund appeared not only to involve a leading role for Britain in the administration of that aid, but seemed to place the Caribbean Part IV countries in a far less favourable position than other groups of Part IV countries as well as the ACP group as a whole in terms of the volume of aid allocated, the CARICOM Council was quick to gather in special session – in October 1975 – and pass an angry resolution, expressing determination to preserve the internal equilibrium of the Caribbean Community.[5] The matter was not finally resolved until early 1977, when a total allocation of aid was made to the region and the CARICOM authorities themselves were allowed to decide on its distribution as between the independent territories and the Part IV states.[6]

From the point of view of the independent territories, the final convention of association, signed at Lomé in Togo in February 1975, constituted a relatively successful conclusion to the negotiations. There is no need to trouble ourselves with the details of the convention, still less to attempt to evaluate its merits and demerits. In respect of the record of the CARICOM countries in co-ordinating their foreign policies, we can mark down the question of association with the EEC as a successful demonstration of the value to small states of pooling their bargaining power. There is little doubt that the concessions they did succeed in winning in negotiation with the EEC exceeded those they were likely to have won if they had each been treating for association separately.

The 'wider' Caribbean

For all its preoccupation with the precise terms of its relationship with Britain and Europe, the Commonwealth Caribbean has increasingly come to realise that it still 'lives within a wider Caribbean'[7] and that it must face up to the reality of its proximity to the other territories of the area – the French and Dutch possessions, Haiti, the Dominican Republic, Cuba and Puerto Rico, and those states of South and Central America which share the heritage of the Caribbean Sea. Until recently, moreover, there were a number of indications that it was also approaching this task on a group basis.

In the first place, the debate about the 'widening' of the integration movement was not allowed to become a cause of intra-regional discord, as at one time appeared possible. All the member governments seem now to have implicity agreed that the consolidation and strengthening of CARICOM is the first priority. When, therefore, Haiti formally applied for membership in May 1974, the heads of government merely noted the application and referred it to the Secretariat for further study,[8] at which point the matter has come to rest.

Secondly, the four independent territories achieved a considerable diplomatic coup in October 1972 by their decision – notwithstanding the objections of the American State Department – to establish diplomatic relations with the Republic of Cuba. The move clearly carried added weight by virtue of being the joint decision of a definite group of territories and, in fact, it proved to be the trigger which led eventually to the ending of OAS sanctions against Cuba in 1974.

Thirdly, a number of foreign policy initiatives towards the wider Caribbean were taken by the Caribbean Community as a diplomatic institution in its own right. For example, at their meeting in St Lucia in July 1974, the heads of government agreed to the establishment of formal relations with the two Latin American economic integration movements on a joint Caribbean Community basis. They instructed the Secretariat to make contact accordingly with the Secretariat of the Central American Common Market and with the *Junta* of the Andean Common Market. Furthermore, in the same month, the Secretary General signed an agreement with the Foreign Minister of Mexico, establishing a joint Mexico–CARICOM commission to explore possible areas of economic, technical and cultural co-operation.

Fourthly, the region has stood solidly by the side of Belize in its continuing dispute with Guatemala.[9] Successive Heads of Government Conferences have repudiated Guatemala's claim to the territory of Belize and reaffirmed their support for the early fulfilment of the Belizean people's right to independence, which has been impeded by the ever-present threat of Guatemalan aggression. The independent territories have also consistently publicised the problem at international gatherings and were instrumental in engineering the overwhelming support given to the Belizean cause at the thirtieth session of the United Nations General Assembly in the autumn of 1975. They also came out in full support of the Belize government in January 1978 when it vigorously opposed a British plan to cede some Belizean territory to Guatemala in exchange for an undertaking that Guatemala would give up the full extent of its claim.[10]

Against these examples of joint action, however, there must be set the angry dispute over Latin American policy which broke out between the Prime Ministers of Trinidad and Jamaica in mid-1975 and which, for a time, transported the Caribbean back to the bitter atmosphere of the latter days of the Federation when it was standard form for regional leaders to air their policy differences in the columns of the press. The rift first appeared in April 1975 in a speech delivered by Eric Williams to a public meeting in San Fernando in Trinidad. He told his audience that many of the important recent advances in the Caribbean integration process were being prejudiced by the way in which other member states of CARICOM were making additional deals in the very same fields with Latin American countries, and observed:

> we talk about Caribbean food, suddenly I hear we are getting that in some arrangement with Venezuela. I say Venezue-who? Venezuela? We talked about aluminium; we hear now that this country has arrangements with Venezuela ... The Caribbean Development Bank where we put in a lot of money, we suddenly hear all sorts of people coming in – Venezuela, Puerto Rico. I begin to look and say, "Ssh ... ssh ... this is Caribbean Development Bank? ... Are you sure there is any Caribbean country still left in the bank? ... We are now trying to develop something, then you suddenly hear that is Venezuela, that is Mexico, that is Colombia. For God's sake, has the Caribbean changed its position? Who is the Caribbean now?"[11]

He then went on to point up what was to his mind the wider lesson of these developments by declaring: 'Ladies and gentlemen, in my opinion the recolonisation of the Caribbean is in full swing today.'[12]

In the ensuing weeks Williams continued to develop his 'recolonisation' thesis. In an address to the PNM General Council (subsequently published under the title *The Threat to the Caribbean Community*) he advanced a lengthy, pseudo-academic analysis of Venezuela's territorial ambitions in respect of the Commonwealth Caribbean,[13] whilst in another speech to a special PNM convention (the first since the momentous convention of January 1962) he denounced in bitter terms the particular deal which had annoyed him most – the economic co-operation agreement signed between the governments of Jamaica and Venezuela in April 1975. In the first place, Williams argued, by accepting Venezuela's offer of inclusion within the oil rebate arrangement worked out in December 1974 with the various states of Central America (by which Venezuela agreed to supply oil at the pre-1973 price in cash, the difference from the world price constituting a soft loan on a deferred payment basis), Jamaica was, in effect, implicitly accepting the other provisions of the so-called 'Declaration of Guyana' in which the oil rebate scheme was enshrined. These included, he pointed out, unreserved support for Guetemala's claim upon the territory of Belize. Secondly, Williams alleged that those parts of the Jamaica–Venezuela agreement which dealt with bauxite placed the first of the CARICOM aluminium smelters 'in serious jeopardy'.[14] According to his sources, Venezuela planned to expand its production of aluminium from the existing level of 55,000 tons to a minimum of 330,000 tons a year: to achieve this, it had arranged in the deal with Jamaica to be supplied with 200,000 tons of alumina for the next ten years, as well as 400,000 tons of bauxite for three years and 500,000 tons for the following seven. Since Venezuela's local consumption of aluminium was only 27,000 tons a year in 1973 – barely half its existing smelter capacity – the planned increase could only mean an enormous increase in exports which would have a disruptive effect upon the viability of the CARICOM smelter project. It was 'simply not possible' to view Venezuelan policy 'as anything but a calculated attack' upon the CARICOM scheme[15] – an attack, moreover, to which one of Trinidad's CARICOM colleagues was a party. Williams's patience was exhausted. 'My friends', he announced, 'one man can only take so much, and I have had enough. To smelt or not to smelt, no big thing as there is no shortage of claims on our gas.'[16]

Manley replied by doubting the validity of Williams's use of the term 'recolonisation' – he could not see how, in any aspect of the arrangement with Venezuela, Jamaica had 'surrendered control of its resources or of its disposition of these resources, which would be the only basis for deciding that a form of colonialist exploitation was at work'[17] – and by implying that 'the Trinidad source'[18] (as he euphemistically termed Williams) was ignorant of the basic facts of bauxite-alumina technology. All that had happened, he argued, was that Venezuela had agreed to contribute 10 per cent of the cost and take 200,000 tons of the output of a new alumina processing plant to be built in the South Manchester area of Jamaica, and had, in turn, offered Jamaica a 10 per cent equity interest in a new aluminium smelter to be built in Venezuela. How could this be seen as colonisation? As for the CARICOM smelter project, was it not realised that the smelter planned for Trinidad would, at full capacity, require less than 10 per cent of Jamaica's existing annual production of alumina and thus could easily be supplied, Venezuelan demands notwithstanding? Nor would there be any problem marketing the output of the Trinidad smelter, as Williams had intimated. According to Manley, a study undertaken by the experts employed by CARICOM to assess the feasibility of the smelter project had predicted that there would still be a world-wide shortage of aluminium by 1979 of 1·02 million tons, even after taking into consideration the 330,000 tons that the expanded Venezuelan plant would be putting on to the market about that time.[19]

It is extremely difficult to arbitrate between the two viewpoints. Within the region, Williams was certainly completely isolated by his stand. The Guyanese government refrained from making any public pronouncements on the controversy, but when Burnham visited Caracas at the end of July 1975 for talks on closer co-operation between Guyana and Venezuela, his was the fifth such visit by heads of government of CARICOM member states within a four-month period. After Manley in April had come the Premier of St Kitts-Nevis, Robert Bradshaw, the Premier of Antigua, George Walter, and the Prime Minister of Grenada, Eric Gairy, all of whom publicly announced their disagreement with Williams's 'recolonisation' charge. And yet, in view of the increasingly close relationship that was developing between Venezuela and many Commonwealth Caribbean territories, illustrated by all these journeys and their fruits, Williams was right to draw the region's attention to the possible consequences of the growing economic penetration of the Caribbean Community by Venezuelan 'petrodollars', which was resulting from the so-called 'co-operative' arrangements concluded at the end of each of these 'pilgrimages to Caracas',[20] as he contemptuously termed them. Against that, it must be said that, on the particular two points on which he took issue with Williams's analysis, Manley's case does seem to be the stronger. On the technical side, it is not immediately obvious that the CARICOM smelter was rendered unviable by Jamaica's other deals in connection with bauxite and alumina, whilst his semantic objections were also fair comment. 'Recolonisation', which is intrinsically a highly emotive concept, is not the most accurate term available to catch the essence of the general process which Williams was describing. As noted earlier, some formulation of the concept of 'penetration' would, perhaps, have been more appropriate.

Both these latter points, however, are very narrow considerations and are not the most important aspects of the affair. The row has much graver implications when looked at from the point of view of the co-ordination of foreign policy within the Commonwealth Caribbean. In this respect it was unquestionably a major lapse – for two reasons. Firstly, it showed nearly all the countries of the region (Trinidad nobly excepted) seeking to make bilateral deals with Venezuela instead of trying to formulate a common regional front on the matter. Jamaica was particularly culpable because the nature of its particular deal with Venezuela – concerned, as it was, with the bauxite-alumina industry – plainly overlapped with CARICOM policy in the same sphere. We can be absolutely sure from the vehemence of Williams's reaction that Manley did not consult the Trinidad government before agreeing to the deal. Mention should also be made of the fact that one of the other equity contributors to the new Jamaican alumina plant was the Mexican government, which agreed to put up no less than 29 per cent of the cost in return for Jamaica contributing 29 per cent of the equity of a new aluminium smelter to be built in Mexico. This deal did not arouse Williams's ire in the same way that the Venezuelan agreement had; but it irritated the technocrats in the Secretariat, since it was with the Mexican government in July 1974 that the Caribbean Community states had, as a group, signed a trade and co-operation agreement. It also illustrated, again, the tendency to bilateralism in Jamaican foreign policy and pointed up, more generally, the diverse interests that were beginning to appear in the external trade policies of the various Community states in direct contravention of the commitment they had given in Article 34 of the Common Market Annex to seek the co-ordination of policy in such matters.[21]

Secondly, the row highlighted the existence of two different and conflicting concepts of the countries that comprise the Caribbean – what might be termed the 'Williams Latin American doctrine' and the 'Manley Latin American doctrine'. The main ingredients of the former are a deep suspicion of the motives of certain Latin American states with regard to the Commonwealth Caribbean and the consequent avoidance of relations with them. In foundation, it rests upon a definition of the Caribbean which firmly excludes the Central and Latin American states, except, of course, for what were once the three Guianas. Williams has accordingly been contemptuous of a Venezuelan plan to call a conference of 'the Caribbean basin' – 'whatever that may be', as he put it[22] – and sees it as his mission to preserve 'the Caribbean personality' and not allow it to be lost in a wider Latin American identity. In May 1975 he succeeded in getting the sixteenth session of ECLA to create within its structure a Caribbean Development and Co-operation Committee, designed to perform just that function. By contrast, the hallmarks of the 'Manley Latin American doctrine' are friendship, co-operation and closer ties with Latin American states in the battle to create a 'new world economic order' in favour of developing countries. It, in turn, is obviously based upon a sense of the Caribbean's geo-political affinity with Latin America. With which of these perspectives the other states of the Commonwealth Caribbean will align themselves is as yet unclear. They are prepared, as we have seen, to look upon Venezuela as a friend, but, on the other hand, they have had much longer than Jamaica to become attuned to the idea of West Indian unity. Although the temperature of the debate has fallen since the angry days of 1975, a resolution of the difference between these two doctrines will not be easily achieved.

International issues

The governments of the region have not made any sustained attempt to take up common positions on international affairs which do not directly affect the Caribbean, and indeed it may well be that differences of stance in regard to the Middle East or China do not matter very much. Having said that, though, it is increasingly hard in an interdependent world to conceive of major international problems which are not likely to bear in some way on the Caribbean. In fact, there is one such issue – the future of Southern Africa – on which the marked failure of the region's governments to co-ordinate their foreign policy may well prove to have the most unfortunate consequences for the general cause of Caribbean integration.

The independent territories of the region have always been in accord in looking forward to the advent of black majority rule throughout Southern Africa, but they have rarely found it so easy to preserve their unity when faced with the need to agree upon practical steps to give effect to these aspirations. In March 1976 a special Summit conference, called principally to discuss the future of the University of the West Indies, broke up in some rancour after the heads of government had turned their attention to recent events in Africa. No statements were made afterwards, but reports had it that the Jamaican and Guyanese governments refused to discuss the questions of aid to Mozambique, which had just announced the closure of its borders to Rhodesian traffic, and sporting links with South Africa as separate matters. They insisted that they be incorporated within an overall discussion of policy towards Africa, including the matter of giving diplomatic recognition to the new Marxist government in Angola, a step readily taken by the governments of Jamaica and Guyana, but not at that stage by Trinidad and Barbados. Williams apparently declined to deviate from his government's policy of withholding recognition of any new government until it had been recognised by the United Nations. Both he and Barrow had also refused permission to Cuba to use their territories to refuel planes carrying troops to Angola, although the Barbados government claimed not to have discovered that the Cuban planes were using its airport until a number had landed and had been refuelled. Both governments based their refusal on a policy of neutrality amongst the various factions fighting for power in Angola, whereas Jamaica and Guyana made no secret of their support for the Marxist cause and their approval of Cuban military involvement in the struggle.[23]

These differences of position, although well known before the special Summit met, nevertheless embittered relations between the heads of government. Not only did they fail to reach agreement on the question of financial and material help for Mozambique; they were also unable to resolve an associated dispute about cricket. A month or so before the conference, a member of the Barbados cricket team, selected to play for his country against Guyana in the regional Shell Shield tournament, was refused permission to play in Guyana because he had once played in South Africa. The Barbados Cricket Association promptly recalled their team and were subsequently supported in this action by the Barbados government. The Commonwealth Caribbean states had previously agreed to boycott sports events in South Africa and those in which South Africa participated, but the Barbados government took the position that the cricketer involved had played in South Africa on his own behalf, not as a representative of Barbados or the West Indies, and that he should be exempt from the ban imposed by Guyana. Guyana, however, refused to make an exception to its boycott policy and was supported by the Jamaican government, which announced a similar entry ban. These decisions open up the possibility that the other major cricket-playing countries will refuse to tour the West Indies, since many of the players liable to be selected, having played in South Africa, would have to be banned from entering Jamaica and Guyana, where two of the test matches are customarily held. Thus the West Indies *could*, paradoxically, find itself as isolated as South Africa from the mainstream of international cricket, and one of the most cherished of all West Indian institutions, the West Indies cricket team, could face dissolution. The matter will almost certainly not be allowed to go that far, but it does highlight the importance of reaching agreement within the region on the stance to be adopted on all major international issues if foreign policy co-ordination is not to become the Achilles heel of the whole integration movement.

External representation

Finally, something needs to be said about the matter of joint diplomatic representation abroad. In this area, the regional record has been distinctly ambivalent. On the one hand, a succession of working parties and intergovernmental committees[24] have failed to make any headway in curtailing the wasteful duplication of resources, both material and human, occasioned by the insistence of each independent Commonwealth Caribbean state that it should have its own diplomatic representatives separately accredited to the major powers of the world. The one experiment in this field – the joint appointment of a High Commissioner to Britain by the governments of Barbados and Guyana in the mid-1960s – lasted less than three years.[25] Since then the possession of an individual voice in London, Washington and other major foreign capitals has been thought to be an indispensable part of the diplomatic armoury. From the point of view of the new nation it not only emphasises its arrival on the international scene but creates a number of high-prestige jobs for disposal. Sustained by both the call of prestige and patronage, it will prove a difficult habit to break. On the other hand, greater success has attached to the efforts of the governments in the Caribbean to cut down on the costs of representation at international institutions. At the International Civil Aviation Organisation, for example, Trinidad is the sole representative of all the states of the region that have membership rights, and even at the more political gatherings – like the UN Law of the Sea Conference, meetings of the Non-aligned movement or the Commonwealth Prime Ministers' Conference – it is no longer as unusual as it once was for one delegate to speak on behalf of the region as a whole. Indeed, in regard to the numerous complex issues raised by the law of the sea, the region sought to develop a unified approach well in advance of the actual opening of the conference, albeit without great success.

Conclusion

What are we to make of the Community's approach to the co-ordination of foreign policy? As we have seen, there have been instances of joint actions being taken and common policies being pursued. Some, indeed, have been in quite crucial areas. Moreover, whenever foreign policy positions have been successfully co-ordinated, the result has either been an increase in the effective bargaining power of the region or an enhancement of the image of the Commonwealth Caribbean internationally or both. Equally, there have been obvious failures and examples of lack of co-ordination, and even of outright conflict, between the positions of different Community members: some of those, too, have been in critical areas. The most important current weakness undoubtedly concerns the growing tendency of the independent countries of the region to negotiate bilateral deals with other countries or groups of countries without prior consultation with their CARICOM partners. External deals inevitably offer opportunities for co-operative arrangements which may be more favourable to a member country than similar arrangements within the region, especially if they are not accompanied by the necessity to contribute to redistributive measures in favour of the LDCs, but they can easily create patterns of interaction which detract from the prospects of regional integration. Some of the larger states seem to have fallen into this trap of late.[26] The establishment of relations with third countries on a regional basis has thus become the crucial test of foreign policy co-ordination in the Caribbean. Demas, indeed, has seen this problem as the possible seed of the erosion of the whole of CARICOM.[27]

In general, though, it is not possible to say much more in evaluation of the movement towards the co-ordination of foreign policy than here it exists and here, as yet, it does not. The approach has been pragmatic and the results reflect this. There are, however, two further observations that might usefully be made by way of conclusion. The first is this: greater success has been achieved in co-ordinating the implementation of foreign policy than its formulation. On the whole, foreign policy is still *made* at national level, even if it is subsequently *articulated* by a single regional spokesman. The second, and perhaps the more important, concerns the efficacy of the Standing Committee of Ministers responsible for Foreign Affairs. In view of the eminence accorded to the co-ordination of foreign policy in the list of the Community's overall aims, it was perhaps surprising that the Committee was not given the status of a principal organ of the Community on a parallel with the Common Market Council.[28] Even so, its impact has been negligible. To date, it has only met four times – inaugurally in November 1973, again after a gap of fully two and a half years in March 1976, again in January 1979 after an even longer interval and most recently in July 1979 – and cannot be said in any of these meetings to have been particularly instrumental in bringing about the extent of policy co-ordination that has actually been achieved. The first was largely devoted to procedural matters and contented itself with taking note of and praising existing attempts to develop joint approaches on foreign policy questions; the second dealt only in general statements of principle; and the third and fourth did little more than reaffirm previously agreed positions and discuss international developments since the last meeting. Such co-ordination of policies as has been developed has been worked out in meetings between heads of government, trade ministers and ambassadors. Thus, in a sense, its evolution has been completely informal – at least in the context of the specific arrangements made in this connection by the Community Treaty.

To sum up, a consensus of opinion is now emerging in the region that the area of foreign policy co-ordination is one of the Caribbean Community's main weaknesses. Demas has consistently urged member states 'to take somewhat more seriously' this aspect of the Treaty;[29] the new Secretary General, Kurleigh King, has admitted that this 'modest goal' has not been reached;[30] the Trinidad White Paper of April 1979 was very critical indeed of the functioning of the Foreign Ministers Committee;[31] and even the Foreign Ministers themselves at their third meeting recognised that, in order to be more effective, they would have to meet more frequently[32].

Notes

1. *Treaty establishing the Caribbean Community*, Chaguaramas, 4 July 1973, Article 17(1).

2. S. S. Ramphal, *Just, Enlightened and Effective Arrangements: New Approach to Relations with the European Economic Community*, Georgetown, 1973, p. 4.

3. E. Carrington, 'CARICOM – After One Year: its Achievements and Prospects', amended version of address given to Trinidad and Tobago Economic and Statistical Society, Port of Spain, 6 August 1974, mimeo, p. 14.

4. See H. J. Geiser, 'The Lomé Convention and Caribbean Integration: a First Assessment', *Revista/Review Interamericana*, vol. VI, no. 1, spring 1976, pp. 23-48.

5. For further details, see *Press Release of the Special Meeting of the Common Market Council*, Georgetown, 1975.

6. See W. G. Demas, *CDB: a Bank and a Development Instrument* (Statement by the President of the Caribbean Development Bank at the

seventh Annual Meeting of the Board of Governors, Port of Spain, 27-28 April 1977), Bridgetown, 1977, p. 30.

7. S. S. Ramphal, *To Care for CARICOM: the Need for an Ethos of Community*, Montego Bay, 1975, p. 11.

8. Caribbean Community Secretariat, *One Year of CARICOM*, Georgetown, 1974, mimeo, p. 45.

9. For the background to this dispute, see C. H. Grant, *The Making of Modern Belize: Politics, Society and British Colonialism in Central America*, Cambridge, 1976.

10. See *Financial Times* (London), 25 January 1978.

11. *Trinidad Guardian*, 27 April 1975.

12. *Ibid.*

13. E. Williams, *The Threat to the Caribbean Community*, Port of Spain, 1975.

14. *Trinidad Guardian*, 16 June 1975.

15. *Ibid.*

16. *Ibid.*

17. 'Michael Manley replies', *Caribbean Contact*, vol. 3, no. 4, July 1975.

18. *Ibid.*

19. *The Jamaica Daily News*, 19 June 1975.

20. *Trinidad Guardian*, 16 June 1975.

21. Axline suggests that an early draft of the CARICOM Treaty, in fact, included an article which went a long way towards a commitment to a co-ordinated external economic policy, but that Jamaica, among others, objected to it so strongly that a much watered-down version eventually appeared as Article 34 of the Annex. W. A. Axline, *Caribbean Integration: The Politics of Regionalism*, London, 1979, p. 203.

22. *Trinidad Guardian*, 16 May 1975.

23. See *Daily Gleaner*, 22 April 1976.

24. For the history of these efforts, see L. Searwar, *Administration of Foreign Relations*, Occasional Paper No. 1, Institute of Social and Economic Research, Cave Hill, Barbados, 1974, pp. 20-3.

25. See L. Luckhoo, 'The Wearing of Two Hats', *Guyana Journal*, vol. 1, no. 2, 1968, pp. 61-5.

26. For example, early in 1977 Guyana and Jamaica expressed a definite interest in applying for some form of associate status with COMECON (the Council for Mutual Economic Assistance) without, it seems, forewarning any of their CARICOM colleagues. More recently, in January 1978, the Trinidad government declared that, in view of the problems being encountered in the Caribbean in connection with the economic integration movement, it would henceforth seek to make new economic alliances with countries such as Brazil and Colombia.

27. W. G. Demas, 'What the Caribbean Community is all about', an interview with the President of the Caribbean Development Bank, 20 June 1977, mimeo, p. 9.

28. For a discussion of this point, see D. E. Pollard, 'Institutional and Legal Aspects of the Caribbean Community', *Caribbean Studies*, vol. 14, no. 1, 1974, p. 53.

29. W. G. Demas, *West Indian Nationhood and Caribbean Integration*, Bridgetown, 1974, p. 73.

30. K. King, 'Statement by the Secretary-General of the Caribbean Community Secretariat to the ninth Annual Meeting of the Board of Governors of the Caribbean Development Bank, 25-26 April 1979', Bridgetown, 1979, mimeo, p. 5.

31. See 'Trinidad's Criticisms of CARICOM Partners', *Caribbean Contact*, vol. 7, no. 1, May 1979.

32. *Press Release. CARICOM Foreign Ministers hold Important Meeting in Jamaica*, Georgetown, 1979.

CHAPTER NINE

The style of regional decision-making

We aim now to consider the style and manner of decision-making within the Caribbean Community. We have, therefore, to turn our attention away from questions of policy and look instead at the institutional structure through which the Community is run. It is simple enough in outline (see Fig 1[1]) and, in large part, will already have emerged from previous chapters. The two principal organs of the Community are the Conference of Heads of Government and the Common Market Council of Ministers, served by a Regional Secretariat, situated in Guyana, and headed by a Secretary General. In addition, there are the 'Institutions of the Community',[2] ministerial bodies charged with the performance of specific functions. Seven are listed in the Treaty, namely the Conference of Ministers responsible for Health and the Standing Committees of Ministers responsible for Education, Labour, Foreign Affairs, Finance, Agriculture and Mining. There are also the 'Associate Institutions'[3] which are, in effect, the bodies responsible for the operation of the various areas of functional co-operation. The main difference between the two is that the Institutions are established under the Community Treaty whilst the Associate Institutions operate under separate legal agreements and have simply been given recognition by the Treaty as bodies also working to achieve the general purposes and objectives of the Community. They include the Caribbean Development Bank, the Caribbean

Figure 1

INSTITUTIONAL ORGANISATION OF THE CARIBBEAN COMMUNITY

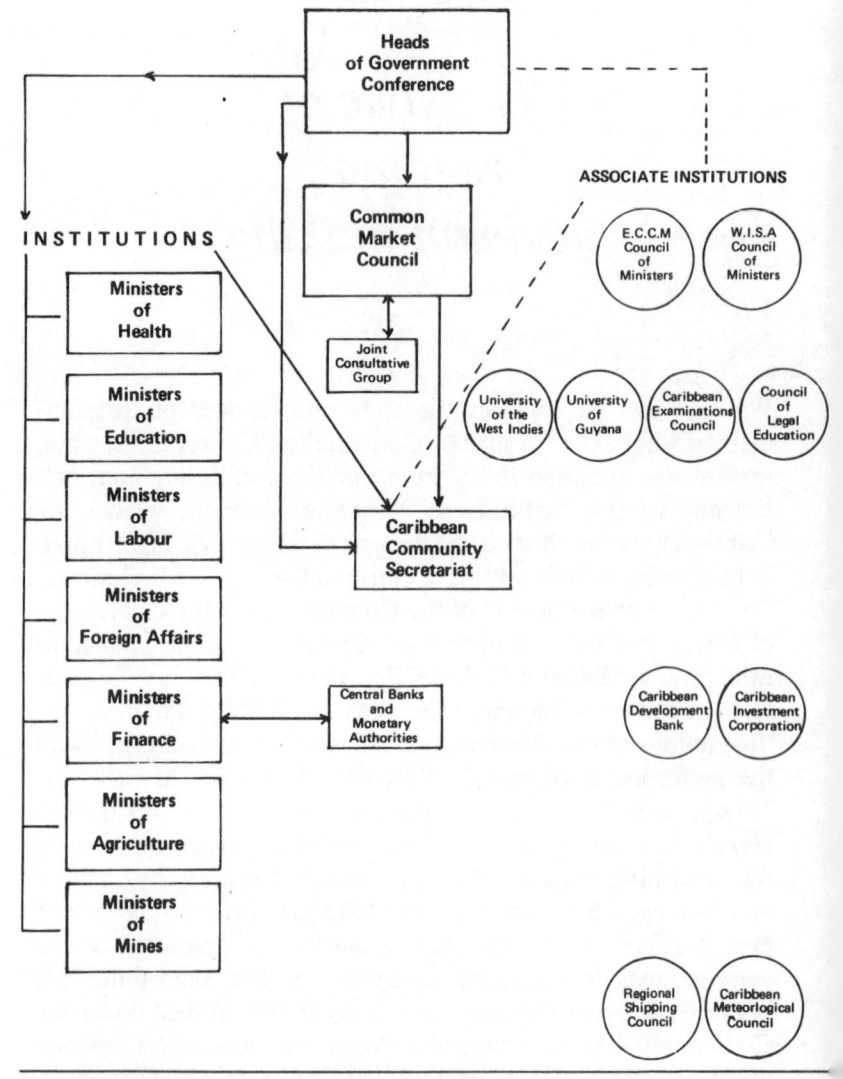

INSTITUTIONS

- Ministers of Health
- Ministers of Education
- Ministers of Labour
- Ministers of Foreign Affairs
- Ministers of Finance
- Ministers of Agriculture
- Ministers of Mines

Heads of Government Conference

Common Market Council

Joint Consultative Group

Caribbean Community Secretariat

Central Banks and Monetary Authorities

ASSOCIATE INSTITUTIONS

- E.C.C.M Council of Ministers
- W.I.S.A Council of Ministers
- University of the West Indies
- University of Guyana
- Caribbean Examinations Council
- Council of Legal Education
- Caribbean Development Bank
- Caribbean Investment Corporation
- Regional Shipping Council
- Caribbean Meteorological Council

LEGEND

⟶ Indicates flow of authority
⟵⟶ Indicates consultation and two-way flow of information
- - - - Indicates a relationship with an Associate Institution

Investment Corporation, the West Indies Associated States Council of Ministers, the Eastern Caribbean Common Market Council of Ministers, the Caribbean Examinations Council, the Council of Legal Education, the Universities of Guyana and the West Indies, the Caribbean Meteorological Council and the Regional Shipping Council (which has since been terminated). Finally, it should be mentioned that, like CARIFTA, the Community has an international legal personality,[4] that is to say, the capacity to negotiate and conclude treaties and agreements with other countries, groups of countries and international organisations which, in turn, have bestowed recognition on the Community.

Even from this brief and summary review of the main institutions of the Community, it is apparent that it has been conceived primarily as an umbrella organisation. The Secretariat has itself stated that, from the legal and administrative point of view, the creation of the Community was 'a tidying-up ... of an on-going process',[5] intended essentially to formalise and amalgamate into one structure the many facets of regional co-operation in existence in the Caribbean immediately prior to its establishment in 1973. The Community is thus a multifarious creature. This chapter does not attempt to analyse the *modus operandi* of every one of the institutions included within the Community's embrace, but concentrates instead upon the four main pillars of the CARICOM decision-making structure – the Heads of Government Conference, the Common Market Council of Ministers, the Community Secretariat and the Caribbean Development Bank.

The Heads of Government Conference

The Heads of Government Conference is the highest policy-making body of the Community. It has the power to issue directions to be pursued by the Common Market Council and the Institutions; it is the final authority for the conclusion of treaties between the Community and international organisations or individual states; and it is the body responsible for the settlement of all questions relating to the Community's financial affairs.[6] In respect of all these functions it can make decisions, which are binding upon member states, and recommendations, which are not. Each member of the Conference is entitled to one vote, regardless of the size, wealth or status of the country represented, and decisions and recommendations can only be made by unanimous vote. Abstentions are not construed as impairing their validity provided that not less than three-quarters of the members, including at least two MDCs, vote in favour.[7]

Although it was first convened in 1963, these powers and procedures were only *formally* conferred upon the Conference by the terms of the CARICOM Treaty. Until the Treaty's signature, it had met as a purely informal arrangement without constitutional status, statutory authority or legal responsibility for the supervision of the regional movement. Even from the outset, though, it was a good deal more than a mere forum for the exchange of ideas between the leaders. As our earlier account of the evolution of the Caribbean Community illustrated time and again, the Conference has been the moving force behind nearly all the major developments in Caribbean integration in the past decade, including the very establishment of CARICOM itself. It also undoubtedly functioned as the supreme policy-making body of CARIFTA, even though there was no juridical basis for such a role in the CARIFTA agreement.

The explanation for the pre-eminence of its role in regional affairs lies, of course, in its membership. From 1967 onwards it was comprised of the heads of government of all the states of the Commonwealth Caribbean – Prime Ministers, Premiers and Chief Ministers. In a region like the Caribbean, in which the political culture is highly personalist,[8] individual leaders have great power to influence the formulation of policy – much more than in the bureaucratic state systems of the developed world. An institution which regularly gathers these leaders together and allows them to operate as a policy-making body is bound, therefore, to sit at the very nub of the political system in which it is located, and so it has been with the Heads of Government Conference.

By its very nature, though, its functioning is dependent upon the smoothness of personal relations between the heads of government, which is a potential flaw. In recent years relations

The style of regional decision-making

have, on the whole, been good, and a substantial measure of personal *rapport* was built up, especially between Forbes Burnham, Michael Manley and Errol Barrow. Burnham showed that at the ceremony to mark the signing of the Community Treaty by the four MDCs in July 1973, when he spoke nostalgically of 'the dream that Michael, Errol and I shared when we were radical undergraduates in the heart of Imperialist London'.[9] But all the leaders know each other well and habitually address each other on a first-name basis. As one observer has commented, 'it would be hard to find a comparable familiarity among a group of political leaders in any other part of the world'.[10] Great store is set on this 'club' approach by the leaders themselves, and for the most part it has worked well, providing an intimacy and opportunity for direct dealing which has proved useful on more than one occasion in resolving difficult problems and settling potentially acrimonious disputes.

At the same time, this face-to-face style has its perils. Clubs, after all, are not immune from rivalries and estrangements. When such characteristics develop in the relations between the heads of government of the Caribbean, as inevitably they have, the result is not just the advent of a slightly tense period of intra-regional diplomacy – which is not, in itself, calamitous – but the swift neutralisation of that harmony on which the integration movement so greatly depends for vitality. And, in the short term at least, there is usually no substitute for their agreement. The row over the smelter project well illustrates the problem. From the very beginning the project was exposed to the dictates òf personalised diplomacy. As Eric Williams explained it, the scheme had been agreed as a joint venture between Trinidad and Guyana when one morning

> there was a telephone call from Jamaica, Mr. Manley; 'What is this I hear about this smelter? Why have you left me out?' This is actually what was said. 'How you mean leave you out? I did not know you were interested.' 'Of course we are interested'. I said – 'What is your interest?' He said, 'we want to come in.' I said, 'Well, look, I am acting on a Cabinet decision between two governments, I have got to go to the second government now and ask them about it.' We agreed, they came in.[11]

Instead of being handled by the appropriate ministers primarily as a technical matter, the directive for the smelter project came straight from the heads of government. This enabled a decision to be taken quickly at the outset (before, one might add, much detailed study of the project's viability had been completed), but it meant that when Manley and Williams fell to bickering publicly over the sort of policy which the Commonwealth Caribbean should adopt towards the leading states of Latin America, the main political thrust behind the project was abruptly removed and the whole plan left hanging dangerously in the air. Even when the row died down, it took several months before serious talks about the smelter were resumed – this time at official and ministerial level.

The row may have had longer-lasting implications for the future of the regional movement. Although a full Heads of Government Conference was held in St Kitts-Nevis in December 1975, this was the last time all the region's heads of government met in formal session. By virtue of Trinidad's good fortune as the only CARICOM country to have a thriving economy and of the political position of Williams as the senior regional statesman, the signal for another such conference can only effectively emanate from Port of Spain. Williams has certainly shown little inclination to travel outside Trinidad in recent years and, despite a number of hints from other heads of government,[12] he has demonstrated just as little interest in hosting a Summit conference. In circumstances such as these the Heads of Government Conference appears as a dangerously fragile institution.

In addition to this inherent weakness, the 'club' approach has one further consequence which has aroused criticism in some quarters. It demonstrably does not allow positive regional intervention in the settlement of *internal* political disputes within CARICOM member states, no matter what breaches of morality may be perpetuated by remaining aloof. For the members of the Heads of Government Conference to attempt to give a regional lead in the resolution of a conflict inside a member territory would be to ride too closely to the question of domestic political prerogative: it would risk arousing the anger and resentment of one of their own colleagues. Williams found this out when his intervention was solicited to defuse the bitter political conflict in British Guiana in 1963. Since then leaders of the Commonwealth Caribbean have generally taken the view that unity at the helm of the integration movement is a prior consideration and have adopted a very low-key line in the face of such disputes. On the occasion of the Anguillan crisis in the late 1960s the four MDCs, Jamaica, Trinidad, Barbados and Guyana, joined in the diplomatic activity which preceded the attempt to set up a Commonwealth peace-keeping force, but then abdicated in favour of the more prudent doctrine that the problem was primarily the responsibility of the British government.[13] At the Heads of Government Conference in February 1969 they gave Britain a blank cheque, urging her to 'take all necessary steps ... to confirm the territorial integrity of St Kitts-Nevis-Anguilla',[14] and never subsequently resumed a major role in the settlement of the conflict. More recently, in 1973-74, the crushing of civil disorder in Grenada by government use of highly repressive methods of doubtful legality was met with what one observer called a 'diplomacy of silence'[15] on the part of the governments of the other member states of CARICOM.

In both these instances, critics have argued, major breaches of principle – in the Anguillan case, the right of self-determination, and in Grenada, the right to demonstrate against and lawfully oppose an elected government – have been allowed to pass without criticism by other governments, just for the sake of maintaining a friendly atmosphere around the Heads of Government Conference table. In the view, for example, of Basil Ince, a member of staff of the University of the West Indies,

> Caribbean cooperation or integration will not be worth the paper it is written on if in the process the fundamental human rights of the Caribbean people are trampled upon. The deafening silence of the Commonwealth Caribbean States has set the tone for the type of Caribbean that Caribbean leaders are prepared to accept in the name of cooperation.[16]

Such a view somewhat oversimplifies the situation. If it is, at heart, a call for the establishment (perhaps within the Community Secretariat) of machinery for the peaceful arbitration of internal Caribbean disputes on a regional basis –

machinery, that is, which can be brought into action at the *request* of the particular head of state concerned (and such a request was, in the end, made by Bradshaw in regard to the Anguillan imbroglio) – then the criticism is sound enough. If, however, it is a call for collective Community interference – for whatever reason – in the internal affairs of a member state without the permission of its government, then it has to be said that on that basis a movement like the Caribbean Community would be utterly untenable, whether or not the heads of government were aloof and unfriendly in their attitude towards each other. The 'club' approach to decision-making favoured in the Caribbean inevitably means that heads of government tend to give a sympathetic hearing to each other's point of view, but it would be an exaggeration to assert that it was a conspiracy hatched by an anti-democratic alliance of heads of government with a view to preserving their collective hold on power.

The Common Market Council of Ministers

The Council is the principal organ of the Common Market and is thus the successor to the CARIFTA Council, which it closely resembles in practically every respect of its functioning. According to the Common Market Annex, it is the body primarily responsible for 'ensuring the efficient operation and development of the Common Market including the settlement of problems arising out of its functioning'.[17] Membership consists of one minister designated by each CARICOM member state. The designated representative is usually the minister in each territory who is responsible for trade, industry and commerce, although two riders have to be attached to that statement. Firstly, Trinidad has established and maintained a Ministry of West Indian Affairs and is the only Caribbean state to do so. Its representative on both the CARIFTA and CARICOM Councils has, therefore, usually been the head of that Ministry, although the Minister of Industry and Commerce has sometimes attended. Secondly, although the Guyanese representative has generally been its Minister of Trade, space was often also found for Shridath Ramphal, the former Guyanese Foreign Minister, who played a leading role in regional affairs until he was appointed Commonwealth Secretary General in 1975. As with the Heads of Government Conference, the decisions and recommendations of the Council are made, for the most part, by unanimous vote, allowing for the application of the same rule concerning abstentions.[18] There are, however, situations where the Council may make authorisations or recommendations by 'majority vote'[19] – and, in the context of the Common Market, this means the affirmative vote of two-thirds of the member states, including at least two MDCs.[20] In terms of voting power, therefore, there is a relatively greater flexibility in the Council's procedures[21] and a very slight loading in favour of the MDCs.

So much for the formal constitution of the Council. Politically, its main function has been to contain the tensions which exist between governments engaged in the pursuit of regional economic integration. Although it meets regularly every few months and its deliberations tend often to be administrative and to possess a rather routine flavour, one must not forget that the Council is the main forum in which member states confront each other over the distribution of the economic benefits of integration. The incorporation of the so-called 'Special Regime for the Less Developed Countries' into the Common Market Annex has certainly not stemmed the flow of complaints from the LDCs that they are not receiving their just deserts from the integration movement, and, given the size of the disparity in the level of economic development which exists in the Commonwealth Caribbean and the political constraints involved in tackling the problem, it is hard to imagine what will. However, so far from threatening the very existence of CARICOM, as it once did, the LDC–MDC division has all but become part of the furniture of Caribbean integration. Both the CARIFTA and CARICOM Councils have been notably successful in controlling the level of tension generated. Disputes about the distribution of benefits have sometimes spilled over into Heads of Government Conferences and soured the atmosphere between the region's leaders, but more often frustrations have been vented in Council and the heads of government then left to smooth over the traces with easy-flowing rhetoric, grand gestures and occasional timely concessions.

Finally, before leaving the subject of the Council, some mention should be made of its power to admit outside observers to its deliberations, a more important provision than may, at first, appear to be the case. In particular, liaison status has been accorded the Joint Consultative Group, a body comprising regional representatives of the Caribbean Congress of Labour (CCL), the Caribbean Consumers' Council (CCC) and the Caribbean Association of Industry and Commerce (CAIC). The group was established by the CARIFTA Council in October 1972, largely as a means of accommodating the demands which were being made by a number of interest groups for a place in the formal machinery of regional decision-making. The business community certainly felt that, having played such a large part in the early moves to create CARIFTA, it was being excluded from the counsels which had come to control the integration movement. As part of the Joint Consultative Group it does at least have a presence within the institutions of the Community. It would be wrong, though, to think that the occasional meetings between the group and the CARICOM Council are anything more than talking-shops where opportunities exist to raise problems and make complaints. Business, labour and consumer interests all know that the way to bring their influence to bear upon the formulation of regional policy is not by means of an exchange of views with the CARICOM Council, but by assiduous lobbying of their own governments at national level. In no sense can local interest groups be said to have transferred the main focus of their activities to the regional arena.

The Community Secretariat

The Community Secretariat is the old Commonwealth Caribbean Regional Secretariat under a different name. Established in principle by the Fourth Heads of Government Conference in 1967 and approved in form by a conference of regional Ministers of Trade in February 1968, the Secretariat operated for five years as the main administrative agency of CARIFTA and the other programmes of regional co-operation. To this end, it was split into two parts with differing responsibilities – a Trade and Integration Division and a

Figure 2

COMMOMWEALTH CARIBBEAN REGIONAL SECRETARIAT'S ORGANISATIONAL CHART
(1971)

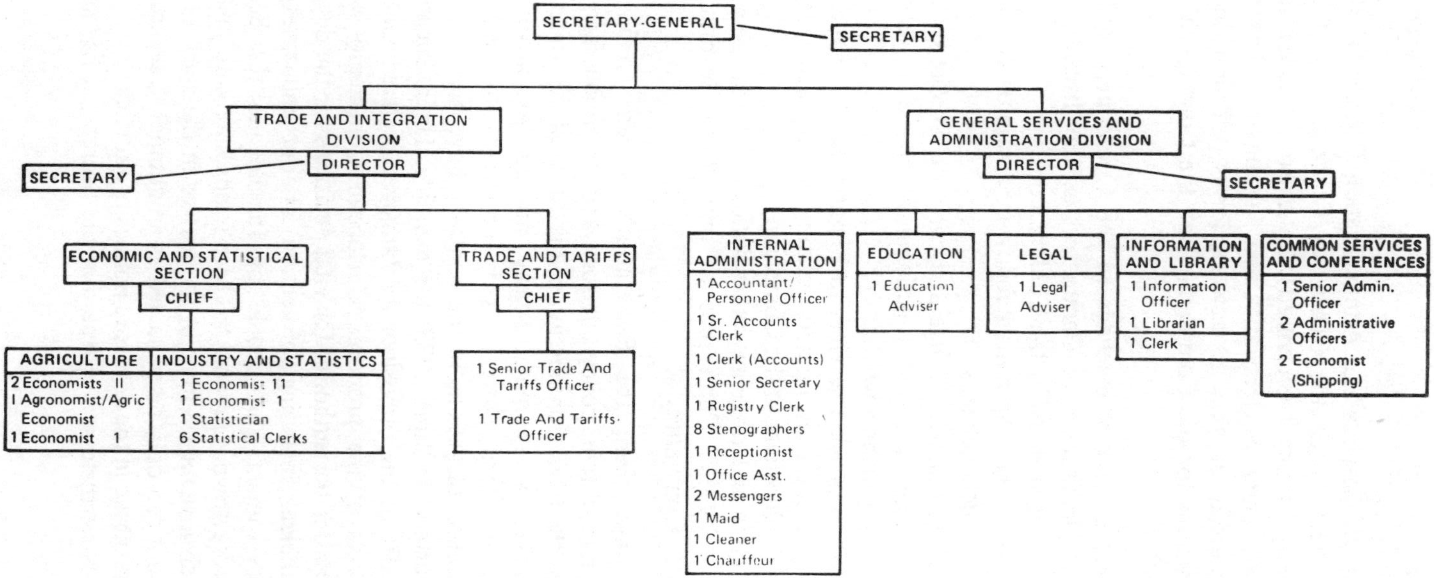

SECRETARY-GENERAL — SECRETARY

TRADE AND INTEGRATION DIVISION
DIRECTOR — SECRETARY

ECONOMIC AND STATISTICAL SECTION
CHIEF

AGRICULTURE
- 2 Economists II
- 1 Agronomist/Agric Economist
- 1 Economist 1

INDUSTRY AND STATISTICS
- 1 Economist: 11
- 1 Economist: 1
- 1 Statistician
- 6 Statistical Clerks

TRADE AND TARIFFS SECTION
CHIEF
- 1 Senior Trade And Tariffs Officer
- 1 Trade And Tariffs Officer

GENERAL SERVICES AND ADMINISTRATION DIVISION
DIRECTOR — SECRETARY

INTERNAL ADMINISTRATION
- 1 Accountant/Personnel Officer
- 1 Sr. Accounts Clerk
- 1 Clerk (Accounts)
- 1 Senior Secretary
- 1 Registry Clerk
- 8 Stenographers
- 1 Receptionist
- 1 Office Asst.
- 2 Messengers
- 1 Maid
- 1 Cleaner
- 1 Chauffeur

EDUCATION
- 1 Education Adviser

LEGAL
- 1 Legal Adviser

INFORMATION AND LIBRARY
- 1 Information Officer
- 1 Librarian
- 1 Clerk

COMMON SERVICES AND CONFERENCES
- 1 Senior Admin. Officer
- 2 Administrative Officers
- 2 Economist (Shipping)

General Services and Administration Division, as illustrated in Fig. 2.[22] When the Caribbean Community was formed, the Treaty simply 'recognised' the existing organisation as the Community Secretariat,[23] and, although it has been much expanded in size, it now performs substantially the same functions for the Community and the Common Market. They are:

(a) to service meetings of the Community and any of its Institutions or Committees as may from time to time be determined by the Conference;
(b) to take appropriate follow-up action on decisions made at such meetings;
(c) to initiate, arrange and carry out studies on questions of economic and functional co-operation relating to the region as a whole;
(d) to provide services to Member States at their request in respect of matters relating to the achievement of the objectives of the Community;
(e) to undertake any other duties which may be assigned to it by the Conference or any of the Institutions of the Community.[24]

In law, then, the Secretariat's powers confine it to an administrative, policy-advisory and co-ordinating role. Unlike, say, the EEC Commission or the *Junta* of the Andean Common Market, it is quite clearly not an executive body with supranational powers. It is important to understand this, because allegations to the contrary have been made in certain quarters. In June 1973, for example, Hugh Shearer, then the leader of the opposition in Jamaica, declared that one of the effects of the proposed Caribbean Community would be to 'transfer the authority for vital decisions for the development of Jamaica, including protection of our industries, from the Government and people of Jamaica to the Secretariat in Georgetown, Guyana'.[25] There is absolutely no justification for such a remark, either in the text or in the spirit of the Treaty, and it can only be explained as an attempt to secure some party advantage in the domestic politics of Jamaica.

Nevertheless, it is true that the Secretariat has succeeded, in practice, in transcending the relatively limited role accorded it on paper. The point hardly needs to be made, since we have already described in some detail the process by which CARIFTA was replaced by CARICOM and the prominent part played in these events by the Secretariat – especially in preparing the way for the decisions that were taken at the Seventh Heads of Government Conference in October 1972. Some explanation is needed, however, of the way it was able to gain so much influence.

There were essentially two reasons. The first was the fact that, after a hesitant start, the Secretariat developed into a highly competent unit, in the efficiency of which the regional governments acquired a good deal of confidence. Even the early doubts felt by the Jamaican JLP government about the dangers of creating a 'neo-federal' institution were steadily reduced over time. The Secretariat was never overstaffed – there were only just over fifty members, including secretaries and clerks, as late as May 1972[26] – but all were extremely hard-working and dedicated to the cause of regional integration, and whenever the necessary expertise was unavailable, assistance was sought from the two regional universities, from the Caribbean office of ECLA, or from other international organisations. The investigations undertaken by the Secretariat invariably resulted in solid, well researched reports which impressed the politicians; so when the Secretariat began increasingly to use its initiating powers to bring items before the Council of its own accord – as, of course, it was formally entitled to do – its recommendations were listened to with respect. Part of the explanation for its influence, therefore, lies in the sheer accomplishment with which it has carried out the basic administrative and advisory tasks it was established to perform. Only part, though, for there is a much more important, second, reason why the Secretariat was able to play such a prominent role in regional affairs – namely the considerable personal prestige of the man who was Secretary General between January 1970 and August 1974, William Demas. The first Secretary General was a Mr F. Cozier, a senior civil servant from Barbados, but he made little personal impact, and at the beginning of 1970 Demas took over. It is probably not too much to say that CARICOM today is Demas's own creation. Certainly, without his presence, one cannot be sure that it would exist at all.

Who, then, is Demas? Born in 1929 in Port of Spain, he first excelled himself by winning an Island Scholarship to Emmanuel College, Cambridge, where he studied economics. Following a period between 1957 and 1958 when he served as an adviser on trade policy to the Commission for the West Indies in London, he returned to the Caribbean and worked as an economist in the Trinidad civil service, rising to the post of Economic Adviser to the Prime Minister. It was whilst he was on sabbatical leave from this position that he entered our story as the author of a book which analysed the causes of economic underdevelopment in the West Indies in terms that prepared the way for the market-widening strategy of regional economic integration subsequently pursued in the Caribbean. Since then he has never left the centre of the stage – dominating the crucial officials' meeting in Georgetown in October 1967 as head of the Trinidad delegation, overseeing the consolidation of CARIFTA as Secretary General from January 1970 onwards, engineering the creation of the Caribbean Community itself, and, when he left the Secretariat in 1974, becoming President of the Caribbean Development Bank, the position he currently occupies. Demas's role as the architect of regional integration has been so critical that when he first announced his intention to resign from the Secretariat, many doubts – albeit exaggerated – were raised about the very survival of the Community. One newspaper said that his intended resignation cast 'a cloud of suspicion and fear of the unknown over the whole of the Caribbean'.[27] This sums up his achievement, for he has, above all, been a reassuring figure who, by virtue of his own clear conception of the needs of the region, has been able to impart a real sense of direction to the integration movement. He has built up unparalleled lines of communication with other political leaders, civil servants and businessmen in the Caribbean and has won the respect and confidence of them all. One academic study of CARIFTA, based on widespread interviewing throughout the region, affirmed that:

> all the politicians interviewed considered that he was doing an

excellent job, even though they might not have agreed with his views of ultimate political integration, or even full economic integration. Very important is the fact that he did not attempt to push the politicians any further than he felt was politically feasible ... One senior civil servant who participated in Carifta meetings stated that meetings often succeeded or failed because Demas was there or not there.[28]

His favoured technique was to propose temporary adjournments at moments when meetings became tense and unproductive and to try and resolve disagreements between ministers, even Prime Ministers, in private, using his skills as a broker and intermediary and, when necessary, the formidable weight of his personality. Despite his frequent assertions that he was merely the servant of the Heads of Govenment Conference, it would be quite wrong to believe that Demas is anything but an operator of great political skill.[29]

The performance of the Secretariat and its Secretary General has undoubtedly been a critical factor in the advance of the integration movement. Indeed, it is probably true to say that the maintenance of the Secretariat's leading role has become a necessary condition of the movement's continued development. How well, then, has this been maintained since Demas's departure? The Secretariat has grown steadily in size in recent years[30] and has lately been reorganised into five divisions, incorporating new Sectoral Policy and Planning and Functional Co-operation Divisions.[31] Its reputation for technical competence has certainly not diminished. However, there has been lacking since Demas's departure the drive and vision which he consistently gave to the integration movement. His successor as Secretary General was Alister McIntyre, who moved to the Secretariat from the University of the West Indies, where he had been Director of the Institute of Social and Economic Research. McIntyre had been associated with the integration movement in an advisory capacity from the very outset, but as a former academic doubts were raised about his ability to show the political sensitivity and cunning required by the job. In the event, the doubts proved to be well founded: McIntyre always seemed ill at ease trying to tease out of reluctant governments the highest common factor of agreement on questions of economic policy, and he resigned in August 1977 to become head of the commodities division of the United Nations Conference on Trade and Development. For the next fifteen months the Secretariat was without a substantive head, McIntyre's deputy being appointed Acting Secretary General on a temporary basis. The failure to make an appointment for so long was a consequence of the difficulties and tensions experienced by CARICOM in 1977 and 1978, but it was at the same time a not insignificant contributor to those problems. More effective action by the Secretariat in this period might have been able to counter some of the crisis talk which came to the fore. At any rate, in November 1978 Dr Kurleigh King, formely head of the industry division of the CDB, took up duties as the new Secretary General and quickly restored a sense of dynamism to the Secretariat's work.[32] However, the events since Demas's departure do clearly show the extent to which, in a region like the West Indies where personal politics is the order of the day, the presence of someone with the ability to reconcile personality conflicts with the minimum of bitterness is a vitally necessary component of a successful integration movement.

The Caribbean Development Bank

The thinking behind the establishment of the Caribbean Development Bank, the controversial circumstances in which it was founded, and the main responsibilities imposed upon it by its charter, have already been described in an earlier chapter and need not be repeated here. We shall, in this section, be attempting to explain how the Bank has actually operated – not so much in the technical sense in respect of the contribution it was designed to make to the economic development of the region (which would involve a discussion of such matters as its financial and capital raising activities), but more in the political sense in connection with its role as an LDC-oriented agent in the politics of Caribbean regional integration. That said, the two aspects of the Bank's function cannot be completely divorced: for it has been the case that the manner in which it has executed its formal responsibilities as a bank has, in some respects, worked to the detriment of its ability to carry out its more

The style of regional decision-making

political role of appeasing the LDCs.

Such a statement requires some explanation. The first point is that the CDB charter, although conceding that part of the Bank's purpose was 'to promote economic co-operation and integration'[33] in the Caribbean, pointedly made no mention of the existence of the other leading institutions of the integration movement – the Heads of Government Conference, the Council and the Secretariat. Whatever may have been the intentions of some of the region's governments, the notion that the CDB should function primarily as an 'integration bank' was firmly rejected by the Bank's directors and staff and certainly by its first president, Sir Arthur Lewis. To underline this, the Bank deliberately kept its distance from the integration movement. Lewis himself never attended Heads of Government Conferences, although he was always invited, and the staff of the Bank had, on the whole, very little contact with the Secretariat despite their overlapping responsibilities – and, furthermore, were not particularly concerned to remedy the situation.

Their concern, above all, was that the CDB should function as a normal regional development bank, operating according to conventional banking criteria, which meant that initially more attention had to be paid to the Bank's ability to borrow money in the international capital markets than to its lending activities. In 1972 Lewis publicly criticised the idea that 'the CDB was created to run at a loss, through subsidising desirable undertakings' and he observed that it would be 'stillborn unless it becomes creditworthy in the eyes of those from whom it has to borrow money'.[34] The overriding priority, in his eyes, was to build up a sound, commercial reputation amongst international financiers, at the expense – if need be – of its standing in the Caribbean itself. Accordingly, the Bank determined, for example, that every project should be thoroughly studied in both its financial and its technical dimension, should be self-liquidating and should be supported up to 20 per cent of its cost by the borrower. It insisted, too, upon the need to build up its reserves: it was, in any case, prohibited by its charter from lending money for purposes for which other finance was available and from purchasing equity in the enterprises it was supporting. Finally, its freedom of action was limited by the long list of rules imposed by the Bank's subscribers. These included, *inter alia*, a ban upon the use of soft loans to purchase land, an insistence that CDB money be spent on new capital formation and that loans from the Bank be used to purchase goods only from countries which had subscribed to the Bank's resources, and the establishment of procedures to prevent loans from being used for party political purposes.[35]

Sound enough procedures, perhaps, except that the LDC governments – who were, after all, intended to be the main beneficiaries of the Bank's operations – found them excessively strict and extremely tiresome to implement. They had neither the staff to perform the required project studies nor the savings to provide the necessary counterpart funds to the Bank's loans. Gradually a situation developed where actual loan disbursements lagged well behind the amounts approved in principle by the Bank's Board of Directors. At the end of 1972, for example, US$16,435,000 had been promised, but only US$446,000 actually disbursed.[36] From the Bank's point of view, this only raised doubts as to whether the region was capable of taking advantage of a multilateral financing institution; the LDCs, for their part, could only see that the Bank was failing to live up to their hopes and expectations, and their disenchantment and anger grew apace.

The confrontation was something of a culture clash. As Lewis observed, it was not surprising 'that people who are not used to dealing with international development banks feel a strong sense of frustration when first they become involved with this type of financial institution ... especially ... if they have been led to believe that an international development bank is going to solve all their financial problems'.[37] And, of course, this was *just* what the LDCs had been led to believe. As we have shown, it was, in the final analysis, the lure of the Bank's funds which persuaded them to participate in CARIFTA and it was again the Bank which acted as the unspoken *quid pro quo* for the establishment of CARICOM. The fact that the Bank's chosen method of operation has prevented it from successfully meeting the political demands placed upon it has, therefore, been a major cause of the existence of LDC–MDC tension within

The style of regional decision-making

CARICOM.

However, responsibility for this situation does not lie solely with the Bank. In this connection we can usefully cite Demas's assessment of the problem in May 1975 shortly after he had assumed duties as president of the Bank. This is part of his address to the annual meeting of the Board of Governors:

> let me admit that before I came to the Bank I shared the view which is widespread in the region that it is the Bank's own procedures that were responsible for delays in loan approval and implementation. My nine months' experience of the working of the Bank from the inside convinces me that there is considerable need to speed up the internal procedures of the *borrowing Governments* and *private firms* for dealing with Bank loans.[38]

Having thus made the essential point that the LDCs themselves have not displayed the urgency and efficiency in their dealings with the CDB which one might have expected from small, developing countries desperately in need of capital inflows, Demas was prepared to go on and also admit that the Bank's procedures were somewhat complicated and that 'the traditional remoteness of the typical Regional Development Bank'[39] was not appropriate in a region such as the Caribbean. On both these counts he can claim, with justification, to have made some improvements, firstly, by instructing that the terms and conditions of a loan be hammered out between the borrower and Bank staff before, and not after, the loan is approved by the Board of Directors, so that disbursement could begin in a much shorter time after the signature of the loan than previously,[40] and, secondly, by encouraging a much closer personal dialogue between the staff and the customers of the Bank.

Furthermore, as one might have expected, Demas has also sought to involve the Bank much more closely in the activities of the Community, of which it is, after all, an Associate Institution. To quote again from the speech which he made to the Bank's Governors in May 1975, his view was that 'one of the central purposes of the Bank must always be to support the strengthening of CARICOM, all the time giving special emphasis to the development needs of the LDCs. This is one reason why we are seeking increasingly to identify and finance regional projects between members of the Caribbean

Community.'[41] Indeed, in his first annual report, delivered shortly beforehand, he was able to refer to the Bank's 'first regional integration project' – a loan of US$ 2,245,877 to the West Indies Shipping Corporation for the purchase of a new vessel for container traffic on the trunk route between Guyana, Trinidad, Barbados and Jamaica[42] – which has been followed since by other such loans. In addition to promoting projects of this kind, Demas has also urged that the Bank be used as the prime channel by which development aid is transmitted to the LDCs, and he must, therefore, have been gratified by Trinidad's establishment in 1974 of a special US$ 5 million fund to help the LDCs meet their counterpart contributions to Bank-financed soft loans or 'mixed' loans and by the fact that the chosen means of helping the LDCs through the current world economic recession was the creation within the Bank of an Emergency Fund for Programme Assistance and Common Services. Finally, under his direction, the Bank has developed a much closer working relationship with the Secretariat in the *planning* of Community policy. It has, for example, been an active participant in the preparation of the Regional Food Plan, has played a key role in the technical work done in respect of industry and transport, and has been represented on a number of working parties and study groups.[43]

In conclusion, then, we can already see evidence of a much greater co-ordination of effort between the two bodies. McIntyre at one stage wondered publicly whether some special form of machinery ought not to be devised to facilitate this process.[44] There would, however, be some difficulty in going this far, since the Bank is open to all member states of the United Nations and four non-Commonwealth Caribbean countries are already members – Britain and Canada as founding members and Venezuela and Colombia, who joined in April 1973 and November 1974 respectively. The latter states did so, however, on the condition that Commonwealth Caribbean members should always have 'a majority of the voting power in the Bank and a majority of the number of Directors',[45] so there is no danger that the Bank will lose its regional character. On the contrary, it seems likely that its role in the Community decision-making structure will become even more crucial, and certainly less covert, in the future.

Conclusion

Having examined, in turn, the major constituent elements in the Caribbean Community system — the Conference, the Council, the Secretariat and the Bank — it remains to look at the structure as a whole. Although it may appear to be a somewhat negative approach, we must begin by making quite clear what the Community is not, and in this respect we must be careful not to be misled by the fact that the word 'community' serves in both the diplomatic and academic vocabulary with major differences of meaning. In particular, it would be wrong to assume that the way in which the term is used in diplomatic practice in the Caribbean is the way in which it is most often used by students of politics, and thus of concluding that the pursuit of integration in the region has culminated in the creation of a *political community* in any of the senses in which the phrase is generally used by academics. There is a fundamental theoretical difference — which the ambiguity of the concept of community conceals — between the relations which exist among states that are engaged in the process of integrating themselves into a political community (which, for the moment, we need not define precisely, but which clearly involves the acquisition of some degree of power and authority by the central political institutions of the system), and those that, however closely they work together, most decidedly are *not*. The difference, as Stanley Hoffmann has explained,

> lies in the conceptual framework suitable for the study of those two types of situations. Once nations are engaged in political community-building, methods derived from the 'group theory of politics' become relevant. Since their borders are being not merely pierced by the very thin holes through which the threads of diplomacy can pass, but to a large extent dismantled, the formation of transnational parties and interest groups, the birth of a 'community viewpoint' that can animate even the separate governments, the development of common institutions with an authority and a legitimacy of their own, the settlement of conflicts by 'upgrading the common interest' rather than by 'splitting the difference' or by 'mimimum accommodation' all

become possible, although not certain. If, on the other hand, one is dealing with a group of states, however friendly, whose statesmen remain in the mental universe of traditional interstate relations, the application of the methods and concepts I have just mentioned will be impossible or misleading. Parliamentary meetings may have an indicative value but no more; parties and pressure groups will try to get their viewpoints endorsed by their respective governments, rather than relying on supranational action; the joint institutions will share the basic ambiguities and weaknesses of general international organizations; and it will be difficult to define a joint rationality or a common interest higher than those of any member. More often than not, those who advocate 'upgrading the common interest' really advocate (deliberately or not) the endorsement by all of the interest of one – usually that of the predominant partner. If an agreement on matters in dispute is reached, it will be by acceptance of the demands of the strongest, or by minimum accommodation, or, at best, by 'splitting the difference.' In other words, we are still in the realms of 'strategic-diplomatic behavior' with its own rules of the game.[46]

These two theoretical poles are, of course, ideal types, and reality usually lies somewhere in between. In the case of the Caribbean Community, it is absolutely clear from everything we have said so far, not just in this chapter but throughout the study, that it is the latter which predominates. We shall be dealing further with the differences between these two approaches in the next chapter. At this stage it is enough to emphasise, by way of summary, three fundamental aspects of the character of regional decision-making, as it has actually manifested itself in CARICOM, all of which illustrate the irrelevance of the 'political community' model.

Firstly, we need to stress again that the Community Treaty was quite deliberately designed to avoid any mention, any hint even, of supranationality. As a result, it does not impugn in any way the legal competence of its participant states. The Community is run by a series of conferences and councils and is only serviced by its Secretariat. With the exception of a few relatively unimportant items, decisions have to be taken unanimously, and then have to be legitimated by each member state in accordance with its own constitutional procedures. There is no regional Cabinet and no regional parliament capable of passing laws that have effect across the region. The Community has no direct powers of economic intervention or taxation, and relies for funds to conduct its affairs on the jointly agreed countributions of the various governments. It does possess the right to negotiate and conclude treaties and agreements with other countries and organisations, but this derives from its status as an international legal personality in its own right and does not depend upon any transfer from the Community's member states of the authority to act in the field of foreign affairs. In short, the Community demands no cession whatsoever of the formal governmental authority of its members.

It is as well to reiterate this point, because a lot of confusion has been caused within the region in this connection by widespread use of the emotive concept of 'sovereignty' in an ill advised way. Even Demas's pronouncements have been slightly ambiguous. He has stated, for example, that 'in agreeing to the establishment of a Common External Tariff and Common Protective Policy' – for the purpose, as he put it, of bringing about a greater degree of effective sovereignty – 'a Member State of a Common Market agrees to share with other Member States of the Common Market its formal sovereignty over its policy on tariffs and quantitative restrictions'.[47] Yet it is apparent that the member states of the Caribbean Community possess at all times the option of contracting out, as it were, and establishing an external tariff of their choosing simply by revising the Act of parliament which legitimated that aspect of the Community's arrangements in their territory. Demas should have gone on to distinguish between a state genuinely conceding its formal sovereignty, as to some central supranational body, which would indeed signify the emergence of a political community, and a state agreeing to share its *exercise* of that sovereignty with other states, as in his example. The distinction, though subtle, is important. In the case of a common external tariff, and generally in the Caribbean Community, what is agreed upon is merely the co-operative use of some of the *instruments* of government which all states have in their armoury.

Secondly, we should underline the fact that the civil servants, professionals, academics and businessmen who regularly take part in regional decision-making have not sought to impose a supra-governmental community viewpoint upon the territorial governments. Naturally they have, over time, developed a much greater awareness of, and indeed sympathy for, the different points of view of their colleagues. Secretariat staff report, for example, that meetings generally proceed more smoothly and expeditiously now than they did in the days of CARIFTA, simply because there is a wider base area of agreement which, as it were, can be taken as read at the beginning of each meeting. This change is due partly to the sheer frequency of contact engendered by the growth and expansion of integration activities; but it owes a lot, too, as Edwin Carrington has pointed out, to the role of the Universities of the West Indies and of Guyana in 'bringing together, training, outfitting and remitting to the same region a cadre of young technocrats finding their way into the professions, the civil service, the academic field and business circles' and thereby creating 'a basis for co-operation and collaboration among these cadres characterised by a personal knowledge and familiarity'.[48] Trained in similar disciplines at the same or related institutions, the scope for interaction amongst these groups has undoubtedly proved to be far greater than amongst their predecessors in the previous generation. Carrington has even suggested that 'the plains of Mona, Cave Hill, St Augustine and Turkeyen [the campuses of UWI and the University of Guyana respectively] may become for the West Indies what the fields of Eton and Harrow were to others'.[49] All the same, one should not exaggerate the influence of this *rapport*, for *rapport* is all that it is. Except for the Secretariat staff, who were formally enjoined in the Treaty to promote the interests of the Community at all times,[50] they are all, in the final analysis, intent upon pursuing their national and sectional interests above and beyond Community considerations. No attempt has been made to forge a coalition of '*técnicos*' capable of assuming control of the integration movement and directing it in accordance with a higher rationality than whatever accommodation can be found between the narrow, political concerns of territorial politicians. Demas's primary concern was always to persuade the politicians, recognising that it was they who controlled the Community decision-making system. The politicians are not, of course, completely unresponsive to the advice of their civil service or of non-governmental bodies; indeed, they often accept without argument the recommendations put forward by the officials' meetings which precede all Community gatherings. They do so, though, only because they know that protection of the national interest (or what is taken to be the national interest) is as much the uppermost priority in the minds of their officials as it is in their own outlook. *Rapport* at elite level does not, therefore, necessarily imply community of interest.

Thirdly, there has *not* developed at mass level the community spirit which might have animated the governments to subordinate national interests before wider regional concerns. Although one would have thought that the validity of this observation could hardly be disputed, there is admittedly no proper survey evidence to hand to support it, except for the responses to one question asked by J. E. Greene about the desirability of Guyana joining CARIFTA during the course of an investigation he undertook into Guyanese political culture in 1968-69. His conclusion, for what it is worth, was that this was 'the one issue on which very few persons had a firm opinion'.[51] It is extremely doubtful if anything has happened since then to afford regional integration a more important place in the minds of ordinary West Indians, except perhaps as a convenient scapegoat on which to blame the ills of the moment. Certainly, no transnational political parties have been formed. The Secretariat has also admitted that it has had very little success in promoting popular understanding of what the Community is about.[52] It has undertaken occasional 'Meet the People' tours and has issued a number of explanatory pamphlets, but it has not, until recently, had the support of a Caribbean News Agency and has consequently been unable to counter effectively the strikingly parochial manner in which news of the integration movement's achievements is usually presented in the national press of each member state. For example, by reading only the Jamaican press one could easily have been forgiven for thinking that the island's Minister of Trade and Industry, P. J. Patterson, was the only Caribbean minister involved in the association negotiations with the EEC, such was the prominence his role was given. One often finds, too, that the amount of space which an island newpaper gives to a routine Council of Ministers meeting will be considerably increased if its national representative happens to be the chairman on that particular occasion, despite the fact that the chairmanship of Council meetings is a purely rotating privilege. Objective commentary upon Community affairs is at a premium in the regional press, and in the last year or so this has given rise to almost a literature of doom in respect of CARICOM's future prospects. Relatively trivial incidents are allowed to assume immense proportions in the public dialogue about integration, and predictions that CARICOM is about to break up are regularly made. Such analyses often miss many of the more substantive realities of the integration movement, but they do underline how tenuous are the roots which CARICOM has established in the collective consciousness of the West Indian people.

The regional decision-making system of the Caribbean is, then, the product of men who remain, as Hoffmann, said, in 'the mental universe of traditional interstate relations',[53] where the concept of national interest still reigns supreme. They have nevertheless – and this is their achievement – successfully systemised those relations within a permanent club-like structure of inter-state, intergovernmental co-operation. The Caribbean Community is not the manifestation of a politically integrated Caribbean, but it is the embodiment of something just as real: a 'Caraibe des patries'.

Notes

1. From Caribbean Community Secretariat, *The Caribbean Community: A Guide*, Georgetown, 1973, p. 67. Reproduced by courtesy of the Secretariat.
2. *Treaty establishing the Caribbean Community*, Chaguaramas, 4 July 1973, Article 10.
3. *Ibid.*, Article 14.
4. *Ibid.*, Article 20.
5. Caribbean Community Secretariat, *op. cit.*, p. 27.
6. *Treaty establishing Caribbean Community*, Article 8.
7. *Ibid.*, Article 9. On the question of voting in the Conference, see also D.

E. Pollard, 'Institutional and Legal Aspects of the Caribbean Community', *Caribbean Studies*, vol. 14, no. 1, 1974, pp. 54-5.

8. See L. Best's analysis of the 'doctor figure' in Caribbean politics in *Tapia*, passim, and A. W. Singham's discussion of the 'hero' in *The Hero and the Crowd in a Colonial Polity*, New Haven, 1968.

9. *Trinidad Guardian*, 5 July 1973.

10. N. Linton, 'Regional Diplomacy of the Commonwealth Caribbean', *International Journal*, vol. 26, no. 2, 1971, p. 407.

11. E. Williams, *The Threat to the Caribbean Community*, Port of Spain, 1975, pp. 5-6.

12. Burnham, for example, made a point of calling for the 're-introduction of dialogue in regional affairs' in his 1978 New Year message to the Guyanese people. *Financial Times* (London), 2 February 1978.

13. See Y. Collart, 'Regional Conflict Resolution and the Integration Process in the Commonwealth Caribbean', in R. Preiswerk (ed.), *Regionalism and the Commonwealth Caribbean*, Port of Spain, 1969, pp. 181-8.

14. *Final Communiqué of the Fifth Heads of Government Conference*, Port of Spain, 1969.

15. B. Ince, 'Grenada: West Indian Dilemma', *Trinidad Guardian*, 10 February 1974.

16. *Ibid.*

17. *Treaty establishing Caribbean Community*, Annex – the Caribbean Common Market, Article 7.

18. *Ibid.*, Annex, Article 8(1)-(4).

19. *Ibid.*, Annex, Article 11(3) and (4), 13(6), 18(5), 28(2) and 29(3).

20. *Ibid.*, Annex, Article 8(5).

21. According to Pollard, the reason for this is to be found in 'the fact that the Council is responsible for the operational efficiency of the Common Market and as such a rigid system of voting was considered to offer undesirable possibilities for the frustration of the economic objectives sought to be secured'. Pollard, *op. cit.*, pp. 55-6.

22. From Commonwealth Caribbean Regional Secretariat, *CARIFTA and the New Caribbean*, Georgetown, 1971, p. 137. Reproduced by courtesy of the Secretariat.

23. *Treaty establishing Caribbean Community*, Article 15(1).

24. *Ibid.*, Article 16. Article 10 in the Common Market Annex sets out the same functions, merely substituting Common Market for Community.

25. *Daily Gleaner*, 8 June 1973.

26. See Commonwealth Caribbean Regional Secretariat, *From CARIFTA to Caribbean Community*, Georgetown, 1972, pp. 154-6.

27. Editorial, *Dominica Herald*, 8 September 1973.

28. R. E. Wiltshire, 'Regional Integration and Conflict in the Commonwealth Caribbean', unpublished PhD thesis, University of Michigan, 1974, pp. 99-100.

29. He has himself said this of his role as Secretary General: 'I am merely an official and, of course, it is for the political leaders of the Region to make the decisions. But ... I try to assist the decision-makers in unlocking the

various doors to the long corridor of closer and fuller regional integration'. W. G. Demas, 'The New Caribbean Community', address to the First Convention of Rotarians, Basseterre, St Kitts-Nevis-Anguilla, 8 June 1973, mimeo.

30. The number of staff employed within the Secretariat at the end of 1976 was nearer 150 than 100.

31. For details, see K. Hall and B. Blake, 'The Caribbean Community: Administrative and Institutional Aspects', *Journal of Common Market Studies*, vol. 16, no. 3, 1978, pp. 226-8.

32. See *CARICOM Bulletin*, no. 2, March 1979, pp. 5-6.

33. *Agreement establishing the Caribbean Development Bank*, Kingston, Jamaica, 18 October 1969, Article 1.

34. W. A. Lewis, *Some Constraints on International Banking*, Bridgetown, 1972, p. 2.

35. *Ibid.*, pp. 3-8.

36. W. G. Demas, 'Address to the fifth Annual Meeting of the Board of Governors of the Caribbean Development Bank, Bridgetown, 26-27 May 1975', mimeo, p. 14.

37. Lewis, *op. cit.*, p. 8.

38. Demas, 'Address to the fifth Annual Meeting', p. 15. My emphasis.

39. *Ibid.*, p. 17.

40. As a result, the ratio of cumulative disbursements to cumulative approvals has increased substantially – from 2·1 per cent in 1972, to 5·6 per cent in 1973, 10·3 per cent in 1974, 33·1 per cent in 1975, 45·9 per cent in 1976, 52·8 per cent in 1977 and 53·8 per cent in 1978. Caribbean Development Bank, *Annual Report 1978*, Bridgetown, 1979, p. 58.

41. Demas, 'Address to the fifth Annual Meeting', p. 29.

42. Caribbean Development Bank, *Annual Report 1974*, Bridgetown, 1975, p. 20.

43. See Caribbean Development Bank, *Annual Report 1974*, p. 21, *Annual Report 1975*, pp. 29-30, *Annual Report 1976*, pp. 39-40, *Annual Report 1977*, p. 45 and *Annual Report 1978*, pp. 52-3.

44. A. McIntyre, 'Statement by the Secretary General of the Caribbean Community Secretariat to the fifth Annual Meeting of the Board of Governors of the Caribbean Development Bank, Bridgetown, 26-27 May 1975', mimeo, pp. 2-3.

45. Caribbean Development Bank, *Annual Report 1971*, Bridgetown, 1972, p. 13.

46. S. Hoffmann, 'Discord in Community: the North Atlantic Area as a Partial International System', *International Organisation*, vol. 17, no. 3, 1963, p. 527.

47. W. G. Demas, *West Indian Nationhood and Caribbean Integration*, Bridgetown, 1974, p. 52.

48. E. W. Carrington, 'Mutual Interaction for Economic Integration in the Caribbean', unpublished paper prepared for the Commonwealth Foundation Seminar on the Professions, Universities and the Civil Service, Kingston, Jamaica, 13–18 January 1975, p. 6.

49. *Ibid.*

50. *Treaty establishing Caribbean Community*, Article 15(4).
51. J. E. Greene, 'Participation, Integration and Legitimacy as Indicators of Developmental Change in the Politics of Guyana', *Social and Economic Studies*, vol. 21, no. 3, 1972, p. 253.
52. Demas, *West Indian Nationhood*, p. 72.
53. Hoffmann, *op. cit.*, p. 257.

CHAPTER TEN

Political integration

Finally, we cannot completely ignore the question of political integration. Although it has not been a major theme of our story, the subject has raised its head on a number of occasions and, in a sense, as a result of the federal experience, it has been in the background throughout. It has also caused a good deal of misunderstanding in respect of its relationship with the Caribbean Community and with the idea of regional economic integration in general. In the concluding section of the last chapter we began the job of trying to explain just where the issue of political integration does, and does not, fit into the recent history of intra-regional relations in the Commonwealth Caribbean, and it is to this task that we now return.

We must establish immediately what meaning is to be attached to the concept of political integration in the discussion that follows. There are, after all, a bewildering number of definitions to be found in the literature of integration theory. By and large, however, West Indians have a very clear idea of what is meant by the term, and we shall follow their understanding of the problem. Political integration, in this view, is a process leading to the formation of a political community or union between a group of states, in which some or all of their *authority* is formally transferred to a new supranational body. In this usage, the term 'authority' denotes the constitutional rights and competences possessed by a state. It is conceptually distinct in meaning from the *capacity* of the state to exercise those rights effectively in the real world, which may in practice be very limited. Authority is seen as an absolute, not a relative, concept: a state either possesses the authority to act in certain governmental areas or it does not. Thus authority cannot be eroded, only extinguished, although a government can, of course, opt to exercise its rights in conjunction with other governments by co-ordinating the actual use of the instruments of government that derive from the formal authority of the state. In such a view, the formation of a political community is seen to depend upon a direct confrontation with a state's authority in a given area, its withdrawal and formal transfer to a new body. In a federal state, for example, the various competences of the state are divided between the centre and the units in a precisely demarcated way, so that each possesses, in Wheare's phrase, 'co-ordinate but independent'[1] powers; in a unitary state all authority is placed at the centre and only devolved powers are granted to the units. In either case, political integration is envisaged as the change from inter-state society to the domestic political system of the new union. The transformation occurs, archetypically but not necessarily, at a constitutional conference where the constituent states strike a bargain on the form of the union and the power to be yielded to it. It is expected too that, in time, elections will be held at the level of the new union. In short, the whole concept of political integration is interpreted in the Caribbean in a very formal and legalistic way. This is the first important point to grasp.

The prospect of automatic political integration

The next stage in the argument takes us back for a moment to the development of economic integration in the region. We know from our earlier account of the origins of that movement that in the mid-1960s, when CARIFTA was launched, no Caribbean government was prepared to risk reawakening the hostilities and bitter memories of the federal period by openly expressing its support for another experiment in regional political integration in the near future; and we know too, from our discussion in the last chapter, that the economic integration movement which the governments did see fit to initiate has not developed into a political integration system. Indeed, it is not too much to say that the construction of the whole of the current integration apparatus has been predicated upon the assumption that there exists an explicit distinction between the concepts of economic integration and political integration. What, however, has not yet been considered is, firstly, whether or not some of the regional governments embarked upon economic integration in the expectation or hope that, in time, it would lead, indirectly as it were, to political integration, and, secondly, whether or not it is even remotely possible that it may still do so.

On the general question of the relationship between economic and political integration there has accumulated a considerable theoretical literature, which is of some relevance to the Caribbean situation. In 1964 Haas and Schmitter put forward the by now well known neofunctionalist thesis

> that under modern conditions the relationship between economic and political union had best be treated as a continuum. Hence definite political implications can be associated with most movements toward economic integration even when the chief actors themselves do *not* entertain such notions at the time of adopting their new constitutive charter.[2]

The essence of their argument was that integration originating in the functional areas of financial, commercial and economic activity would create crises and imbalances in the economy, which would be resolved in ways that upgraded common interests and created pressures for further integration in other sectors with more pronounced political implications. The original purposes of the actors would thus be gradually 'politicised' until eventually economic integration was transferred by this 'expansive logic of sector integration', or spill-over, into some species of political union. Haas and Schmitter identified nine variables that seemed to characterise the process more or less consistently: four background conditions, two conditions at the time of economic union, and three process conditions.[3] In an organisation scoring high in these categories, or one in which suitable 'functional equivalents' were found for some of the favoured conditions, progress towards a political union was said to be virtually automatic, 'even if some of the members are far from enthusiastic about this prospect when it is argued in purely political terms'.[4] The practical political attractions of the theory were obvious. It was, as one metaphor had it, 'a strategy for attacking the castle of national sovereignty by stealth, with interest groups as mercenaries and technocrats as agents within the walls to open the gates quietly'.[5]

In the mid-1960s just such a process seemed to be working in Western Europe, where the chances of the automatic politicisation of the European Economic Community had been rated as 'good' by Haas and Schmitter.[6] There is evidence that some governments and other interests in the Caribbean, undoubtedly impressed by the EEC experience, were hopeful that political resistance to the formation of a new federation in the West Indies could be overcome via the operation of spill-over. Guyana's Prime Minister, Forbes Burnham, has written that his government 'spoke of economic integration because we felt that after the establishment of a free trade association, by stages perhaps, we should be aiming at achieving full economic integration *and subsequently political integration*'.[7] The Trinidad government also implied as much in a pamphlet about CARIFTA, in which it asserted that one reason why the Federation failed was that it had embarked upon political integration before economic integration.[8]

Whatever expectations there may have been along these lines have, of course, been disappointed. In their defence, however, it should be mentioned that Haas and Schmitter did point out that the Caribbean was an unpropitious setting for the activation of an 'unseen' process of political integration. Of the ten different unions they considered in their article, the West Indian Federation was judged to have had the least chance of automatic politicisation and thus of evolving into a political union. In this respect its overall prospects were marked 'poor' and most of the variables scored 'low'.[9] Transactions between the participant governments were not high, and the governments themselves were primarily concerned to protect their own territorial interests. The pluralist type of interest-group politics, on which the prospects of spill-over and the dynamics of the theory rested, did not exist in the Caribbean, and the politicians, the dominant actors, were still highly suspicious, in the aftermath of the federal *débâcle*, of the motives of their colleagues in neighbouring territories. In short, in such a setting the theory of sector integration was always a non-starter.

It is doubtful, moreover, if the region currently merits a much more optimistic assessment in respect of the variables identified by Haas and Schmitter. Not that it matters much any more, for academic critics have subsequently exposed several flaws in the basic methodology of neofunctionalism, which have almost completely destroyed belief in its efficacy, at least in the form in which it was first conceived. In the first place, as Hansen has argued, the dynamics of spill-over may often be limited by the achievement of substantial economic benefits without the need for excessive movement towards supranational jurisdiction.[10] It further transpired that the range of actor involvement had been set too narrowly. In the neofunctionalist model, national decision-makers were all assumed to be 'economic incrementalists': that is, they were seen as actors who by their outlook would inherently be responsive to the demands of spill-over and who would be able to bypass the so-called 'support politicians' and the force of public opinion, until sector integration had at least proceeded far enough to make radical changes in the pattern too costly. This approach omitted a significant set of actor variables, as Hoffmann demonstrated by drawing the distinction between 'high' and 'low' political actors. He pointed out that where 'high politics' – defined as 'the vital interests of national diplomacy and strategy' – were concerned, the key neofunctionalist actors, the 'incrementalists', were virtually irrelevant.[11] Finally, in a telling adaptation of this criticism, Nye pointed out that, in the underdeveloped world, much that in Europe would pass as simple, almost invisible, welfare politics becomes tinged with emotive, symbolic and 'high political' content, and that the problem was thus more usually one of 'premature over-politicisation'.[12] However, like old soldiers, neofunctionalists never die. Nye himself has revised and comprehensively reworked the original Haas–Schmitter statement[13] in an attempt to overcome the naive over-simplicity of the early formulations of neofunctionalism. In doing so he has had to retract many of the sweeping claims which gained the theory such exaggerated attention. We need only note this one example:

> in the short run of decades, the prospects for micro-regional economic organisations leading to federation or some sort of political union capable of an independent defense and foreign policy do not seem very high.[14]

Proposals for a political union

What have we learnt so far? Despite theoretical prognostications, political integration has not simply followed economic integration as night follows day. Nor is it likely to do so in the future. The theoreticians of integration now accept this, and, in the particular case of the Caribbean, Demas has argued that 'it is doubtful whether the Caribbean Community, however effectively it may work, will ever automatically develop into a political union'.[15] His judgement is widely shared. Proponents of a political union, of which he is one, have come to realise that the achievement of political integration in the Caribbean is an objective that has to be consciously and explicitly pursued *dehors* the economic integration arrangements. This lesson has been well learnt. It was the foundation for the emergence between 1971 and 1974 of what can virtually be called a 'political union movement' in the Caribbean. A number of different schemes of political union were advanced in this period, of which four in particular stand out.

The most substantial was the Grenada Declaration, signed on 25 July 1971 by the heads of government of six West Indian states, in which they announced their intention 'to seek to establish out of their Territories a new State in the Caribbean'.[16] The Declaration arose out of a meeting of regional leaders in St Lucia at the end of June 1971, called principally to consider Colombia's application to join the Caribbean Development Bank. The Guyanese government was at the time disturbed by the unilateral action Britain was taking to resolve the Anguilla incident (the British government had only recently proposed that the island revert to full colonial status) and it clearly saw the St Lucia meeting as an opportunity to sound out regional opinion on the implications of the whole Anguilla issue. In Burnham's own words, 'during the course of those discussions the question arose not so much as to whether there should be political integration but what should be the stages towards this political integration — and there was some discussion as to the form this integrated group should take in Constitutional terms'.[17] Ominously, the Jamaican government was unrepresented at the meeting, whilst the Trinidad and Barbados delegates arrived after the informal talks about political union had finished. Nevertheless, sufficient enthusiasm was engendered for the Guyanese government to be asked to prepare certain constitutional models for consideration at a subsequent meeting in Grenada in July.

Out of this emerged the Grenada Declaration, described by Burnham as 'the first practical step toward political unity taken since the dissolution of the Federation of the West Indies in 1962'.[18] It was published simultaneously in all the territories of the region on 1 November 1971 and set out a procedure for the formation of the new West Indian State. A Preparatory Commission, funded by the participating territories, was to be established by 30 November and staffed with technocrats. On questions of general policy, it was agreed that the Commission would have to defer to a Council of Ministers, representing all the territories, which would meet periodically to give political direction to the preparatory work; and, further, that a Constituent Assembly should be established by 1 January 1972, consisting of at least one and not more than three nominated members from each territory. The Assembly was charged with drafting the constitution of the new state and given just twelve months to complete the task, in which time it had to tour the region, hearing views, taking evidence and generally ensuring 'the fullest participation of the people'.[19] Finally, the territorial governments had to secure parliamentary approval for the proposed structure in time to allow the new constitution to be promulgated by late April 1973 and elections to be held by the end of June that same year.

Although the whole plan smacked of zeal and urgency, and aspired to include within its ambit 'all the people of the West Indies',[20] only six heads of government actually signed the

Political integration 261

declaration at the July meeting – Le Blanc of Dominica, Burnham of Guyana, Compton of St Lucia, Gairy of Grenada, Bradshaw of St Kitts-Nevis-Anguilla and Cato of St Vincent. The combined population of these six states represented only a quarter of that of the states belonging to CARIFTA. Despite hopes to the contrary, a three-month delay in publication failed to elicit any new signatures; the Premier of Antigua remained uninterested and the Chief Minister of Montserrat preferred to reserve his position. In October Barrow also let his opposition to the scheme be known. Barbados, he said, was not interested in political integration at this stage, believing instead that the region's energy should be concentrated for the time being on economic integration, and that some form of political association should be left to follow naturally, perhaps in some ten to fifteen years.[21] He did, however, ask for observer status on both the Preparatory Commission and the Council of Ministers. The Jamaican government was absent from the Grenada meeting and made no official response to the declaration.[22] But its position was unlikely to have been much different from that expressed in a letter from Leslie Ashenheim, published in the *Daily Gleaner* on 10 October 1971. It merits quoting at some length:

> I hope our Government and our opposition will both take early opportunity to make it crystal clear both to the public of Jamaica and to the peoples of the Eastern Caribbean that, as far as Jamaica is concerned, any kind of political association is a complete non-starter ... I have many good friends in the Eastern Caribbean and I have great respect and admiration for many Eastern Caribbean personalities ... but ... we hardly ever get a fair deal in any matter that comes to a vote ... The problems are threefold. First, the devotion to so-called 'democratic procedures' leads to a one-country-one-vote set-up under which territories with a small fraction of Jamaica's population, size and resources and which moreover make insignificant financial contributions (when they pay the contributions at all) as compared with Jamaica's, have the same voting power as Jamaica has. Secondly, the Eastern Caribbean territories form a tight geographical group, being comparatively near to each other and far away from Jamaica and thirdly, there is in the entire Eastern Caribbean a feeling of jealousy and fear

of being dominated by Jamaica which inevitably leads to their (consciously or unconsciously) combining together against Jamaica. The result is that in every matter which I can recall in which a vote has been taken, the vote had invariably been against Jamaica, and we have time and again in negotiations by very weight of numbers been constrained to fall in with arrangements which are disadvantageous to us and unsound on any objective consideration of the facts.[23]

Whether or not the letter was inspired from government circles we obviously cannot say, but Ashenheim *was* a leading member of a wealthy commercial family which supported the Jamaican Labour Party and he carried considerable influence within Shearer's JLP government.

The key to the success of the initiative lay, therefore, with the attitude of Dr Williams. Trinidad's representative at the Grenada meeting, Senator Prevatt, had not signed the Declaration; but, although expressing his reservations on certain procedural points, he had been generally cordial about the initiative as a whole. This, and Williams's own long-standing and frequently restated commitment to the broad unity of the Caribbean, raised hopes that Trinidad would eventually accede. In a statement issued on 1 November, however, the Trinidad government declared its intention not to participate – on the grounds that, having appointed a 'Caribbean Task Force' and a Constitutional Commission only that July, it was committed to its own re-examination of Trinidad's constitutional status and relationship with the rest of the Caribbean.[24] The ritual reiteration of Trinidad's 'firm and irrevocable commitment to the goal of economic and political unity in the Caribbean', and the offer of the sum of TT$15,000 and the services of a technocrat to assist in the work of the Preparatory Commission, could not conceal the rebuff.

Indeed, the Trinidad disclaimer proved fatal. Within forty-eight hours of the publication of the declaration Gairy was admitting that he had never envisaged the concept of political integration without the participation of Trinidad and Barbados,[25] while Compton declared that his government would not join any group that included only Guyana and five Associated States. Compton felt that it would be easy for Guyana to absorb the rest one by one, 'like a shark swallowing sardines', and, somewhat histrionically, he expressed a fear of potential Communist domination. 'If there were a general election in Guyana', he was reported as saying, 'and Cheddi Jagan assumed power, the Associated States could easily become satellites not only of Guyana but also of the Soviet Union and other Communist countries'.[26] At all events, St Lucia sent no representative and Grenada only its Minister of Health to a follow-up meeting in Georgetown on 8 November. The other leaders, although placing on record their unflagging determination to pursue the goal of political unity, postponed by two months the date on which the Preparatory Commission was to have been appointed, and deferred indefinitely the establishment of the Constituent Assembly. In a reference to Williams's notorious piece of arithmetic after the Jamaican referendum in 1961 in which he avowed that ten minus one equals zero, Bradshaw was reported to have wryly asked how many were left when two were taken from six.[27] The answer again proved to be nil, for despite Ramphal's call 'to stop the chat and begin the work'[28] and Burnham's promise to get 'the message to the people',[29] not even the Preparatory Commission was ever established. The whole scheme, tragic or comic according to point of view, was quietly allowed to fade away.

It was soon replaced as the focus of interest in political union by a new plan, the second initiative we have to consider. In June 1972, without any prior warning, 'A Group of West Indians Meeting in Tobago', as they styled themselves, issued a statement entitled *Towards An Eastern Caribbean Federation*.[30] Amongst the fourteen signatories only two possessed region-wide reputations, and the press, at least, immediately assumed that the document was their work. They were Sir Arthur Lewis, then President of the Caribbean Development Bank and one-time adviser to the Prime Minister of the West Indies Federation, and Sir Hugh Wooding, then Chancellor of the University of the West Indies. The proposal was for a federation, initially confined to the eastern Caribbean, but leaving the door open for Jamaica and other Commonwealth Caribbean countries to join at a later stage. The statement described Trinidad as 'the centre of so many of the region's activities'[31] and considered her participation to be absolutely essential. It did not favour a prior federation of the Associated States, for the 'reason that they have greater commercial, cultural and social links with Barbados and Trinidad than they have with each other'.[32] Although concerned 'not to be identified as preferring a loose rather than a strong federation',[33] the signatories were mindful of the contentious history of the former Federation – a nightmare which seemed to cloud the spirit of the whole document – and argued in consequence that the proposed federal government should not at the outset have any authority over the previously controversial fields of industrial and agricultural development, social service financing, income tax and inter-territorial freedom of movement. Their primary objective was 'to rally public opinion'[34] in the hope that it would crystallise in support of the creation of the Eastern Caribbean Federation they themselves favoured. However, no programme of action was outlined to arouse interest in the blueprint, and the hope of an excited, popular response soon subsided. The air of mystery about the statement, especially the failure to disclose how the plan originated, and at whose bidding, probably militated against its ready acceptance. It was essentially a piece of kite-flying by a group of people who admitted to thinking of themselves as West Indians, but who never convinced West Indian governments of the practicality of their proposals.

A year later Dr Williams made the third major contribution to the debate. In the July–September 1973 issue of the British journal *The Political Quarterly* he expressed his willingness to consider (to quote the title of his article) 'A New Federation for the Commonwealth Caribbean'.[35] In the light of his professed belief that the timing of the Grenada and Tobago initiatives was wrong, Williams's approach was academic: to provide a 'dispassionate appraisal of the possibilities and prospects'.[36] One could count on Guyana's participation, but not that of Jamaica. 'Jamaicans', he revealed,

> frequently express the hope that the Leeward and Windward Islands could be persuaded to form one single unit, thus reducing the number of 'States' in any new political grouping. So far, however, all efforts to form such a single unit have been unsuccessful ... The regrettable alternatives might therefore be:

a Federation similar to the former in form, with Guyana but without Jamaica (at least to start with), or even, as some suggest, a Federation of the larger independent countries to begin with, leaving room for the subsequent accession of the smaller islands, preferably as a single unit.[37]

Williams accepted what he portrayed as the Jamaican position, and insisted that in meetings between the future Federal Prime Minister and the heads of unit governments the Leeward and Windward Islands should be represented by only one person. In constitutional terms, he favoured a powerful federal centre, having control over defence, agriculture, central banking, customs revenue and, in time, income tax, and further suggested that 'the Federal Government should have the power to suspend the constitution of a State Government in such clearly defined cases as the total breakdown of law and order in the Unit, the illicit assumption of power over a State Government, or the refusal of a State Government to recognise the orders of a Federal Court'.[38] What his proposal amounted to was a call for the revival of the classical notion of federation, tempered only by care not to repeat the tactical mistakes of the previous effort. Perceiving rightly that many of the controversial issues of the past, notably the questions of a common external tariff and the harmonisation of fiscal incentives, had been subsumed within the Caribbean Community experience, Williams seemed to believe that the conception of the 1958–62 Federation had been right, and that with the application of more sensitivity in the management of centre–unit relations, it could, this time, be made to work.

Lastly, we must consider the thinking and ideas of Demas. Throughout 1973 and 1974, he regularly made known his judgement that 'there exists a very strong case for the formation of a political union outside the Community arrangements among all the English-speaking countries in the Eastern Caribbean',[39] in which the Leeward and Windward Islands would participate as one unit. More important, in his view, than the question of the desirability of political unity in the eastern Caribbean was the form it should take. In this regard, he looked not to a classical federation or a unitary state, but to a constitution that divided powers between the central and individual governments in a unique way. He contemplated, for example, 'an arrangement under which for the first five years or ten years of the life of the new Union there is no rigid separation between the two layers of Government. The Central Cabinet could consist entirely of Heads of Government of the individual territories'.[40] He did stress, however, the importance of building into the arrangements 'procedures for an automatic transfer in predetermined stages of power over different subjects to the Central Government and for a progressive separation of the two layers of government'.[41] The essential requirement was that, from the very beginning,

> all diplomatic and economic dealings with the outside world should be 'centralised' in order to achieve the preservation and enhancement of the effective sovereignty of the new union. There would be no point in establishing a Union unless from the very inception it was possible to have not merely a *common* but a *single* policy on all aspects of external relations, both economic and non-economic.[42]

The balance of impediment and inducement

The most important comment to be made about these various proposals for some sort of Caribbean political union is that they all came to nothing. The Grenada Declaration and the Tobago Statement have passed into history. And there is no reason to believe that any formal intergovernmental attention has been given to either Williams's or Demas's ideas. In short, the political integration movement has been distinguished above all by its lack of success. But why has this cause, to which so many influential men in the Caribbean have been, and still are, attached, failed to make any headway? Why have all these four initiatives fallen so flat? The answer lies, we believe, in the nature of the balance between, on the one hand, the impediments that militate against the formation of a political union and, on the other, the inducements by which governments are encouraged to take the plunge. In the Caribbean in recent years it has been the case that the latter have been as weak as the former have been strong.

Take, first, the area of impediment. In the years since the

dissolution of the Federation, it has become almost a commonplace in the Caribbean to propound the need to be liberated from the traditional, federal stereotypes of political integration. Ramphal, whose speeches contain much of the most thoughtful and eloquent recent advocacy of a political union, declared that for him the primary lesson of the Federation was that 'we must never again mistake the forms of unity for its substance and that, by the same token, we must never dogmatise about those forms lest they become our masters and cease to be responsive to our needs and our situation'.[43] In the same vein Demas proposed what he called 'a unique constitution',[44] and those still attached to the federal form — the Tobago signatories and Williams — did pay some heed to past experience in regard to the particular division of powers they recommended.

Yet one cannot but wonder how well the lesson drawn by Ramphal and others has been learnt, and whether it has actually been fully understood. The four proposals for political union considered in this chapter were all oriented towards constitution-building. All demanded — as indeed by definition they had to, given the sense in which political integration is generally conceived in the West Indies — that the constituent states of the union should formally give up some of their governmental authority. That was certainly true of the two schemes for a new federation, whilst Demas argued that the conduct of external affairs should be formally placed in the hands of a central Cabinet. The signatories of the Grenada Declaration never committed themselves to a particular blueprint, but Burnham has admitted that, as early as the St Lucia meeting in June 1971, 'it was unanimously agreed that whatever state should come out of the political integration, should have a strong centre'.[45] Three centuries of colonialism and the experience of decolonisation via a series of precisely demarcated 'stages of self-government' have left West Indians with an intense concern for constitutional form and the exact location of authority. It may be that it was originally a psychology engendered by the *lack* of authority, but as these four models of political integration clearly indicate, it has proven to be a legacy hard to shake off in the post-colonial period.

It follows from this preoccupation that the construction of a political union will be as difficult as the governments of the region are adamant in the defence of their legal and political authority. Here surely is the most important lesson of the Federation experience viz. that in the West Indies, as elsewhere, governments are very reluctant to relinquish their formal authority in *any* area in which their writ runs. We saw earlier, for example, that the attempts of the federal government to acquire some degree of meaningful authority in its own right were frustrated by the fact that many rights of self-government had been granted to Jamaica and Trinidad in the years between 1947 and 1958. Since then, of course, the range of authority conceded to the territories of the West Indies has been virtually total.

As Vaughan Lewis has reminded us, the central fear of all forms of political union in such settings is:

> that the 'power' to plan in response to electoral promises, and the power to exercise patronage, will be removed from the local island-level, away from the real political brokers of the island societies to some locus and set of institutions, which whatever the potential benefits they may confer, take on the appearance of an *imposition* on the local systems. Or that these institutions will, by some process of osmosis, draw the local political brokers away more and more, from their political bases, divorcing them from the day to day political concerns of their island societies, leaving a vacuum for new political brokers to fill and to challenge them, eventually cutting away their original political bases.[46]

Yet it would be wrong to attribute this feeling entirely to the selfishness of the politicians. The phenomenon has much deeper, historical roots. A vivid sense of insular self-consciousness played havoc for three centuries with the best laid plans of the British Colonial Office to rationalise its administration of the Caribbean, and that insularity has become no less robust for having been clothed with all the paraphernalia of governmental authority. Island self-government is now the kernel of the political culture of the region. It is the characteristic psychology of the little islands of the Leewards and Windwards as much as it is of Jamaica, the familiar big bad wolf of eastern Caribbean demonology. *All* the states of the West Indies are reluctant to surrender any of their authority, and 'surrender' is not too emotive a word to use. It matters not at all in this context that the possession of constitutional competence cannot guarantee the capacity to make policy effectively. It does at least place the levers of political power in the hands of the island governments, and that is a prerogative often undervalued by political analysts, but never lightly conceded by the governments in question.

Supporters of political union have, therefore, been confronted with what is essentially 'the Hobbesian question': by what means are states that possess certain governmental rights and competences brought voluntarily to concede some or all of this formal authority? It is obvious that very compelling inducements indeed have to be offered. The leaders of the states concerned must jointly agree that certain important problems can be solved, and certain important goals attained, *only* within the dramatically restructured framework of a political union — and here we stress the word 'only'. It is an inescapable conclusion from the evidence of the past two decades — indeed, it is something of a truism — that, however logical they may seem in theory, the arguments adduced in recent years in favour of the political unity of the Caribbean have not succeeded in generating this conviction in enough of the region's leaders.

In this regard there is no doubt that the major weakness of recent pleas for a Caribbean political union has been their failure to make a clear distinction between economic integration and political integration. Often the case for political integration has been phrased in a vague and ambiguous way. Burnham, for example, would ask: 'Can the Caribbean as we know it today ... really improve the lot of its people if it remains a number of separate and little entities for whom independence, in most cases, is an expensive undertaking?'[47] Or Ramphal would assert that only through political unity 'can we maximise our all too slender chances of meeting the demands for change, including as they do the demands for employment and a better quality of life, that lie behind the protest movements of the Region'.[48] These arguments might possibly have proved more effective as a spur to political integration if there had not already been well founded within the Commonwealth Caribbean a movement for regional economic integration. Its existence has effectively absorbed many of the more general calls for political unity. The governments of the West Indies believe — with justification — that what they have laboriously created in the Caribbean Community is potentially, at least, a means of improving the lot of the West Indian people and of meeting their demands for employment and a better quality of life. It is incumbent, therefore, upon the advocates of political integration to establish that there is a need to go *beyond* the Caribbean Community arrangements. Reiteration of the potential of economic integration is insufficient. Something more is needed to justify the surrender of authority which is concomitant with the embrace of political integration.

With this in mind, then, we now review the arguments which have been most frequently used by protagonists of political integration in their recent attempts to induce Caribbean governments to surrender that authority.

1. *The argument that only thus could a sense of West Indian nationhood be genuinely satisfied.* 'Intuitively,' wrote Demas,

> one feels that the peoples of the English-speaking Caribbean are one people, be they from the North-western part of the Caribbean, the Eastern Caribbean Islands, or from Guyana; be they of Indian or African origin; be they of white or Chinese extraction. Therefore, to refuse to institutionalise through political unity this feeling of oneness is to leave the people of the Region psychologically diminished and unfulfilled.[49]

It is a difficult thesis to deal with. Objectively, one can see that the territories of the region share a common history, a common language, common institutions and values, and many contemporary problems. Yet, subjectively, do these shared features add up to a sense of nationhood? After all, the countries of Scandinavia share many similar bonds without there being much talk of the existence of a Scandinavian *nation*. All we can say in the Caribbean case is that there are some who do genuinely feel members of a single nation — the Tobago signatories, for example, Ramphal, Williams, Demas, the educated and travelled for the most part, those in a position to sense the broad cultural unity of the region, and maybe (although only fleetingly) the crowds which have over the years supported the West Indian cricket team. It can hardly be denied, either, that the formation of a West Indian state would most effectively institutionalise such a feeling.

It is difficult, however, to avoid the conclusion that this sense of West Indianism is declining and has probably been doing so since 1947, when the Montego Bay Conference in Jamaica excited what, in the event, proved to be the height of the enthusiasm for the West Indies Federation. Many of the recent calls for the fulfilment of West Indian nationhood have been characterised by an air of urgency, deriving, in the main, from a perception that the last chance to translate the emotional feeling of West Indianism into political reality may very well be upon the region. It was felt that the longer each island continued to govern itself the stronger would become its own sense of nationhood. Although Trinidad and Guyana are exceptional cases by virtue of the racial division of their populations, one's impression is certainly that the inhabitants of the other islands of the region are becoming increasingly aware that they are St Lucians, Barbadians, Jamaicans first, and West Indians – if at all – second; and, further, that the disparity between the insular and regional levels of kinship is growing wider, and is likely to continue doing so in the coming years. There is little doubt but that, of the two, insularity is the more easily politicised: the apparatus of self-government exists, after all, to give it voice. Politically, West Indianism does not punch its psychological weight. It may even be that the Caribbean Community arrangements, if extensively presented as the working manifestation of West Indian brotherhood, will in time prove to be enough to satisfy what is left of the sentiment of West Indianism. In this light, Ramphal's talk of 'a new West Indian released from the inhibitions of a thwarted island nationalism and well equipped, or at least better equipped, to adjust to the need for a more mature West Indian Nationhood'[50] seems extravagantly optimistic. Is West Indian nationhood a 'myth, mirage or mandate?' he has asked, concluding rather questionably, one would have thought, that it is the latter.[51] If so, it is a mandate for which neither he nor anyone else has yet been able to mobilise much political thrust.

2. *The argument that the region could only effectively*

conduct external negotiations and protect itself against external threats by articulating its foreign policy from the solid base of a political union. The argument implicity accepted that the regional territories – including the Associated States – possessed the right to operate alone in the international arena, but held that individually they did not have the resources to do so in a meaningful, self-respecting way; and that, even if they had, the rest of the international community would scarcely appreciate the task of dealing with them all separately, especially when very often they would likely be advancing essentially similar views. Putting the point, as Demas has, in commonsense terms, it is to say that

> to deal with giants a lot of pygmies have to get together because, even if the giants are not bad people, they are so gigantic that they inadvertently crush the pygmies. So that, if the pygmies get together, at least the giants would notice them and be very careful not to step on them.[52]

It may sound like a fairy tale, but it does contain a plausible argument. The rest of the world does view the Commonwealth Caribbean as a *group* of states and does expect to hear them expressing ideas with one voice. The question is: does this necessitate political integration? What is the advantage of a single foreign policy, as envisaged by political integrationists, over a common foreign policy, as agreed by governments? The former extinguishes the participant's formal 'right to act' in a way the latter process of consultation and co-ordination does not, arguably without adding significantly to the effectiveness of the policy that is in the end articulated. Within the rubric of the Caribbean Community the four MDCs have been able to take the important step of jointly re-opening diplomatic relations with Cuba and have, moreover, acted very effectively as a sub-group within the African–Caribbean–Pacific alliance formed for the purpose of negotiating an association agreement with the EEC. The Lomé Convention – or at least the extent to which it is regarded as a favourable outcome to the association negotiations – is a powerful argument against the need to form a political union in order to conduct an effective foreign policy.

From the opposite point of view, it is true that the Caribbean

Political integration

states have not been able to settle upon a common stance on every issue of foreign policy, failing notably to agree upon the appropriate reaction to the growing economic and diplomatic activity of Venezuela in the Commonwealth Caribbean. Yet, equally, whilst non-unanimity persists on such issues and whilst there is at the same time a forum in the Caribbean Community for working out compromises, it is unrealistic to expect the various governments to surrender all right to disagree to some central body, established purposely to hammer out and conduct a single foreign policy. It might just become a possibility if the region as a whole were to be threatened by armed attack. Some West Indian states have been encouraged, at times, to seek a closer relationship with their regional neighbours by a threat to the integrity of their borders − as Guyana was, for example, throughout the 1960s by virtue of the long-standing Venezuelan claim to part of its land area, and as Belize has been, and still is, whenever Guatemalan military activity is escalated in pursuit of a similar ancient claim to much of Belizean territory. These are, however, exceptional cases: there is no prospect in the foreseeable future of there being any threat of external aggression against the West Indies as a whole, and no certainty that, even if there were, it would lead to the creation of a West Indian union.

There did, however, develop a corollary to this whole argument about the pooling and centralisation of the authority to act on the international stage. It concerned, in particular, the constitutional responsibility still held by Britain for the defence and external affairs of the Associated States. Critics contended that the very institution of Associated Statehood represented 'a challenge to regional ambition', and yet conceded that even 'the most ardent nationalists' had to 'pause before promoting independence in isolation for any of the Associated States'. It was alleged that they just did not have the wherewithal to sustain independence and that, in consequence, the British presence could only be removed by 'such a measure of agreement on political association that the exercise of the separate options for independence by each Associated State will produce a West Indian community'. So at least Ramphal, for one, could argue.[53] And for a while this sort of thinking did seem to grip the minds of a number of Caribbean leaders. The Anguillan secession and the melodramatic British reaction (paratroopers and London policemen) underlined both the region's vulnerability to metropolitan intervention – under 'constitutional cover',[54] as Ramphal put it – and the fragility of each Associated State's control of its own internal security. The first problem could be overcome by an independent union of the Associated States, but the second – the danger of secessionism and fragmentation – applied equally to the independent states of the region. The Guyanese government, from whom these views were most often heard, was especially aware of the possibility in the light of its experience of the Rupunini rising in January 1969.[55] It therefore proposed that both problems could be solved by the assembly of machinery for regional peace-keeping under the roof of regional political unity: hence the activity that led up to the Grenada Declaration of July 1971.

Since that time, however, this analysis has lost much of its appeal: not because the Associated States are now any more capable of sustaining effective independence or of maintaining themselves against the forces of fragmentation and intervention, but primarily because independence has come to be seen in a different light. It is now perceived much more as a formal *status* in international society, an expression of self-determination, and not so much as a reward for the achievement of 'viability' in some practical sense. In sum, the idea that there is some equation relating size and sovereignty has been exposed as a myth.[56] It has become increasingly apparent, for instance, that even the larger states of the West Indies – those which have been independent a decade or more – are just as much lacking in the capacity to exercise effectively the rights that stem from their independence, and are similarly vulnerable to the possibility of external interference. 'There is a fundamental similarity', as Lewis observed, 'between the recent British intervention in the state of St Kitts-Nevis-Anguilla, and the virtual intervention of the United States and Venezuela in Trinidad during the recent crisis there'.[57] In addition, a number of international institutions have grown up – not least the Caribbean Development Bank – whose existence serves to sustain small, economically unviable states. The result has been that individual island independence,

Political integration 275

which Britain has always been willing to concede to the Associated States, is now seen as a realistic option. Or, to put the point another way, the leaders of the Associated States have at last acquired the confidence to cash the independence cheque given them in the 1967 arrangements. Grenada was the first to break the psychological hold, becoming fully independent in February 1974. Gairy, the island's first Prime Minister, demonstrated his understanding of the changes that had taken place by taking as his maxim the slogan 'Independence will support Grenada, the people of Grenada do not have to support independence'.[58] Dominica and St Lucia followed suit by becoming independent in November 1978 and February 1979 respectively, and they were joined by St Vincent in October 1979. It is likely now to be only a matter of time before all the Associated States graduate in this way. All this is a turn of events, or rather a change of perceptions, that Ramphal and many others in the independent states completely discounted. It does not, of course, reduce the possibility of secessionism – it may very well increase it – but it does mean that a solution to the problem is less likely to be sought within the embrace of a West Indian political union.

3. *The economic integration argument*. Throughout this chapter we have gone out of our way to make a clear distinction between economic integration and the movement for political integration in the recent history of the Caribbean. But there is alleged to be an important link between them which constitutes, at least potentially, the most telling of all the inducements that have been put forward as necessitating a political union. This was *the proposition that the identified limitations and failings of the economic integration programme could only be overcome by the advent of political integration*. It was most often heard in connection with the complaints of the LDCs that they had not received an equitable share of the benefits of economic integration. The comments of Ronald Armour, the Minister of Finance, Trade and Industry of Dominica, just before the ninth CARIFTA Council meeting in October 1971 are typical:

> My frank opinion is that if we want to get closer economic integration we cannot hide our heads in the sand and expect us

to come at this stage closer without political association. We must start making a decision towards this end. We can't have all these so-called visionaries of the Caribbean talking of closer economic unity and at the same time denying political unity.[59]

From a similar concern that the economic integration movement was stagnating, Ramphal also added his weight to the view

> that the demands of economic integration reinforce the case for political unity; that the realities of separation and the political constraints which they place on regional decision-making require us to evoke appropriate forms of political unity or face the erosion of the institutions of mutual assistance we have so far established.[60]

There is some logic in all this. In view of the common commitment which all the governments of the Commonwealth Caribbean, in their differing ways, have made to regional economic integration, one would indeed expect them to consider very seriously any course of action that purported to rescue the integration movement from failure. That said, the difficulties in the thesis begin to emerge. Not everybody agrees that economic integration has been a failure and those who do, do not necessarily agree on the reasons why. More important, those who advocated political integration as the means of revival failed to explain in any detail how it would achieve that end. Presumably the LDC leaders felt that as representatives of the underdeveloped parts of a unified whole, rather than as weak partners in an intergovernmental alliance, they would be better able to direct benefits to their islands; presumably Ramphal, too, anticipated that a unified *form* of government would somehow break down the stubborn '*realities* of separatism',[61] of which he talked. Perhaps, in the long run, they would have been proved right, but it is difficult to see how the entrenched and insularist attitudes that currently exist could have been altered in the short run. And in the short run, as the governments undoubtedly perceive, they are more likely to secure the desired reforms within the structure of the economic integration movement itself. The relevant barrier is not the lack of political integration but the lack of political will.

4. *The advantage derived from the ending of the wasteful*

duplication of political and administrative activity in the region. The diagnosis is uncontroversial: for its population, the Caribbean is one of the most over-governed areas in the world. In 1973, for example, the Leeward and Windward Islands, with a combined population of 476,000, were serviced by no fewer than forty-seven ministries, compared to Barbados, which with half the population, 238,000, budgeted for just twelve.[62] The prescription offered is not, however, very realistic. In practice, government ministers are unlikely to legislate themselves out of their jobs or be advised by their civil servants of the need for less administration; and, from the administrative point of view itself, there is actually no reason why a regional public service, eliminating waste, saving money, sharing talent and resisting the 'brain drain', cannot be achieved without the creation of a political union.

5. *The civil liberties argument*, as trenchantly expressed in the mid-1960s by Arthur Lewis in his pamphlet *The Agony of the Eight*, and revived (at his instigation, perhaps) in the Tobago Statement in 1972. Caribbean societies are small, it ran, 'a charismatic leader can exert undue influence on those who disagree with him',[63] and civil liberty can be thus prejudiced. The wider dispersion of power in a federation is thought more likely to provide greater safeguards. There is not much to be said about this plea. Clearly, the primary guarantee of civil liberties is moral, not a particular structure of government; nor can there be said to be a correspondence between size and liberty in the world as a whole. It may be, though, that a political union can make available to defendants in courts of law more experienced and less easily cowed legal representatives than local attorneys from the same island. Equally, something of this sort can be arranged without the need for political integration. Either way, it is an inducement unlikely in itself to move governments to action.

Conclusion

Let us now try to sum up. The arguments advanced in favour of a political union in the Caribbean must be judged a very mixed bag. They have manifestly not carried sufficient political weight to compel a response. Despite a prolonged period between 1971 and 1974 when the subject of political integration was a prominent issue, a regional political union is nowhere in sight today. It is not, at present, a practical option, and, as far as one can anticipate the future, it is unlikely to become one. Indeed, it has been possible lately to detect a mood of pessimism and resignation on the part of those long attached to the goal of political integration. In an interview given in 1975 Robert Bradshaw, the former federal Minister of Finance and a man with a long record of support for a political union of the West Indies, completely dismissed the prospect,

> because it couldn't happen in the foreseeable future unless there was some world catastrophe which forced us willy nilly together. Other than that, people are going their own and remain their own way ... Look at the situation. Everybody is seeking independence. They are having their flags, their anthems and their everything.[64]

Since 1974 there has certainly been a marked diminution in the number of calls for a political union, and a feeling has arisen that its continued advocacy has become counter-productive. Many of the incentives are — as we have shown — less compelling now than when they were widely propounded at the height of the political integration movement in the early 1970s. By comparison, an increasing number of the governments of the region, by seeking independence, are in the process of adding to their range of formal rights and competences. At the moment, therefore, the balance of impediment and inducement is tipped heavily against a political union.

The fundamental reason why this should be so is the existence of the Caribbean Community, which cuts much of the ground from underneath the political integrationists but avoids confrontation with the main obstacles they must inevitably face. In other words, the implication of our analysis is that the 'live trend' in Caribbean regional integration is not towards the supranational implementation of regional policy via a political union, but towards — and not beyond — the co-ordination of governmental policy on a regional basis. The difference is crucial and can be usefully restated. The first involves the assumption of full constitutional responsibility for certain governmental functions by a central, supranational body; the second means that island governments retain ultimate, constitutional authority over that function, but agree to pursue a common policy in that particular area and, where appropriate, consent to its articulation by a single spokesman. The latter strategy in legal and constitutional terms only involves the co-operative use of the instruments and mechanisms by which governments seek to make effective the legal authority of the states they represent. In a manner which political integrationists scorn, it takes account of the fundamental feature of regional politics in the Commonwealth Caribbean, namely the fact that individual territorial governments want *to be seen* to possess the right to make policy on their own initiative and to legitimate whatever co-operative policy is thought to be necessary. As Lewis has observed, the relevant principle is: '*Decentralise* the bases of political power, authority and therefore initiative; *centralise* the mechanisms for performing such tasks and functions as the local or international environment induce or impel us to perform cooperatively.'[65] A form of regional integration which seeks to breach this principle will make no headway, as may be seen in the various attempts to establish a West Indian political union; a form of integration which respects it is likely to make at least some progress, as in the Caribbean Community.

Notes

1. K. C. Wheare, *Federal Government*, London, 1953, p. 11.
2. E. B. Haas and P. C. Schmitter, 'Economics and Differential Patterns of Political Integration: Projections about Unity in Latin America', *International Organisation*, vol. 18, no. 4, 1964, p. 707. Their emphasis.
3. They were: Background Conditions – (i) the size and power of the units, (ii) the rate of transaction among the participants before they proceed to liberalise restrictions, (iii) the degree and kind of pluralism within and among the member states, (iv) the mutual complementarity of national elites; Conditions at the Time of Economic Union – (i) the purposes and aims of the governments, (ii) the powers invested in the union; Process Conditions – (i) the decision-making style which develops among the units, (ii) a re-examination of the rate of transaction, (iii) the adaptability of the chief actors, governmental and private. *Ibid.*, pp. 711-16.

4. *Ibid.*, p. 717.
5. J. S. Nye, *Peace in Parts: Integration and Conflict in Regional Organization*, Boston, 1971, p. 54.
6. Haas and Schmitter, *op. cit.*, p. 720.
7. F. Burnham, 'The Case for Caribbean Political Integration', in The Critchlow Labour College, *Some Aspects of Caribbean Integration*, Georgetown, 1972, p. 3. My emphasis.
8. Government of Trinidad and Tobago, *CARIFTA and the Caribbean Economic Community*, Port of Spain, 1968, p. 8.
9. Haas and Schmitter, *op. cit.*, p. 720.
10. See R. Hansen, 'Regional Integration: Reflections on a Decade of Theoretical Efforts', *World Politics*, vol. 21, no. 2, 1969, pp. 255-6, and 'European Integration: Forward March, Parade Rest, or Dismissed?', *International Organisation*, vol. 27, no. 2, 1973, p. 231.
11. S. Hoffmann, 'Discord in Community: the North Atlantic Area as a Partial International System', *International Organisation*, vol. 17, no. 3, 1963, pp. 521-49. See also 'European Process at Atlantic Cross-purposes', *Journal of Common Market Studies*, vol. 3, no. 2, 1965, pp. 85-101, and 'Obstinate or Obsolete? The Fate of the Nation-State in Western Europe', *Daedalus*, vol. 95, no. 3, 1966, pp. 862-915. The definition of 'high politics' quoted was originally given in *Gulliver's Troubles, or The Setting of American Foreign Policy*, New York, 1968, p. 404, note 12.
12. J. S. Nye, 'Patterns and Catalysts in Regional Integration', *International Organisation*, vol. 19, no. 4, 1965, p. 872.
13. Nye, *Peace in Parts*, pp. 55-107.
14. *Ibid.*, p. 97.
15. W. G. Demas, *West Indian Nationhood and Caribbean Integration*, Bridgetown, 1974, p. 59.
16. *The Grenada Declaration*, Grand Anse, 25 July 1971. The Declaration has been published in full in *Caribbean Quarterly*, vol. 18, no. 2, 1972, pp. 48-50.
17. Burnham, *op. cit.*, p. 5.
18. *Guyana Journal*, vol. 1, no. 5, 1971, p. 10.
19. 'The Grenada Declaration', *op. cit.*, p. 49.
20. *Ibid.*, p. 48.
21. *Barbados Advocate-News*, 6 October 1971.
22. For information about other official reactions see E. Le Blanc, *The Grenada Declaration* (statement by the Premier before the Parliament of Dominica, 13 December 1971), Roseau, 1971.
23. *Daily Gleaner*, 10 October 1971.
24. *Trinidad Guardian*, 1 November 1971.
25. *Ibid.*, 3 November 1971.
26. *Ibid.*, 4 November 1971.
27. *Guyana Graphic*, 8 November 1971.
28. Ramphal, *Dialogue of Unity*, p. 22.
29. Burnham, *op. cit.*, p. 13.
30. A Group of West Indians Meeting in Tobago, 10-11 June 1972, 'Towards an Eastern Caribbean Federation', reprinted in *Caribbean Studies*,

vol. 12, no. 3, 1972, pp. 98-102.
31. *Ibid.*, p. 100.
32. *Ibid.*, p. 100.
33. *Ibid.*, p. 101.
34. *Ibid.*, p. 98.
35. E. Williams, 'A New Federation for the Commonwealth Caribbean?', *The Political Quarterly*, vol. 44, no. 3, 1973, pp. 242-56.
36. *Ibid.*, p. 242.
37. *Ibid.*, p. 252.
38. *Ibid.*, p. 253.
39. Demas, *op. cit.*, p. 55.
40. *Ibid.*, p. 57.
41. *Ibid.*
42. *Ibid.* Demas's emphasis.
43. S. S. Ramphal, *West Indian Nationhood: Myth, Mirage or Mandate?*, Georgetown, 1971, p. 6.
44. Demas, *op. cit.*, p. 57.
45. Burnham, *op. cit.*, p. 6.
46. V. A. Lewis, *The Idea of a Caribbean Community*, New World Pamphlet No. 9, Kingston, Jamaica, 1974, p. 8. Lewis's emphasis.
47. Burnham, *op. cit.*, p. 10.
48. Ramphal, *Dialogue of Unity*, p. 16.
49. Demas, *op. cit.*, p. 26.
50. Ramphal, *West Indian Nationhood*, pp. 8-9.
51. *Ibid.*, p. 26.
52. Demas, *op. cit.*, p. 7.
53. Ramphal, *West Indian Nationhood*, p. 11.
54. *Ibid.*, p. 10.
55. For details of this rising, see *Guyana Journal*, vol. 1, no. 3, 1969, pp. 39-46.
56. For the source of these remarks and an elaboration upon them, see V. A. Lewis, 'Small States in the International Society: with Special Reference to the Associated States', *Caribbean Quarterly*, vol. 18, no. 2, 1972, pp. 36-47, and 'Commentary' in Institute of International Relations, University of the West Indies, *Independence for Grenada – Myth or Reality?*, Port of Spain, 1974, pp. 53-5.
57. Lewis, *Caribbean Quarterly*, p. 42. The crisis referred to was the threat to the stability of the Trinidad government brought about in 1970 by numerous Black Power demonstrations.
58. *Trinidad Guardian*, 1 November 1972.
59. *Trinidad Guardian*, 4 October 1971.
60. Ramphal, *Dialogue of Unity*, p. 15.
61. *Ibid.* My emphasis.
62. The Constitutional Commission, 'The Political Economy of Independence for the Leeward and Windward Islands', mimeo, 1975, pp. 43-4.
63. A Group of West Indians, *op. cit.*, p. 100.
64. Caribbean Broadcasting Union, 'Transcript of Interview with Hon. R.

Bradshaw, Premier of St Kitts-Nevis-Anguilla on the Occasion of the First Anniversary of the Inauguration of the Caribbean Community', Georgetown, mimeo, 1975, p. 3.
65. Lewis, *Idea of a Caribbean Community*, pp. 11-12. Lewis's emphasis.

CONCLUSION

The politics of regionalisation

We have now arrived at an understanding of how the Caribbean Community originated and how it has operated to date; we know what it is and what it is not; we are familiar with its strengths and weaknesses and we have set out its successes and failures. The aim of these few concluding pages is not to reiterate the various conclusions of earlier chapters, but to attempt to draw together the threads of the preceding discussion and to point the direction in which the study of regional integration amongst new states ought perhaps now to move.

Looking back across the years which have passed since the announcement of the result of the Jamaican referendum in September 1961, one's initial impression cannot but be of the immensity of the change which has come over the character of inter-island relations since that moment. Out of collapse and disintegration has emerged the framework of a new Commonwealth Caribbean community. Regional institutions exist and function, ministers meet regularly in a variety of forums and just about everyone is in favour of West Indian integration in one form or other. Of course, there are still arguments and recriminations between member territories of the Community — sometimes bitter ones — but they occur now as between members of the same club. It is probably fair to say that the achievement of these years has been to transpose the question of regional integration in the Caribbean 'from one of concept to one of function – from "if" to "how" '[1] – and that is no mean achievement. Probing more deeply, though, into the actual way the contemporary situation does differ from the severe economic and political fragmentation which we argued was the predominant characteristic of the Caribbean as a region in September 1961, one is perhaps less sure of what has, in fact, been achieved. Obviously there is a considerable difference today: it would be a nonsense to suggest otherwise when the pattern of fragmentation has so clearly been modified in so many ways. The fact nevertheless remains that it has not been completely eradicated. The *underlying* pattern is essentially the same: each territory still pursues its own political and economic interests and still retains faith in its right to operate as a political and economic unit. The difference is that, elevated above that enduring base, there now exists the elaborate structure of regional intergovernmental organisation, which it has been the purpose of this study to describe and analyse. What the Caribbean Community has done is to promote the coexistence of regional integration at one level with regional fragmentation at another. It has, in other words, rendered workable and relatively stable the interaction of the two forces which have pulled the West Indies apart for three centuries or more.

The Community cannot, however, be said to have completely resolved that conflict. Maybe that is to expect a reconciliation of the irreconcilable, but certainly no more than a *modus vivendi* of the two opposing forces of integration and fragmentation has been established. As such, CARICOM inevitably remains intrinsically a prey to interruptions of that fragile coexistence. Perceiving this only too clearly, Ramphal has warned that one consequence of the relative success experienced by the Caribbean integration movement over the last few years has been 'a readiness to believe that unity is our natural state'.[2] A history of colonialism and the geography of a scattered archipelago deny the validity of that assumption: 'without constant effort, without unrelenting perseverance and discipline in suppressing instincts born of tradition and environment it is to our natural state of disunity that we shall return'.[3] Integration is thus still only a tender plant, and one would be foolish to discount the possibility that the structure that has been so laboriously created might suddenly collapse.

The encapsulation of this endemic conflict within the Community has also determined the type of movement that it has become. The Community is not a structure designed, in the first instance, to secure the economic and political integration of the Caribbean; it is a structure created by national governments to make nationalist policies more effective by pursuing them within a regional framework. This is surely the point which, again, Ramphal was making when, in asking why Caribbean integration had not succeeded in fully coming to grips with the reality of the region's fragmentation, he wrote:

> I suggest that the explanation lies in the fact that while we have passed resolutions that promote integration, some of us have made no national commitment to it. We have not made that commitment because we have not developed an ideology of regionalism. Pragmatism and expediency have their places in national and regional affairs; but there is a level of collective endeavour – whether at the level of the community, of the State or of the Region – that needs to be supported by belief and by faith; for it is only out of such belief, out of such faith, that will come the type of commitment that produces fundamental change. What we have lacked is that ideology of regionalism.[4]

The word 'regionalism' has not been used in this study – quite deliberately – until this moment, because we believe, with Ramphal, that the concept is only properly applicable to a process of regional integration, in which policies are regularly assessed during the course of their formulation against the needs of the region as a whole. Countries have to be prepared to accept that the greater regional good must predominate over national concerns even if this means that, on occasion, their national interests, as they perceive them, are damaged. For good or ill, this has never been the case with the Caribbean Community. It is simply not concerned with integration in that sense. Indeed, strictly, it is not an *integration* movement at all, if the term 'integration' is considered to have anything to do with the emergence of a new and separate community into which previous identities are submerged. This, of course, again underlines the irrelevance to our concerns of conventional integration theory, which is preoccupied with precisely that sort of process.

From a theoretical point of view what, in fact, may best describe the way in which the values and beliefs of Commonwealth Caribbean governments have been translated into practice in respect of the Community is the concept of 'regionalisation'. We define regionalisation as a method of international co-operation which enables the advantages of decision-making at a regional level to be reconciled with the preservation of the institutions of the nation state. For what has been created in the Caribbean is not a regional economy in the sense advocated by the UWI economists, but a regionalised economy exemplified by the existence of a coherent web of economic relationships between the various national units; nor is it a regional polity in the sense advocated by political integrationists, but a regionalised polity exemplified, in the same way, by the existence of a similar web of political relationships, albeit more tangled, between the various national units of the region. The term 'regionalisation' is, therefore, designed to catch the essence of an international political structure, which cannot be said to have secured the economic and political integration of the region, but in which the constituent states clearly no longer make policy solely as national units. What we have on our hands is neither nationalism nor regionalism, but a hybrid creature consisting of elements of both. Regionalisation is not, however, a process by which a neat half-way position is reached between nationalism and regionalism: it is much more an artefact of the nation state than the regionalist community. Of the two perspectives, the nationalist one is undoubtedly uppermost, the regional connection being conceived primarily as a support. Regionalisation in the Caribbean is not, therefore, a means to the complete elimination of the problems of fragmentation. It has been aimed, not at the replacement of national economic and political action, but at the very opposite, its reinforcement. This is the heart of the matter, because it draws attention to the crucial difference between the reality of regional integration amongst new states, as illustrated by the experience of the Commonwealth Caribbean, and the conventional theory of regional integration amongst developed countries. In the final analysis, the latter is concerned with the demise and disappearance of the nation state, the former with its preservation and enhancement.

The final point to be considered is whether this assessment of the politics of integration amongst new states has a validity beyond the experience of the Caribbean Community, from which it has been derived. Unfortunately, there is no way of answering that question until further research has been done. It would certainly be unscientific to advance a general theory on the basis of one case study, and we have no intention of making that mistake. However, it is perhaps possible to say this much. The states of the Commonwealth Caribbean are no doubt different in many ways from those of East and West Africa, Central and Latin America and Asia; but they do have in common one very important characteristic – namely, an attachment to the concept of the independent nation state which sits increasingly uneasily with the capacity of that state to meet the demands placed on it. We have argued that it was the conflict inherent in this situation which led Caribbean governments to embark on the process of creating the intergovernmental structure of co-operation currently embodied in the Caribbean Community. It would not, therefore, be unreasonable to wonder whether the concept of regionalisation, as we have explained it, is not one which may fit the experience of other new states better than the various ideas derived from neofunctionalist theory about Western Europe. It is to be hoped that other scholars will alight upon these conclusions and test them in other settings. In the meantime they may perhaps be considered as interesting hypotheses capable, in time, of sustaining a theory of regional integration which has been derived from, and is thus genuinely relevant to, the world of new states.

Notes

1. S. S. Ramphal, *To Care for CARICOM: The Need for an Ethos of Community*, Georgetown, 1975, p. 5.
2. *Ibid.*, p. 7.
3. *Ibid.*
4. S. S. Ramphal, *West Indian Nationhood: Myth, Mirage or Mandate?*, Georgetown, 1971, p. 20.

APPENDIX
Basic data on the Caribbean Community States

The following notes contain brief comparative data on the countries that comprise the Caribbean Community. The information is derived from various publications of the Community Secretariat. The population figures are estimates for early 1979. The figures concerning the economy are for gross domestic product at factor cost for 1970, and are given in Eastern Caribbean dollars.

Antigua
Area, 170 sq. miles. *Population*, 71,420. *Capital*, St John's. *Economy*, GDP EC$40,673. Per capita, EC$581. *Political Status*, Associated State.

Barbados
Area, 166 sq. miles. *Population*, 247,200. *Capital*, Bridgetown. *Economy*, GDP EC$273,500. Per capita, EC$1149. *Political status*, Independent.

Belize
Area, 8,866 sq. miles. *Population*, 143,500. *Capital*, Belmopan. *Economy*, GDP EC$100,286. Per capita, EC$836. *Political status*, Colony.

Dominica
Area, 305 sq. miles. *Population*, 81,753. *Capital*, Roseau. *Economy*, GDP EC$33,856. Per capita, EC$484. *Political status*, Independent.

Grenada
Area, 133 sq. miles. *Population*, 104,387. *Capital*, St George's. *Economy*, GDP EC$42,118. Per capita, EC$443. *Political status*, Independent.

Guyana
Area, 83,000 sq. miles. *Population*, 793,000. *Capital*, Georgetown. *Economy*, GDP EC$460,640. Per capita, EC$645. *Political status*, Independent.

Jamaica
Area, 4,411 sq. miles. *Population*, 2,072,800. *Capital*, Kingston. *Economy*, GDP EC$2,339,520. Per capita, EC$1254. *Political status*, Independent.

Appendix

Montserrat
Area, 32 sq. miles. *Population*, 12,162. *Capital*, Plymouth. *Economy*, GDP EC$11,847. Per capita, EC$987. *Political status*, Colony.

St Kitts-Nevis-Anguilla
Area, 101 sq. miles. *Population*, 49,100. *Capital*, Basseterre. *Economy*, GDP EC$28,417. Per capita, EC$617. *Political status*, Associated State.

St Lucia
Area, 233 sq. miles. *Population*, 114,400. *Capital*, Castries. *Economy*, GDP EC$62,858. Per capita, EC$622. *Political status*, Independent.

St Vincent
Area, 150 sq. miles. *Population*, 108,009. *Capital*, Kingstown. *Economy*, GDP EC$37,022. Per capita, EC$416. *Political status*, Independent.

Trinidad and Tobago
Area, 1,980 sq. miles. *Population*, 1,098,200. *Capital*, Port of Spain. *Economy*, GDP EC$1,717,000. Per capita, EC$1817. *Political status*, Independent.

SELECT BIBLIOGRAPHY

This bibliography contains the major published works that have contributed to the interpretation of the Caribbean Community advanced in this study. Readers are referred to the notes at the end of each chapter for detailed references and citations.

Axline, W. A., *Caribbean Integration: the Politics of Regionalism*, London, 1979.
Balassa, B., *The Theory of Economic Integration*, Homewood, 1961.
Beckford, G. L., *Persistent Poverty: Underdevelopment in Plantation Economies of the Third World*, New York, 1972.
—(ed.), *Caribbean Economy: Dependence and Backwardness*, Kingston, 1975.
Best, L., and Levitt, K., *Externally Propelled Industrialisation and Growth in the Caribbean since the War*, Montreal, 1969.
Brewster, H., and Thomas, C. Y., *The Dynamics of West Indian Economic Integration*, Kingston, 1967.
Chernick, S. E., *The Commonwealth Caribbean: the Integration Experience*, Washington, 1978.
Crassweller, R. D., *The Caribbean Community: Changing Societies and U. S. Policy*, New York, 1972.
Demas, W. G., *The Economics of Development in Small Countries with Special Reference to the Caribbean*, Montreal, 1965.
—*West Indian Nationhood and Caribbean Integration*, Bridgetown, 1974.
Geiser, H., et al., *Legal Problems of Caribbean Integration: a Study on the Legal Aspects of CARICOM*, Leyden, 1976.
Girvan, N. (ed.), *Dependence and Underdevelopment in the New World and the Old*, Kingston, 1973.
Girvan, N., and Jefferson, O. (eds.), *Readings in the Political Economy of the Caribbean*, Kingston, 1971.
Greene, J. E., *Race vs. Politics in Guyana*, Kingston, 1974.
Jefferson, O., *The Post-war Economic Development of Jamaica*, Kingston, 1972.
Lewis, G. K., *The Growth of the Modern West Indies*, New York, 1968.
Lewis, S., and Mathews, T. G. (eds.), *Caribbean Integration: Papers on Social, Political and Economic Integration*, Rio Piedras, 1967.
Lewis, V. A., *The Idea of a Caribbean Community*, Port of Spain, 1974.
—(ed.), *Size, Self-determination and International Relations: the Caribbean*, Kingston, 1976.

Lowenthal, D., *West Indian Societies*, London, 1972.
Manley, M., *The Politics of Change: a Jamaican Testament*, London, 1974.
Mordecai, J. S., *The West Indies: the Federal Negotiations*, London, 1968.
Munroe, T., *The Politics of Constitutional Decolonisation: Jamaica 1944–62*, Kingston, 1972.
Parry, J. H., and Sherlock, P. M., *A Short History of the West Indies*, London, 1956.
Preiswerk, R. (ed.), *Regionalism and the Commonwealth Caribbean*, Port of Spain, 1969.
Ramphal, S. S., *The Prospect for Community in the Caribbean*, Georgetown, 1973.
—*West Indian Nationhood: Myth, Mirage or Mandate?*, Georgetown, 1971.
Ryan, S. D., *Race and Nationalism in Trinidad and Tobago: a Study of Decolonisation in a Multiracial Society*, Toronto, 1974.
Segal, A., *The Politics of Caribbean Economic Integration*, Rio Piedras, 1968.
Singham, A. W., *The Hero and the Crowd in a Colonial Polity*, New Haven, 1968.
Smith, M. G., *The Plural Society in the British West Indies*, Berkeley, 1965.
Stone, C., *Class, Race and Political Behaviour in Urban Jamaica*, Kingston, 1973.
—*Electoral Behaviour and Public Opinion in Jamaica*, Kingston, 1974.
Wallace, E., *The British Caribbean: from the Decline of Colonialism to the End of Federation*, Toronto, 1977.
Williams, E., *Capitalism and Slavery*, Chapel Hill, 1944.
—*From Columbus to Castro: the History of the Caribbean, 1492–1969*, London, 1970.

Index

Adams, Sir Grantley, 16, 27, 33
African, Caribbean and Pacific (ACP) Countries, 209–10, 272
Agreement on the Harmonisation of Fiscal Incentives to Industry, 92, 105, 127–31, 143, 145–6, 154, 179
Agricultural Marketing Protocol (AMP), 105, 121, 125–6, 144, 182
Air Jamaica, 115, 198
Alcan, 131
Andean Common Market, 212
Anglo-American Caribbean Commission, 10–12, 32
Antigua, 51, 121, 134, 261; joins CARIFTA, 65, 76, 91, 108; rejects Georgetown Accord, 153, 157–9, 162
Antigua Labour Party (ALP), 157–8
Armour, Ronald, 148–9, 275–6
Arusha Agreement, 135
Ashenheim, Leslie, 261–2
Axline, W. A., 182

Bahamas, The, 100–1, 103, 111–12, 119, 145, 181
Balassa, B., 166–7

Barbados, 1, 21, 30, 82, 94, 167; colonial administration of, 2–3, 5–8; contributes to functional co-operation, 196–8, 200, 204; favours 'deepening', 129; foreign policy, 218–20; opposes BWIA as regional air carrier, 115–6; participates in renewed regional collaboration after Federation, 39–40; road to independence, 13, 15–16, 33–4, 49, 74; role in Common Market, 174, 190–2, 186, 188; role in establishment of CARIFTA, 62–5, 70, 83, 91, 93, 101–3, 108, 119; signs Georgetown Accord, 153; trade, 120–1, 168–72; views on political integration, 260–1
Barrow, Errol, 39, 43, 45, 101–2, 229, 261; on BWIA, 116–17; on LDCs, 158–9; role in establishment of CARIFTA, 62–5, 70; role in Eastern Caribbean Federation attempt, 33, 49, 65
Basic Materials List, 66, 170–1, 189–90
Beckford, George, 76, 79

Index

Belize (formerly British Honduras), 1, 4, 103, 111–12, 132, 153; dispute with Guatemala, 212, 214, 273
Best, Lloyd, 41–2, 189
Bird, Vere, 65, 157
Bookers, 188
Bradshaw, Robert, 162, 215, 232, 261, 263, 278
Braithwaite, Lloyd, 11
Bramble, Austin, 148
Brewster, Havelock, 77–85, 186, 188
Britain, 94, 103, 119, 244, 273–4; colonial administration, 2–5; EEC policy, 37, 71, 74–5, 133, 210; handling of British Guiana crisis, 43–4, 49; response to Anguillan secession, 162, 259, 274; solution for Belize, 212; support for federalism, 5–16, 19–21, 29–30, 33–5
British Overseas Airways Corporation (BOAC), 114–15
British West Indian Airways (BWIA), 42, 46, 114–17, 198
British West Indies Sugar Association, 11
Brussels Tariff Nomenclature (BTN), 171
Burnham, Forbes, 43, 73–4, 215, 229; gives impetus to renewed regional collaboration, 49–51; role in establishment of CARIFTA, 62–5, 70, 75, 83, 128; views on political integration, 257, 260–3, 267, 269
Bustamante, Alexander, 14–15, 17, 38, 40, 43, 45, 48–50, 131

Canada, 17, 94, 119, 244; gift ships, 35, 195; holds trade conference with West Indies, 48, 50, 71–4, 94
Caribbean Association of Industry and Commerce (CAIC) (formerly the Incorporated Commonwealth Chambers of Industry and Commerce), 6, 11, 68–70, 83, 234
Caribbean Broadcasting Union, 202
Caribbean Common Market, 143–6, 148–55, 160–2, 232–3; coordinates economic policies, 179–83; establishes common external tariff, 174–5; general evaluation, 186–90; promotes intra-regional trade, 167–73; provides for factor mobility, 176–9; sets out framework for production integration, 183–6; theory of, 166–7
Caribbean Congress of Labour (CCL), 11, 234
Caribbean Consumers' Council, 234
Caribbean Development Bank (CDB), 146, 213, 225, 227, 238, 274; dispute over location of, 97–102, 106, 112–13, 118–19; functioning of, 120, 148, 156, 196, 240–5; origins of, 93–6
Caribbean Economic Community, 29, 32, 62, 67; attempted implementation, 36–9, 45–6; evaluation, 51–2
Caribbean Examinations Council, 201, 227
Caribbean Festival of Arts (CARIFESTA), 202
Caribbean Food Corporation (CFC), 186
Caribbean Free Trade Association (CARIFTA) (1965), 62–8, 70–1, 73, 76, 83–4, 157
Caribbean Free Trade Association (CARIFTA) (1968), 167, 234; dispute over BWIA, 114–17; division over EEC policy, 133–7; establishment of, 80–5, 90–109; fragility of, 112–14; impasse over 'deepening', 127–32, 136–7;

implications for political integration, 255–7, 275–6; LDCs complain about, 120–7; MDCs gain from, 119–20; negotiations to advance beyond, 140–62
Caribbean Investment Corporation (CIC), 225–7; establishment of, 146–8, 151, 154–6; performance, 177
Caribbean Meteorological Council, 198–9, 227
Caribbean News Agency, 202, 249
Caribbean Union of Teachers, 11
Carlisle, Earl of, 2
Carrington, Edwin, 176, 248
Cato, Milton, 261
Central Americal Common Market (CACM), 62, 93, 212
Charles, George, 26
Cipriani, A. A., 6
Colombia, 213, 244, 259
Colonial Development and Welfare Organisation, 35
Common External Tariff (CET), 91, 128–31, 143–6, 154, 156, 174–5
Common Market Council of Ministers, 171, 175, 200, 210, 225, 227; discussion, 232–4
Common Services Conference (1962), 35
Commonwealth Caribbean Technical Assistance Programme, 156, 199–200
Commonwealth Development Corporation, 95
Commonwealth Immigration Act (1962), 40, 72
Commonwealth Prime Ministers' Conference, 38, 47–8
Commonwealth Sugar Agreement, 15, 42, 134
Compton, John, 51, 199, 261–3
Corkran, Herbert, Jnr., 10
Council of Legal Education, 207, 227

Court Lines, 197
Cozier, F., 237
Cuba, 40, 76, 211; diplomatic relations with Caribbean, 146–7, 218, 272

D'Aguiar, Peter, 43
Daily Gleaner (Jamaica), 71, 97, 117–18, 152, 261; 'Political Reporter', 97, 103
Davson, Sir Edward, 6, 9
Demas, William, 94, 170, 184–5, 201, 222, 247; argues theory of economic integration, 56–62, 69, 78, 90, 187, 189; at officials' conference (1967), 83–5; President of CDB, 238, 243–4; report with McIntyre, 187–8; Secretary General, 129, 138, 142–4, 148, 155–6, 237–40; views on political integration, 259, 265–7, 270, 272
Democratic Labour Party (DLP), 27
Dominica, 2, 5, 31, 130, 148, 153; independence, 275
Dominican Republic (formerly Santo Domingo), 40, 80, 211

Eastern Caribbean Common Market (ECCM), 151, 154, 157, 227; establishment of, 106; fifth bloc, 162; general performance of, 126; trade, 168, 172
Eastern Caribbean Currency Board, 42, 181
Eastern Caribbean Federation, 33–4, 49, 51–2, 62–3
Economic Commission for Latin America (ECLA), 84, 92, 105, 127–8, 130, 157, 217, 237
Economics of Nationhood, The, 17, 27–8
Economist Intelligence Unit (EIU), 151, 154, 163
Etzioni, A., 17

Index   295

European Economic Community
  (EEC), 37–8, 71, 75; Jamaican
  attitude towards, 96, 99; regional
  negotiations with, 116–17, 133–7,
  143–4, 154, 160, 208–11, 249–50
European Free Trade Association
  (EFTA), 67

Federal Development Loan and
  Guarantee Fund, 36
Federation of Civil Servants of the
  West Indies, 11
Federation, The (1958–62), 5–19,
  26–33, 96; automatic
  politicisation, 257–8; lessons of,
  267–8
Foreign Affairs, 141
France, 3, 10, 38, 46–7, 133

Gairy, Eric, 33, 215, 261–2, 275
Georgetown Accord (1973), 153–8,
  162
Girvan, Norman 26, 79–80
Gomes, Albert, 15
Greene, J. E., 249
Grenada, 3, 121, 153, 231;
  independence, 275; support for
  political integration, 261–3;
  unitary state with Trinidad, 31,
  33–4, 36, 51
Grenada Declaration, 130–1,
  259–63, 266–7, 274
Guadeloupe, 37–8, 46, 211
Guatemala, 212, 273
Guscott, M. H., 79
Guyana (formerly British Guiana),
  4, 8, 37, 57, 80, 82, 135, 174, 181,
  249; constitutional crisis in, 42–5,
  47, 49–50; contributes to
  functional co-operation, 196–7,
  200, 204; establishes College of
  Arts and Sciences, 35–6, 39;
  favours 'deepening', 129, 132;
  foreign policy, 215, 218–20, 231;
  independence, 74; participates in
  renewed regional collaboration
  after Federation, 39–41, 49–50;
  racial division of, 81, 271; radical
  economic policies, 131, 182,
  185–6, 188; role in establishment
  of CARIFTA, 62–4, 76, 91, 93,
  100–2, 108; signs Georgetown
  Accord, 153, 155; support for
  political integration, 257, 259–64,
  273–4; trade, 106, 120, 168–73,
  180; urges migration, 73–4; U.S.
  support for, 102
Guyana Airways Corporation, 114

Haas, E. B., 256–8
Haiti, 40, 80, 211
Hansen, R., 258
Heads of Government Conference,
  225, 241; First, 39–43; Second,
  42–5; Third, 48–51, 64; Fourth,
  90–6, 98, 105, 114, 127, 201;
  Fifth, 113–14, 118; Sixth, 127–8,
  203; Seventh, 144–8, 202–5;
  Eighth, 149–55; Ninth, 182, 184,
  204, 212; as institution, 227–32
Hoffmann, Stanley, 245–6, 250, 258
Hunte, Senator Kenneth, 68

Imperial College of Tropical
  Agriculture, 9
Ince, Basil, 231
Inter-American Development Bank,
  102
International Caribbean Airways
  (ICA), 137, 198
International Civil Aviation
  Organisation, 197

Jagan, Cheddi, 43–5, 47, 49
Jamaica, 1, 4, 28, 57, 73, 80, 82,
  115, 178, 237; contributes to
  functional co-operation, 195–7,
  200, 205; favours Yaoundé-type
  agreement with EEC, 136; foreign
  policy, 212–19; gives new impetus

to integration, 140–2; independence, 36; opposes 'deepening', 129–32; participates in CARIFTA, 63, 67, 70, 75, 93, 95–109, 112–13, 118–19; participates in renewed regional collaboration after Federation, 39–40, 48, 50, 64; provokes 'Rodney incident', 112–13; role in Federation, 13, 15–19, 21, 26, 35–6; role in Common Market, 174, 180–1, 185, 188; signs Georgetown Accord, 153; trade, 117–18, 120–1, 168–73; views on political integration, 260–2
Jamaica Labour Party (JLP), 96, 118, 131, 140, 262
Jamaica Manufacturers' Association, 99–100
Jefferson, Owen, 136
Jonckheer, E., 46

King, Kurleigh, 222, 240

Land-Water Highway, 10
Lastra, Dr, 46
Latin American Free Trade Area (LAFTA), 62, 93, 104
Le Blanc, Edward, 107, 261
Leeward Islands, 1, 15, 19; early links, 2–3, 7–8; *see also* Less developed countries (LDCs)
Leeward Islands Air Transport Company (LIAT), 197–8
Less developed countries (LDCs), 197–8, 233; definition of term, 92–3; discontent with CARIFTA, 113–14, 119–30; hesitancy over joining CARIFTA, 103–8; negotiation of CARICOM, 143–55, 159–62; position in Common Market, 167–8, 171–2, 174, 177–9, 182, 188; position on EEC association, 133–6, 210; view of CDB, 95–7, 240–5

Lewis, G. K., 20
Lewis, Vaughan A., 159–61, 268, 274, 279
Lewis, W. Arthur, 263, 277; after Federation, 27–8, 30, 34; industrialisation policy, 15, 69–70; President of CDB, 120, 241–2
Lightbourne, Robert, 99–100, 113–14, 131–3, 136
Lomé Convention, 210–11, 272
London Conferences (1953 and 56), 16
Luke, Sir Stephen, 35

McIntyre, Alister, 67, 122, 178, 244; report with Demas, 187–8; Secretary General, 239–40
Macleod, I., 19
Manley, Michael, 140–2, 214–7, 229–30
Manley, Norman, 13–14, 17–19, 140
Marryshow, T. M., 5, 21
Martinique, 38, 46–7, 211
Maudling, Reginald, 29, 33
Mexico, 212, 216
Millette, James, 19
Mirror, The, 47
Mohammed, Kamaluddin, 75, 126
Montego Bay Conference (1947), 13–4, 20, 271
Montserrat, 2, 51, 108, 261; paper, 148–53; unique position of, 155–7
Mordecai, Sir John, 16, 31, 33
More developed countries (MDCs), 228, 233; association with EEC, 134–7; attitude to CARICOM, 159–62; definition of term, 93; relationship with LDCs, 97–8, 125–6, 147–8, 152–3, 155; trading gains, 117, 119–21
Moyne, Lord, 7–8
Multilateral Clearing Facility, 181
Myrdal, G., 89–90

Index

Nation, The, 49, 51, 116
Netherlands, 10, 38
Netherlands Antilles, 37, 46, 48
Nye, J. S., 258–9

Oils and Fats Agreement, 125, 182
Organisation of American States (OAS), 50, 102, 147, 211

Patterson, P. J., 249–50
Pengel, J. A., 46
People's National Congress (PNC), 73

People's National Movement (PNM), 49, 51, 213; attitude to federation, 27–34, 36–7
People's National Party (PNP), 140–2
People's Progressive Party (PPP), 43, 47, 73–4
Petit St Vincent Agreement (1972), 178
Pico, R., 94
Pine, Sir Benjamin, 2
Political Quarterly, The, 264
Port of Spain Agreement (1976), 180
Prevatt, Senator, 262
Process List, 66, 171–2
Progressive Labour Movement (PLM), 157
Public Service Agreement (1972), 200
Puerto Rico, 46–8, 58, 64, 71, 211

Quarantine conference (1904), 9

Rampersad, George, 157
Ramphal, Shridath, 129, 132, 136–7, 209, 232–3, 285–6; views on political integration, 263, 267–9, 270–1, 273–6
Regional Economic Committee (REC), 11–13, 50

Regional Food Plan (RFP), 186, 244
Regional Transportation Council, 196, 198
Rodney, Walter, 112

St Kitts-Nevis-Anguilla, 2, 121, 134, 148, 186; secession movement, 231–2, 274; signing of CARICOM Treaty, 153, 162
St Lucia, 3, 26, 31, 51, 103, 153; independence, 275; signs Grenada Declaration, 261–3
St Vincent, 3, 65, 121, 153; considered for CDB, 97, 100–2; independence, 275
Sanderson, James, 3
Sangster, Donald, 13, 40, 47, 50, 70
Schmitter, P. C., 256–8
Schooner, Pool, 10
Seaga, Edward, 99–100, 113; views on CDB, 100–3
Secretariat, The, 123, 167, 209, 211, 231, 248; establishment of, 93, 96, 102; evaluation, 225–7, 234–40; involved in negotiation of CARICOM, 142–4, 148, 155; promotes functional co-operation, 195–6, 198–9, 202–5, 249; quoted, 104–5, 120, 124, 154–6, 184–5; relationship with CDB, 241, 244; relationship with other integration movements, 212, 216; services CARIFTA, 117, 127–9; services Common Market, 171, 178, 183–5
Selvon, Samuel, 21
Shearer, Hugh, 100, 107, 112–13, 118, 131, 262; on powers of Secretariat, 236
Smelter project, 185, 214–16, 229–30
Solomon, Dr, 49
Southern Africa, 218–19
Southwell, Paul, 148–9
Springer, Sir Hugh, 14, 16–17

Standing Closer Association Committee (SCAC), 16
Standing Committee of Ministers responsible for Foreign Affairs, 208, 221–2, 225
Stanley, Oliver, 8, 13
Stapleton, Sir William, 2
Surinam, 37–8, 46, 80

Thomas, Clive, 77–85, 186, 188
Thunder, 73
Tobago statement, 263–4, 266, 277
Tinindad and Tobago, 1, 57, 82, 129, 135, 152, 232; colonial administration of, 3, 7–8; contributes to functional co-operation, 195–8, 200, 204–5; favours 'deepening', 129; foreign policy, 212–18, 220, 222; independence, 36; participates in Federation, 13, 15–19; policy in aftermath of federal collapse, 27–36; promotes idea of Caribbean Economic Community, 36–52; proposes BWIA as regional air carrier, 114–16; racial division of, 81, 271; role in Common Market, 174, 180–1, 185–6, 188, 244; role in establishment of CARIFTA, 63–5, 67–8, 70, 75–6, 83–4, 103, 108; signs Georgetown Accord, 153; trade, 120, 142, 168–73; views on political integration, 257, 260, 262–4
Trinidad Guardian, 136, 147
Tripartite Report, 94

United Nations, 38–9, 47, 199, 212, 218; UNCTAD, 240; UNDP, 94–5; UNESCO, 202; UNIDO, 127–8
United States of America (USA), 10, 17, 73–4, 94; and Guyana, 49, 102; and Puerto Rico, 46, 58, 71
University of Guyana, 35–6, 39, 227, 248
University of the West Indies (UWI), 21, 26, 42, 227; contributes to functional co-operation, 200–1, 205, 248; disagreements over, 35–6, 50, 103, 142, 218; economists, 67, 70, 76–85, 183–4, 189; establishment of, 9; 'Rodney incident', 112–13
'University' of Woodford Square, 46

Venezuela, 40–2, 197, 244, 273; dispute over, 213–17
Viner, Jacob, 59–60

Walter, George, 157–8, 215
Warner, Thomas, 2
Webber, A. R. F., 6
West Indian Bar Association, 11
West Indian Court of Appeal, 9, 203
West Indian Trade Commissioner Service, 9, 11
West India Trans-Atlantic Steam Ship Lines (WITASS), 196–7
West Indies Assiciated States Council of Ministers, 227
West Indies Federal Labour Party, 20
West Indies Shipping Corporation (WISCO), 35, 46, 48, 50, 195–6, 244
Wheare, K. C., 255
Williams, Eric, 18, 74, 158, 229–30; attitude to UWI, 36, 142; idea of Caribbean Economic Community, 36–9, 51–2, 62; initiation of Heads of Government Conferences, 39–40, 42–9, 230; lectures on federation, 20; reaction to Jamaican referendum,

Index

27–33; 'recolonisation' thesis, 212–7; role in CARIFTA, 63–5, 67–71, 93; views on political integration, 262–5, 270

Windward Islands, 1, 15, 19; early links, 3, 7–8; *see also* Less developed countries (LDCs)

Wood, the Hon. E. F. L., 6–7

Wooding, Sir High, 263

World Bank, 93

Yaoundé Convention, 135–6